About Island Press

Island Press is the only nonprofit organization in the United States whose principal purpose is the publication of books on environmental issues and natural resource management. We provide solutions-oriented information to professionals, public officials, business and community leaders, and concerned citizens who are shaping responses to environmental problems.

In 1994, Island Press celebrated its tenth anniversary as the leading provider of timely and practical books that take a multidisciplinary approach to critical environmental concerns. Our growing list of titles reflects our commitment to bringing the best of an expanding body of literature to the environmental community throughout North America and the world.

Support for Island Press is provided by Apple Computer, Inc., The Bullitt Foundation, The Geraldine R. Dodge Foundation, The Energy Foundation, The Ford Foundation, The W. Alton Jones Foundation, The Lyndhurst Foundation, The John D. and Catherine T. MacArthur Foundation, The Andrew W. Mellon Foundation, The Joyce Mertz-Gilmore Foundation, The National Fish and Wildlife Foundation, The Pew Charitable Trusts, The Pew Global Stewardship Initiative, The Rockefeller Philanthropic Collaborative, Inc., and individual donors.

About the Greening of Industry Network

The Greening of Industry Network stimulates, coordinates, and promotes research of high quality, relevance, and usefulness toward ensuring that the activities of industry—including business, labor, consumers, and government—are consistent with building a sustainable future.

Guided by an international advisory board and working through two coordinating centers, the Network comprises over 1000 individuals representing academia, business, public interest, labor, and government from 49 countries. These participants work together to build policies and strategies toward creating a sustainable future through many vehicles—coordinated research efforts, co-authored publications, workshops, public forums, and conferences.

The Network is a space to work in, creating a dialogue and providing an opportunity for all stakeholders—with equal voice—to develop research and policy agendas on issues of industry, sustainability, and society.

Kurt Fischer and Johan Schot are the Network's coordinators and can be contacted using the information provided in the back of this book.

The Greening of Industry Resource Guide and Bibliography

Titles published by Island Press in the GREENING OF INDUSTRY
NETWORK SERIES include:

Kurt Fischer and Johan Schot (editors), *Environmental Strategies for Industry:
International Perspectives on Research Needs and Policy Implications,* 1993.

Peter Groenewegen, Kurt Fischer, Edith G. Jenkins, and Johan Schot (editors), *The Greening of Industry Resource Guide and Bibliography,* 1995.

Series Editors

Berit Aasen
Norwegian Institute for Urban
  and Regional Research
Oslo, Norway

Kurt Fischer
The George Perkins Marsh
  Institute
Clark University
Worcester, Massachusetts

Nigel Roome
Haub Program in Business and
  the Environment
York University
Toronto, Canada

Johan Schot
Centre for Studies of Science,
  Technology and Society
University of Twente
Enschede, the Netherlands

This book series embodies and strengthens the mission of the Greening of
Industry Network. It includes works that will be appreciated by people
working in business, government, nongovernmental organizations, and
academia—cross-cutting books covering concepts, theory, analysis, and
actionable ideas. The books in the series are interdisciplinary, drawing
mainly on three areas of strategic management and organizational studies,
innovation studies, and environmental studies, but also extending to
such areas as urban studies, philosophy, political studies, and ecology.
Working with Island Press, the Network develops book concepts that are
aimed toward an international readership. The series helps to build and
strengthen the emergent field of greening of industry studies by including
resource guides, textbooks, and trade books that make the various issues
and themes accessible to a wide, general audience.

The Greening of Industry Resource Guide and Bibliography

Edited by
Peter Groenewegen, Kurt Fischer,
Edith G. Jenkins, and Johan Schot

Published as part of
THE GREENING OF INDUSTRY NETWORK SERIES

ISLAND PRESS

Washington, D.C. ■ Covelo, California

Library of Congress Cataloging-in-Publication Data

The greening of industry resource guide and bibliography/edited by
    Peter Groenewegen . . . [et al.].
        p.   cm.
    Includes bibliographical references and index.
    ISBN 1-55963-396-4. — ISBN 1-55963-397-2 (pbk.)
    1. Industries—Environmental aspects. 2. Industries—
Environmental aspects—Bibliography. 3. Environmental policy.
4. Environmental policy—Bibliogaphy. I. Groenewegen, P.
HC79.E5G6924   1996
658.4'08—dc20   95-19088
                                                                        CIP

Printed on recycled, acid-free paper ✇

Manufactured in the United States of America
10 9   8   7   6   5   4   3   2   1

Contents

Acknowledgments   *ix*

Introduction   *1*
Peter Groenewegen, Kurt Fischer, Edith G. Jenkins, and Johan Schot

Chapter 1
Strategic Choices and Sustainable Strategies   *9*
Sue Hall and Nigel Roome

Chapter 2
Organization and Human Resource
Management for Environmental Management   *37*
Ulrich Steger

Chapter 3
Strategic Cooperation and Life Cycle Analysis   *63*
Julie L. Hass and Peter Groenewegen

Chapter 4
Industry Relationships with
Communities: Business as Usual?   *87*
Caron Chess and Frances Lynn

Chapter 5
Environmental Performance Measurement   *111*
Peter James and Walter Wehrmeyer

Chapter 6
The Greening of Corporate Accounting   *137*
Mark Gijtenbeek, Johan Piet, and Allen L. White

Chapter 7
Clean Technologies   *169*
Kenneth Green and Alan Irwin

Chapter 8
Transnational Companies and
Industrial Pollution in the South: An Overview   *195*
Jan Hesselberg

Chapter 9
Greening of Small and Medium-sized Firms:
Government, Industry, and NGO Initiatives   *213*
Kenneth Geiser and Marcel Crul

About the Contributors   *245*

Name Index   *249*

Subject Index   *255*

Acknowledgments

As editors of the *Greening of Industry Resource Guide and Bibliography* we find that there are so many individuals whom we need to thank and acknowledge for their dedication and cooperation in bringing this project from concept to publication. First, all of the contributing authors deserve special thanks for their teamwork across many kinds of boundaries—and for working with four volume editors.

We extend thanks as well to the following researchers for their invaluable assistance and insightful commentary in reviewing chapters: Frank Belz, John R. Ehrenfeld, J.C.M. van Eijndhoven, Susse Georg, Manfred Kirchgeorg, Peter Simmons, and Monika I. Winn.

We wish to thank research assistants Amy Cotter, Erica Curran, and Lorelei Prevost and acknowledge their persistent work in tracking the chapters in progress, checking the citations, and compiling and verifying the editing; the members of the Network's advisory board for their support and guidance throughout; and the many participants of the Greening of Industry Network who volunteered ideas and references, adding diversity and richness.

Introduction

Peter Groenewegen
Kurt Fischer
Edith G. Jenkins
Johan Schot

Only recently has research on the greening of industry begun to blossom. The greening of industry is a strategic research area where many paradigms converge, not a new field or discipline, nor a specialty of an existing discipline. These paradigms all share the assumption that industrial firms wi!! play a vital role in the needed transition to a sustainable society. And they share the view that the transition will change firms in a profound way, influencing their strategies and instruments, identities, and relationships with their stakeholders. Issues that are now the focus of research range from corporate strategies to operational changes, from environmental communication and reporting to collaborative decision making between firms and their stakeholders, from management of cleaner technologies and clean production to changing the organizational structures and cultures of firms.

Like the firms themselves, the research community was slow to recognize the strategic importance of these issues. However, many researchers, like some pioneer firms, find the greening of industry to be an exciting and crucial area that needs further work and articulation. Within their own disciplines, they push important new agendas that require a new language to explore new metaphors such as eco-efficiency, environmental co-makership, sustainability strategy, carrying capacity of the Earth, life cycle analysis, integral chain management, extension of product durability, recyclability, and full-cost accounting. These new metaphors cover some changes well underway and at the same time open new avenues of thinking. They create space for yet unknown horizons and connect the greening of industry agenda to the sustainability imperative.

This imperative extends to the broader issues of employment, equity, and development, and these issues are entering the research agenda. There is a growing realization that firms need to become creative and innovative on how to satisfy human needs and maintain quality of life with much less resource consumption. Efficiency gains cannot provide all the answers because the sources of wealth production are polluted: More growth is not the answer.

Some of the pioneering researchers and firms are seeking ways to develop a new vision and practice that starts with accepting limits and moves on to explore the implications of the sustainability agenda for the organization of the entrepreneurial function in our societies. One of the crucial questions for the coming years is whether the new networks and coalitions, such as the Coalition for Environmentally Responsible Economies (CERES) and the European Partners for the Environment (EPE), will create opportunities to develop new kinds of corporate actions for sustainable development.

Addressing a Need

For people working within business, research, government, non-government organizations (NGOs), and the many other organizations involved in the changing course of our industrial system, quick and easy access to relevant information is central to progress and success. But access is not easy because of the diverse nature of the subject and the steep growth in the volume of literature within the realms of various disciplines and across countries around the world. It is hard to track relevant and high-quality research results and to separate them from superficial work. It is easy to overlook critical information pertinent to the questions asked. This bibliography and resource guide aims to be a road map of the most critical and salient research published to date of the greening of industry as a part of the transition to a sustainable society.

We believe this bibliography will serve to

- Provide a valuable resource guide to the most respected and useful cutting-edge research pertinent to the strategic research area of the greening of industry.

- Coordinate and disseminate quality research results and stimulate new thinking.

- Provide a basis and challenge for effective policies, strategies, and actions for policymakers in business, government, NGOs, and other organizations.

- Enhance communication among researchers across disciplines and between researchers and the users of research.

- Provide a distilled volume of references valuable to those already contributing to the development of this new area of research and action, easily accessible to those newly exploring the issues.

Process of Writing This Book

The team that produced this guide began with 20 authors and four editors. Although the project had been brewing for many months, the first meeting of authors and editors took place in Boston at the second international Greening of Industry Network conference, Designing the Sustainable Enterprise, November 14-16, 1993. Participants wanted to work collaboratively with scholars and professionals from other fields. Just as important was the idea of finally bringing together the disparate literature on the issues. This meeting jumpstarted the subsequent process of collaborative teamwork that came to include not only the authors and editors, but also many others who contributed as reviewers and advisors of the chapters under development. (See "Acknowledgments.") This broader process ensures that the literature collected in this volume represents what is considered the most insightful, well-grounded, and important literature available. Of course, the judgments reflect the bias of the authors, editors, and reviewers involved. Many disciplines and research produced in non-English-speaking countries are not well represented. However, as a start, we made a genuine effort to include literature from the Scandinavian countries, from the Netherlands, and from Germany, as is reflected in the references available in the various chapters.

We decided to focus on the relevance and quality of the literature rather than the source. Since such literature is produced by many institutions, including universities, consultants, NGOs, business networks, and governments, this bibliography presents a mixture of academic peer-reviewed and nonacademic literature. Since we were seeking quality, we have restricted the number of references and have asked authors to be selective. We have additionally concentrated on literature that is accessible to everyone. And we have tried to strike a balance between generic literature and specialized literature. We have included in most chapters some of the seminal and most important works on specific issues under discussion. For example, chapters on management contain some references to general management literature along with works discussing specific problems for environmental management.

Using This Resource Guide

This book has a number of fundamental features that make it more than a bibliography. In both its production and use, this resource guide is designed to facilitate bridging across research disciplines and country barriers to practical applications. In addition, each chapter contains not only a list of selected annotated references but also insightful introductory essays. These put the bibliographic references into the context of their fields and give the reader an overview of both the literature and the authors' reasons for choosing the references they did. The essays have two story lines. The first describes the current state of the field and historical description of thoughts and events that led to this state. The second covers the challenge for future research.

Creating a bibliography is difficult, especially when it is known that as soon as it is published, the latest relevant works will be missing. This is most certainly the case in a booming field such as the greening of industry. While we will consider additions to future editions of this volume, we believe that because of our focus on future challenges, and because of the broad participatory process involved in producing this book, many of the collected references will be valuable for years to come and will turn out to be seminal works. They will be read in the staff and board rooms of companies, governments, and other organizations, discussed and read in students' classes, and found on the desks of many future researchers of the greening of industry.

Structure of the Book

The greening of industry is a complex and multifaceted process, a challenge to disaggregate into separate issues. All of the chapters need to be considered as inroads into a complex whole. This led to some overlap between chapters, which we embrace since it offers the opportunity to discuss research findings from different perspectives.

We start with chapters by Sue Hall and Nigel Roome on "Strategic Choices and Sustainable Strategies" (Chapter 1) and Ulrich Steger on "Organization and Human Resource Management for Environmental Management" (Chapter 2), both of which deal with strategic management. Hall and Roome have collected references that describe three strands of discourse (or story lines) running through the literature to depict corporate response to the environmental challenge. The first one, compliance, deals with strategies that ensure that companies will stay in the agreed-upon legal and jurisdictional domain. Second is eco-efficiency, including concepts such as total quality environmental management and industrial ecology, which tries to identify win-win solutions by reducing environmental impacts and costs. A third set of references in Hall and Roome's chapter employs some of the ideas current in modern management literature as it is applied to the environmental challenge. In addition, they cite works that suggest some new, emergent themes, such as the importance of systems thinking, stakeholder involvement and learning, and needed cultural and value changes.

Steger moves the strategic management theme further by focusing on literature that provides insight into the requirements and tensions in the transition to what he calls an integrated, innovation-oriented environmental approach. He has brought together literature that provides insight into practical questions of "how-to-do-it." He focuses on ways to create organizational learning processes and to include environmental requirements into human resource management. From these first two chapters, it is clear that a genuine response to the environmental challenge will entail a change of organization and the creation of new networks and learning processes with a variety of stakeholders, both internal and external to the firm. Stakeholders are seen as partners in helping create solutions.

Two kinds of networks are discussed in Chapters 3 and 4. Julie Hass and Peter Groenewegen guide the reader through references on the networking between suppliers and user firms, including the vital role of life cycle analysis. Then Caron Chess and Frances Lynn introduce the literature on industry relations with communities.

Changing strategies and relationships require new data as well: Change needs measurement. Environmental costs and opportunities present special and unique challenges to traditional accounting practices and performance measurement. Chapters 5 and 6 focus on literature that defines the nature and quality of data needed and the kind of accounting and reporting systems to be developed to get these data. Peter James and Walter Wehrmeyer introduce the literature on environmental performance measurement; and Mark Gijtenbeek, Johan Piet, and Allen White discuss the greening of corporate accounting.

Technological change is considered highly important to the process of greening of industry. In fact, many actors are putting all their hopes into the development of a new generation of cleaner technologies that will, in their view, solve the problems in the Western world. And further, many believe that these new technologies should be transferred to countries in the non-Western world to help prevent their going through a similar disastrous process of environmental damage.

As Kenneth Green and Alan Irwin argue in their contribution (Chapter 7), technical change cannot be perceived as such a cure-all. Technical change is a social process and thus requires an understanding of the economic, political, and social factors that will shape the content of new technology. Green and Irwin have, therefore, collected and discussed two kinds of resources that explore the concept of clean technologies—focusing on incentives and barriers to introducing such technologies at the level of the firm; and they have provided an opening to the literature that discusses clean technologies from a social-shaping perspective.

Discussions on greening of industry have a compelling international dimension. Jan Hesselberg (Chapter 8) has assembled references on behavior of transnational companies in the South. Do firms use the South as a pollution haven? What kind of environmental management practices are deployed in developing countries? He also touches on broader issues, such as international trade and industrialization.

Much greening of industry literature is based on research within large firms, while in most economies small and medium-sized enterprises (SMEs) make up the largest share of most industrial sectors. The environmental impacts of SMEs is significant, justifying a separate chapter on those firms. In Chapter 9, Marcel Crul and Kenneth Geiser discuss three types of literature: case studies, manuals and guides, and government and nongovernmental organization reports on SMEs.

Of course, some important topics have been left out of this volume. A focus on consumerism, changing life styles, and greening of marketing is missing; regional development is another important theme. While most chapters introduce literature on various manufacturing sectors (chemicals, paper, steel), other sectors, such as agriculture, electricity production, and the service industries, are missing. But the selection also reflects the current state of the art; literature is simply not available in many areas.

Chapter 1

Strategic Choices and Sustainable Strategies

Sue Hall
Nigel Roome

Introduction

This chapter reviews literature that examines how companies have addressed environmental concerns within their broader strategic choices to determine the extent to which their actions could be described as deriving from "sustainable strategies." This discussion seeks to identify the main streams of thought within the business strategy–environment domain, delineating three main approaches— compliance, eco-efficiency, and environmental strategy. Although much has been written about how companies can improve their environmental performance and strive toward more-sustainable practices, this chapter suggests that we currently lack an integrated, holistic approach on which to found truly sustainable businesses. Although current thinking provides us with some valuable pointers, there still exists a vacuum surrounding what comprises "sustainable strategies"—in terms of both definition and process.

Sustainability: Definitions, Conditions, Assumptions

The ideas contained in this review are based on key assumptions about sustainability. The position presented here follows from views expressed by the World Commission on Environment and Development (Brundtland 1987) and developed in work by the Business Council for Sustainable Development (Schmidheiny 1992).

- Sustainable development provides a framework for the integration of environment policies and development strategies.

- Sustainable development seeks to meet the needs and aspirations of the present without compromising the ability to meet those of the future.

- Sustainable development is a process of change. . . .

- No single blueprint of sustainability will be found, as economic and social systems and ecological conditions vary widely. . . . Irrespective of these differences, sustainability should be seen as a global objective.

- Sustainable development stands at the center of a global economic, technological, social, political, and cultural transformation that is redefining the boundaries of what is possible and what is desirable.

Taken together, these ideas suggest that sustainable development is a search for new ways of thinking and acting. It is a process of change guided by four principles:

1. The need for a better balance between traditional notions of economic progress and the maintenance of environmental wealth and natural capital.

2. The need to improve intragenerational equity in terms of economic and environmental wealth.

3. The need to improve intergenerational equity in terms of economic and environmental wealth.

4. The need to work out the meaning of sustainability in ways that are meaningful and relevant locally as well as globally.

Strategic Choices: Three Main Approaches for Addressing Environmental Concerns

Much has been written about how business strategies have begun to address environmental concerns. Three main strands of thinking have emerged to date.

A first strand of thinking sees companies as creating compliance strategies to address environmental issues, seen largely as internal legal and liability concerns. A second strand sees companies as concerned with eco-efficiency, primarily seeking to modify their operations to reduce both environmental emissions and costs—creating operational strategies largely based on total quality management principles or building on the principles of environmental management systems. A third strand of thinking sees companies as experimenting with various forms of environmental business strategy. These companies "borrow" mainstream business strategy frameworks in ways that enable them to respond to environmental concerns across a fuller spectrum of their business activities.

This latter approach integrates competitive and revenue-building opportunities to build on the cost-based foundations of eco-efficiency. Although none of these approaches seems to offer an integrated vision of truly sustainable strategies, they do offer distinct world views which—in their differences—provide some important pointers toward the foundations on which sustainable strategies may be created. (See Table 1-1.) This review outlines these three approaches and offers some tentative early opinions about the form that sustainable strategies of the future might assume.

Compliance

At the most fundamental level, companies formulate compliance strategies to ensure that their businesses operate within pre-agreed legal and jurisdictional domains. Management approaches to ensure compliance have been reviewed in the works of Arthur D. Little (1988, 1990). Compliance objectives are to minimize liabilities—designating business economics as the principle driver of their actions to

Table 1-1
Strategies to Address Environmental Concerns

	Compliance	Eco-efficiency	Environmental strategy
Values / Intentions	Legal	Economic	Business/ Ecological
Objectives	Minimize liabilities	Reduce costs	Build competitive advantage
Change paradigm	Business as usual	Incremental change	Discontinuous change
Management mode	Regulatory	Operational	Business strategy
Frameworks		TQEM Industrial ecology	Portfolio management Scenario planning Strategic intent and core competence
Organizational focus	EHS/Auditing	Operations Manufacturing	Marketing Planning Executive committee
Relational frame	Conflict	Compromise	Interconnected
Stakeholder mode	Minimize impact	Engagement	Learn and innovate
Contextual frame	Utilitarian	Anthropocentric	Eco-centric

which other value systems, particularly environmental, are entirely subordinate. Business economics and environmental performance are therefore largely seen as in conflict, paralleling the relationship between companies and other external environmental stakeholders who are often viewed as "part of the problem." This anthropocentric approach places the company as central in the universe and establishes compliance strategies to ensure the continuation of the corporation's legal right to operate. A utilitarian mindset sees resources solely as the means for companies to profit from their operations.

Discussion of compliance initiatives has largely subsided since the early 1990s as focus has shifted toward environmental management systems. Earlier compliance discussions centered for the most part on the policy decisions and operating systems for environmental health and safety departments. Management approaches were outlined by several consulting companies, notably Arthur D. Little (1988, 1990).

Roome (1992) argues that compliance efforts cannot be considered a strategic response to environmental challenges because they address only a limited domain comprising particularly offensive emissions, toxic pollutants, and products. Compliance efforts address only the environmental issues that are required by law, and therefore such efforts usually fall short of meeting society's broader expectations. Since they tackle only the "tip of the iceberg," a "compliance strategy" cannot be considered a sustainability strategy (Sethi 1975).

However, Porter (1991) argues that countries' regulatory policy can impact companies' competitiveness, suggesting that more stringent policies in the long term encourage companies'—and nations'—competitiveness. The Management Institute for Environment and Business (MEB) (1994) reviews this set of hypotheses with Porter and the U.S. EPA in a set of six industry case studies.

Thus, within compliance-based strategies, business strategy drives and environmental decisions follow in a pattern that seeks to minimize change to fundamental business and operating practices. Only Porter (1991) and the MEB (1994) have reviewed the competitive implications of regulatory policies for countries and companies beyond this relatively compliance-oriented approach.

Eco-Efficiency

A second set of literature reviews companies' actions within the context of eco-efficiency. Much of the thinking and terminology of the Business Council for Sustainable Development (Schmidheiny 1992) and the U.S. President's Council for Sustainable Development (PCSD) draw heavily on this concept. Again, three main strands of thought have been explored to date within this domain: total quality environmental management (TQEM), implementation of environmental management systems, and industrial ecology.

Total Quality Environmental Management and
Environmental Management Systems

Extending the span of organizational management to incorporate the environmental impacts of industry has led to the extension of conventional management systems such as total quality and environmental management systems. Management systems such as ISO 9000 have gained currency in organizational management because of the demands in the value chain for an assured level of product quality and the importance of meeting customer satisfaction requirements. Total quality systems have taken this notion further by emphasizing the value to the business of continuous improvement toward the goal of zero defects as well as continuous product innovation. These approaches require a cultural commitment to quality within the organization. They emphasize the importance of cross-functional teams involved in design, manufacture, and marketing and place value on the measurement of performance.

Incorporating environmental performance and quality in management systems (CSA 1993) or total quality programs (GEMI 1991) has become a new challenge for companies and standards-setting institutions. Significant questions remain about the association between product quality and environmental performance. For example, it cannot necessarily be assumed that improvements in product quality always lead to improvements in environmental performance (Walley and Whitehead 1994). Making this linkage requires mechanisms to resolve conflicts of purpose between performance in the product and process domain and performance in the environmental domain.

Industrial Ecology

Industrial ecology offers an organic model of industrial and business practice. Historically, industrial engineers have viewed industrial systems as engineering systems involving the transformation and flow of materials within separate businesses or industrial units. Industrial ecology or industrial metabolism seeks to develop an ecological model of industrial systems (Frosch 1992; Allenby and Richards 1994). Using this concept, the industrial system is seen as a web of interconnected production units linked by the flow of energy and material. These flows are governed by physical and ecological principles. The challenge for industrial ecology is to take a more systemic view of these interconnections and to manage the system as a whole in order to close the material and energy loops. The approach emphasizes the need to understand the flows of energy and material and to retain energy and material within a series of interconnected systems rather than losing or dissipating them outside the system. The approach places emphasis on the application of techniques such as life cycle analysis, full-cost accounting, and design for the environment.

These strands provide largely operational frameworks to create more-efficient businesses, as defined from both an economic and an environmental perspective. Thus they differ in important respects from compliance strategies. Business and environmental decisions are no longer largely assumed to be in conflict, but rather can provide opportunities for mutually beneficial cost savings and operational improvements as resources are managed in more efficient ways. They recognize business and environmental flows as being more interconnected—extending management's decision-making domain beyond the company's internal, formal boundaries to encompass a more interdependent world view. Management also begins to recognize the importance of stakeholders—particularly internal company employees and value chain partners—in achieving more eco-efficient operations. Overall, companies concerned with eco-efficiency seek primarily to modify their operations to reduce both environmental impact and costs, creating an operational strategy that benefits the company's cost structure.

Environmental Strategy

A third set of literature suggests that companies can address environmental concerns in a more integrated way by employing some of the ideas current in modern management thought and applying them to environmental challenges. Here again, three main strands of thinking have emerged: portfolio analysis, drawing on Porter's work; scenario planning, as originally expounded by the Shell Corporation and elu-

cidated further by Schwartz; and strategic intent and core competence, as originally envisioned by Hamel and Prahalad (1989) and
developed by Hall and Ingersoll (1994) and Hall (1995).

Portfolio Analysis

Portfolio analysis provides a tangible strategic tool for business to
use in shaping its response to environmental issues. In this approach
business organizations base their decisions about product and service
development on an analysis of the external threats and opportunities
provided by the marketplace within the context of the core technological and managerial competence of the organization (as it is, or as
it might become). These ideas are found in a number of books and
papers, but Steger (1993) presents them in the context of environmental management in German companies. Under this analysis
companies make strategic choices about market niche and/or cost
differentiation. Companies develop offensive or innovative strategies
for competition or develop more defensive positions, depending on
their place in the market and given their technological competence
and the position of their competitors.

Scenario Planning

Work in scenario planning suggests that companies can improve
their performance by understanding the trends that will impact and
restructure their markets over the long term—and by shaping their
strategic direction to anticipate these changes. Originally developed
by the Shell company, this approach has been covered in more detail
by Schwartz (1991). It has since been adopted in other corporate settings, as documented by Stokke et al. (1992) at StatOil. Several environmental commentators have drawn on this body of thinking. The
"backcasting" approach was expounded by several presenters at the
second Greening of Industry Network Conference, Boston 1993.
This approach attempts to project back from future scenarios to
determine the present requirements of business for achieving a sustainable way of living. However, to date, none of this work has
resulted in practical tools that can guide the formulation of business
strategy.

Hall and Ingersoll (1994) and Hall (1995) also suggest that environmental problems represent comparable long-term trends that are capable of restructuring markets, as demonstrated by several major shifts in market over the last three to five years. Lovins (1994) also draws on this thinking in his analysis of industry responses to environmental concerns, principally in the U.S. auto and energy industries, suggesting that environmental trends are now profoundly shaping company strategies.

The original strategic intent and core competence work by Hamel and Prahalad (1989) establishes a framework that lends itself to the formulation of more-advanced environmental strategies. They suggest that a corporation's strategic intent establishes fundamental long-term intentions that can enable them to gain competitive advantage if these commitments are leveraged to transform markets. They also suggest that to deliver on these commitments a company will need to invest in or develop core competencies that serve as wellsprings for innovation to create new products and services capable of catalyzing these market transformations. Their work draws heavily on a series of Japanese case examples. Hall and Ingersoll (1994) and Hall (1995) recognize the potential that this management framework holds to explain the competitive advantage that some companies have gained by establishing a commitment to "lead the change" toward more sustainable practices. They suggest that these companies develop a strategic intent to be "part of the solution" and a core competence in stakeholder learning. This work also draws on the insights of Senge (1992), who emphasizes the central importance of learning and systems thinking in an organization's success. For Senge, learning organizations oblige managers to become systems thinkers and to engage in adaptation through action-oriented research and continual experimentation.

Value-based Strategies

There is another group of authors, founded on Ansoff's thinking (1979), who have begun to raise questions regarding the role that values play in companies' strategic decision making. These authors argue that decisions surrounding the fundamental values of a corporation need to be made in an explicit fashion, and that these decisions comprise the only strategic choices that a company makes. Decisions concerning "what to do" are regarded as essentially tactical choices. In this way, these authors articulate a theme that underlies all the strategic approaches outlined to date, namely that value choices are being made—implicitly or explicitly—by companies all the time.

Some of the strategic approaches outlined above integrate this thinking—particularly the strategic intent framework oriented toward being "part of the solution" from an environmental perspective (Hall and Ingersoll 1994). Values, as a critical ingredient of organizational strategy, have been addressed in the literature on enterprise strategy (Ansoff 1979) and the field of corporate social responsibility (Carroll 1989). These authors represent the view that businesses are not simply part of systems of production but are components of social and resource systems. They argue that there will be an increasing need for organizations to make explicit choices to retain their social legitimacy over time. The maintenance of legitimacy will, therefore, become an increasingly dominant strategic issue for business.

The idea of legitimacy is extended by ethicists such as Freeman and Gilbert (1988), who argue that business increasingly has to make explicit the values that guide organizational activities. These approaches place emphasis on the importance of ethical systems in judging the suitability of different organizational choices as they affect the interests of different stakeholders in a business. Others have argued that industry cannot secure sustainability without bringing into play other values based on respect, or justice, for people and the environment (Roome 1995). In a similar way, Gladwin (1993) reminds us that the "greening of industry" goes beyond economic analysis to involve feelings as well as thinking and behaviors, expanding the range of values on which a company's strategic decisions must draw. For an excellent review of the many different perspectives on environmental ethics and values, see Armstrong and Botzler (1993).

Summary

The latter three strands of thinking share certain common assumptions, which differentiate them from eco-efficiency and compliance strategies. They seek to integrate and leverage environmental concerns across the full business spectrum, influencing not only a company's cost structures but the ways in which it is positioned strategically, formulates its business policies, generates revenues, or develops new products. Environmental concerns are thus integrated not only into companies' operational strategies, but into their broad business strategies, producing transformations that can encompass discontinuous as well as incremental change. These three approaches view business and environmental objectives as potentially even more synergistic and seek to make decisions based on a more balanced set of economic and ecological values. Correspondingly, these "environmental strategy" approaches view the corporation as part of a far more interdependent universe, seeking to integrate stakeholder concerns and contributions into the business decision-making process. Environmental challenges are viewed as opportunities—and stakeholders as partners in helping to create business-based solutions.

Emerging Themes

Across these strands of business strategy and environmental thinking, distinct differences arise in world view and assumptions, differences that can serve as pointers as we seek to understand what a sustainable enterprise comprises and how to design truly sustainable strategies.

First, the importance of systems concepts (Boulding 1956) is becoming increasingly critical to much of the literature and practice of environmental management, particularly those practices that move beyond a compliance approach. A number of authors have sought to develop more organic models of industrial and business practice based on systemic frames of analysis. This thinking underpins the work of authors in industrial ecology (Frosch 1992; Allenby and Richards 1994), eco-centric management (Shrivastava 1992), and strategic intent (Hall and Ingersoll 1994 and Hall 1995). These systems concepts emphasize the understanding of interdependencies between organizations and environments as complex, ambiguous, and dynamic. Some focus more on the interdependence of organizations with biological and physical systems (Shrivastava 1992), others on the energy and material flows among organizations involved in the process of production (Frosch 1992). These works develop Ansoff's

(1979) view that business is not simply part of the system of production but is integral to social and resource systems.

Paralleling the increasing emphasis on interdependencies between business organizations and the environments of which they are a part, another strong emerging theme is the concern for stakeholders and the role of partnerships in the form of collaboration, alliances, and networks. These structures can fulfill a variety of functions. They may provide a means to reference the values and metrics that business uses to make decisions when business is engaged with local communities or environmental groups to gain trust and credibility (Simmons and Wynne 1993; Lynn and Chess 1994). They can also provide the basis for the technological partnerships needed to effect environmental improvement across value chains, as well as the basis for value and supply chain initiatives between businesses (or between business and the public sector) (Schmidheiny 1992; Gray 1989). Some of these collaborations are developed on the basis of strengthened business relationships through strategic alliances or on the ideas of partnership sourcing (where businesses build long-term relationships with their suppliers to ensure the maintenance of product quality). Others are provoked by a recognition of the need to reduce turbulence in the organizational environment, which cannot be controlled by individual organizations acting alone (Trist 1983).

Others recognize stakeholders as powerful sources of learning and innovation, which can more directly contribute toward discovering and creating more-sustainable business strategies (Hall and Ingersoll 1993). Both of these emerging themes point toward the possibility and necessity of more fundamental change in both the mindsets and practices of the corporation. Systems thinking introduces entirely new management tools and world views. Stakeholder learning offers the opportunity to redefine the mission and operations of the corporation in ways that are more consistent with the sustainability challenges we face. To embrace change of such orders of magnitude requires engagement at the level of the corporation's culture and organizational fabric. To integrate environmental concerns, particularly in ways that could lead toward truly sustainable practices, will affect the visions, mission, symbols, and myths on which organizations are grounded, as well as their structures, systems, and activities.

Another body of literature addresses this organizational change component of environmental strategy, particularly the works of Bartunek and Moch (1987) and Stead and Stead (1992). They suggest that organizational change can be characterized as first order, second order, and third order, depending on the extent to which it impacts the culture of an organization. In their view third-order, or discontinuous, change is change that reshapes organizational culture. Second-order change, in contrast, involves shifting organizational practices at the margin by creating altered structures and systems to implement actions. It does not involve reshaping culture. First-order change requires new mechanisms for action that reinforce existing culture and values. Stead and Stead's view broadly parallels the three main strands of strategic environment/business thinking that have been set out above, suggesting that organizational and cultural change are critical to the development of more-sustainable environmental business strategies.

Sustainable Strategies: The Real Challenge Remains

The three main environmental business approaches outlined in this chapter are capable of improving a company's environmental performance. However, none of them are designed to create or achieve a sustainable strategy. For example, although TQEM may be an important contributor toward sustainability, it is not, of itself, a necessary or sufficient condition to achieve a sustainable strategy. What then might a sustainable strategy involve?

Several commentators, founded on the original works of Ansoff (1979), have raised questions regarding the values on which companies' strategies are to be based if they are to be more sustainable. (See section "Value-based Strategies," above.) However, although these approaches are founded on more-sustainable value systems and/or precepts, they have not yet been able to provide the kind of practical "hands-on" guidance of the strategic approaches outlined above. Hawken (1993) comes closest to attempting to bridge this gap, setting out precepts and founding principles to guide sustainable business practice. Although Hawken puts forward a hypothetical "utility" model for the restoration of natural capital, he stops short of providing a practical implementation framework that can translate such principles into practice. His model still cannot answer the question, "How do we do it, how do we operationalize our understanding of sustainable values and principles?"

In sum, what all of the strategic approaches outlined in this chapter fail to incorporate is a practical management system that can integrate sustainable values into strategic planning and operations to govern what a company produces and how it produces it. This leaves something of a vacuum in the domain of practical "sustainable strategies" and decision making.

In part, this vacuum reflects the way in which we have not yet been able to develop a systematic value system to integrate our different answers to even more fundamental questions of "What do we value and for whom? Profit? Biodiversity? Social justice? Intergenerational equity?" To date, the strategies advanced either use economics to delimit and constrain environmental value or seek to bring economic and environmental value systems into balance. In neither case have practical business-based frameworks been advanced, founded on an integrated set of sustainable values or a process capable of creating sustainable ways of living.

To a large degree, business can improve its environmental performance without jeopardizing the working assumption of a utilitarian system of values—that environmental resources are a means to human satisfaction and that business is driven by profit-maximizing motives. However, industry cannot hope to strive for sustainability without constraining these utilitarian motives by other values based on our respect for justice for the generations not yet born, and for the interests of the physical and biological process and resources of the Earth (Roome 1995). (This argument is based on the view that utilitarianism alone does not incorporate the interests of future generations, nor does it capture the full work of environmental systems.) Until we can create such a value system—and integrate it as the foundation for a decision-making process to guide our business strategies—it is unlikely that any of our strategies will be called truly sustainable.

Moreover, the establishment of a values system to guide decisions does not by itself necessarily ensure sustainability, since this is a shifting goal. For what is regarded as sustainable now will change as future generations express their needs, as new environmental challenges arise, and as our knowledge evolves. Strategies for sustainability will need to reflect these dynamics and emphasize the importance of learning together with a readiness to redefine and transform organizations and their activities as the future unfolds. Such an approach would draw on Morgan's (1986) ideas of organizations as being in a state of flux with the environments of which they form a part. In striving for sustainability, managers are therefore likely to recognize that it is their knowledge (about the transformation of resources into products and services) as well as their ongoing relationships with stakeholders that will ultimately deserve and reward their sustained investment and attention—rather than particular competencies in any one given technology that might be considered sustainable at that time. (See Table 1-2 for a comparison of environmental strategies versus sustainable strategies.)

Table 1-2

Comparison of Environmental Strategies versus Sustainable Strategies

	Environmental strategy	Sustainable strategy
Values/intentions	Business/Ecological	Sustainability
Objectives	Build competitive advantage	Learning and relationships for economic and ecological success
Change paradigm	Discontinuous change	Continuous redefinition
Management mode	Business strategy	Knowledge and relationship strategy
Frameworks	Portfolio management Scenario planning Strategic intent and core competence	Values management Learning Developing capabilities in the transformation of knowledge and relationships
Organizational focus	Marketing, Planning, Executive committee	Total organizational redefinition and transformation
Relational frame	Interconnected	Systemic
Stakeholder mode	Learn and innovate	Relational and innovative
Contextual frame	Eco-centric	Autopoesis

Overall, until we can fully address the critical questions of "What do we value? For whom?" and "How do we embody these values in sustainable management systems?" our strategies will remain focused on improving environmental performance rather than sustainability. Sustainable strategies will clearly need to simultaneously incorporate all the strengths offered by the approaches outlined in this chapter. For example, until we can build as practical and powerful a set of management frameworks to guide strategic decision making as those offered by Porter and Hamel *et al.*, our "sustainable" strategies will not be robust or widely adopted. Until we can also incorporate grounded operational approaches, such as those offered by TQEM and industrial ecology, our sustainable strategies will remain theoretical constructs.

Sustainable theory becomes sustainable (and conventional) practice when the profitable reply to the questions "What do we value?" and "For whom?" is "Posterity." That we strive for the tools to achieve such a transformation is abundantly evident in the rich and rapidly expanding body of literature that addresses this complex and essential responsibility. Social and educational innovation, the process of continuous learning and relationship building, accelerates the renewal of management systems and encourages the "re-invention" of ever more sustainable strategies. Therein lies the challenge.

Annotated Bibliography

Allenby, B., and D. Richards (eds.). 1994. *The Greening of Industrial Ecosystems.* Washington, DC: National Academy Press.

Allenby and Richards edit a series of papers on industrial ecology. The book contains papers by the leading proponents of this approach to industrial systems, including work by Ayres, Frosch, and Allenby. The book is illustrative of the approach industrial ecology brings to the analysis of industrial systems. Unfortunately not all the papers demonstrate well-developed thinking and analysis.

Ansoff, H.I. 1979. "Strategy and Strategic Management: The Changing Shape of the Strategic Problem." In *Strategic Management.* D. Schendel and C. Hofer (eds.). Boston: Little, Brown and Company.

This paper anticipates the need for companies to redefine and reframe their strategic concerns. Ansoff argues that over time the framing of strategy for organizations has moved from tactical questions about products and market technologies to more-complex questions of the legitimacy of the organization within its social and environmental context. This reorientation of strategy places decisions about products and market technology in the context of the need for greater organizational flexibility, alignment with sociopolitical changes, and the retention of social legitimacy. This work established the concept of "enterprise strategy" as a process of identifying organizational values.

Armstrong, S., and R. Botzler (eds.). 1993. *Environmental Ethics: Divergence and Convergence*. New York: McGraw-Hill, Inc.

An excellent and comprehensive review of the many strands of thought about environmental ethics and values. The editors bring together multiple perspectives drawing on historical and contemporary writings from secular as well as Judeo-Christian and other religious settings.

Arthur D. Little, 1988. *Environmental, Health, and Safety Policies: Current Practices and Future Trends*. Cambridge, MA: Arthur D. Little.

————. 1990. *European Environmental Management Trends in the 1990s: Implications for Management*. Cambridge, MA: Arthur D. Little.

Review (1988) of some of the better EHS compliance practices drawing on a series of chemical industry case studies, organized into a framework to help managers become more effective. Review (1990) of the process by which the European regulatory systems are beginning to make their policies and requirements more consistent with one another. Profiles policy changes on a country-by-country basis.

Bartunek, J., and M. Moch. 1987. "First-Order, Second-Order, and Third-Order Change and Organization Development Interventions: A Cognitive Approach." *Journal of Applied Behavior Studies* 23 (4) 483–500.

This paper examines the nature of change and the process of organization development. It categorizes change in terms of the significance of intervention in reframing organizations.

Blumenfeld, Karen, Ralph Earle III, and Frank Annighofer. 1992. "Environmental Performance and Business Strategy." *Prism* (Fourth Quarter). Cambridge, MA: Arthur D. Little.

Paper reviews how environmental performance is becoming an increasingly important criterion by which stakeholders, such as governments and local communities, view companies. Outlines how management can learn to identify the strategic environmental issues that will affect their operations and design a response.

Boulding, K. 1956. "General Systems Theory—The Skeleton of Science." *Management Science* 2 (3): 197–208.

This paper considers different forms of systems in the world and the capacity of humans to understand and model these systems. The paper draws the conclusion that models based on mechanical systems have often been used inappropriately as the basis for interpretation of human organizational systems.

Brundtland, G. 1987. "Our Common Future." In *The Report of the World Commission on Environment and Development*. New York: Oxford University Press.

This report for the United Nations articulates the concept and implications of bringing environment and development issues together under the integrating concept of sustainable development. No discussion of sustainable development or the sustainable enterprise can progress without an appreciation of the span and vision of this report.

Carroll, A.B. 1989. *Business and Society: Ethics and Stakeholder Management.* Cincinnati: South Western Publishing Co.

Carroll uses this book to link ethics, stakeholder management, and corporate social responsibility. It is intended as a course text for students of business and society or similar courses. Even so, its value is in articulating how a corporate responsibility approach to business is essentially a strategic position on ethics, which obliges the explicit use of techniques like stakeholders analysis and management.

Cramer, Jacqueline, Kurt Fischer, and Johan Schot. 1991. "Summary Report: First International Research Conference." *The Greening of Industry Network.* Tufts University, Medford, MA: Greening of Industry Network.

Summary of proceedings of the first Greening of Industry Network Conference, The Greening of Industry: Research Needs and Policy Implications. The summary contains an excellent review of the papers presented, along with future challenges for research and corporate and governmental policy.

Canadian Standards Association (CSA). 1993. *A Guideline for a Voluntary Environmental Management System.* CAN/CSA Z750. Toronto: CSA.

This draft discussion document sets out the general principles for an environmental management system that links quality and principles of environmental thinking and management. Presents the front end of a series of guidance documents on the more detailed aspects of environmental management systems.

Dechant, Kathleen, and Barbara Altman. 1994. "Environmental Leadership: From Compliance to Competitive Advantage." *Academy of Management Executive* 8 (3): 7–20.

Discusses the integration of environmentalism in leading companies and focuses on the more proactive examples. Forces for greening (defined as staying ahead of regulations, stakeholder activism, and competitive pressures) and best practices for environmental leadership are identified. The practices that are discussed are either outwardly oriented—reaching out to local communities and stakeholders—or focus on internal organizational processes such as quality management and green product and processes redesign. The article ends with an appeal for environmental leadership instead of defensive reactions to environmental issues.

Deloitte, Ross, Touche. 1991. *The DRT International 1991 Survey of Managers' Attitudes to the Environment.* Amsterdam: DRT.

———. 1990. *The Environmental Transformations of U.S. Industry: A Survey of U.S. Industrial Corporations.* Amsterdam: DRT.

DRT's review of corporate responses to the environment, based on a questionnaire completed by 250 mainly European companies covering 16 countries (1991) and 80 U.S. companies (1990). Reviews how attitudes vary between different countries and industries, internal company attitudes, the factors that shape company environmental policies, and how companies deal with environmental issues.

Fischer, Kurt, and Johan Schot. 1993 (eds.). *Environmental Strategies for Industry: International Perspectives on Research Needs and Policy Implications.* Washington, DC: Island Press.

This book brings together a number of essays based on papers given at the first conference of the Greening of Industry Network, held in the Netherlands in 1991. The chapters range from theoretical explorations of the meaning of greening, through the internal reorganization of firms in the face of environmental change, and on to discussion of the firm as part of social, public policy, and industrial networks. The book takes care to identify the research and policy agenda to emerge from the essays and the conference from which they were drawn.

Freeman, R.E., and D.R. Gilbert. 1988. *Corporate Strategy and the Search of Ethics*. Englewood Cliffs, NJ: Prentice Hall.

This book places the issue of values and ethics at the center of the strategic management process. It argues the inadequacy of mechanical models of strategy making and suggests the need to have values more explicitly focused in strategic decision making and strategy implementation.

Frosch, R.A. 1992. "Industrial Ecology: A Philosophical Introduction." In *Proceedings of the National Academy of Science 1992*. Washington, DC: National Academy of Science.

This paper sets out ideas about the interdependencies of industries through the flow of material and energy. Frosch argues that a new mindset is needed for the analysis and operation of industrial systems that are linked through flows of materials and energy. This industrial–ecological mindset is necessary to help firms work together to reduce their total environmental impact through more-efficient use of resources.

GEMI. 1991. *Corporate Quality/Environmental Management*. Proceedings of the First Conference of the Global Environmental Management Initiative. Washington, DC: GEMI.

This proceedings of the first Global Environmental Management Initiative explores the relationship between environmental management and total quality programs across the range of corporate functions. It offers a total quality management practitioner's perspective.

Gladwin, Thomas. 1993. "The Meaning of Greening: A Plea for Organizational Theory." In *Environmental Strategies for Industry*. K. Fischer and J. Schot (eds.). Washington, DC: Island Press.

An analysis of the greening of industry drawing on practical and conceptual ideas. The chapter sets out and examines different theoretical views of greening. The author relates these ideas to concern about the nature of the sustainable enterprise.

Gray, B. 1989. *Collaborating*. San Francisco: Jossey-Bass.

This book examines the process and basis for collaboration among organizations. The book is less focused on business collaboration and more on multiparty, multisector collaboration, although it does set out generic principles.

Hall, Sue, and Gemini Consulting. 1992. *The Environment: A Strategic Growth Opportunity.* Underwood, WA: Strategic Environmental Associates.

Analysis of the environmental market restructuring in the U.S. chemical industry, and the opportunities this offers companies to gain competitive advantage. Draws on findings from a comprehensive survey undertaken by Gemini Consulting of the U.S. chemical industry to outline the extent to which companies have recognized this opportunity. Founded on the work of Hamel and Prahalad with their strategic intent and core competence approach. Presented at the Chemical Week Conference, October 1992.

Hall, Sue. 1995. "Sustainable Partnerships." *In Context* No. 41.

Hall, Sue, and Eric Ingersoll. 1994. "Leading the Change: Competitive Advantage from Solution-Oriented Strategies." In *EcoTech Conference Proceedings, 1994.* Snowmass, CO: Rocky Mountain Institute.

Outlines a paradigm linking companies' abilities to gain competitive advantage from environmental market restructuring to their abilities to develop learning relationships with stakeholders. Analysis of the competitive benefits arising from this approach and the longer-term transformation of industry practices that these leading companies catalyze. Founded on Hamel and Prahalad's strategic intent and core competence approach and Senge's insights on learning networks.

Hall, Sue, and Malcolm Salter. 1992. *Conoco's "Green" Oil Strategy.* Cambridge: Harvard Business School.

————. 1993. Block 16: *Conoco's Green Oil Strategy.* Cambridge: Harvard Business School.

Detailed analysis of the role that complex stakeholder relationships play in the formation of company policies and competitive positioning. Designed as a role-play learning exercise among the four principle constituency groups—Conoco, environmental groups, indigenous communities, and the Ecuadorian government. Participative, experiential learning exercise.

Hamel, G., and C. Prahalad. 1989. "Strategic Intent." *Harvard Business Review* (May-June): 63–76.

This paper argues the need for new strategic management that harnesses ideas and ambitions arising throughout a company. "Strategy" in this approach is defined as strategic intent that provides a leadership vision and a framework within which the whole organization can respond.

Hawken, Paul. 1993. *The Ecology of Commerce*. New York: HarperBusiness.

Offers a vision on which to found sustainable business practices, based on the creation of the "restorative economy." Suggests that we will need to design an economy that acknowledges and embraces nature's laws, since we cannot break them. Draws on a systematic understanding of the ecological economic system to provide a road map for businesses to move toward sustainability "based on a radical vision from a hardnosed business man."

Hutchinson, Colin. 1992. "Corporate Strategy and the Environment." *Long-Range Planning* 25: 9–21.

Addresses the changes that occur in environmental strategy when the move is made from threat to opportunity. Assesses the challenge as companywide, and proposes steps for companies to develop sustainable strategies. An important point brought forward is the necessity of asserting company values by involving all levels of employees. Product strategy as an element of sustainable development is also discussed. Stresses the need for integrated change of organizational processes.

Kahane, Adam. 1992. "Scenarios for Energy: Sustainable World *vs.* Global Mercantilism." *Long-Range Planning* 25: 38–46.

This article outlines two scenarios, or alternative presentations of the future, prepared in the Group Planning Coordination of Shell International Petroleum Company. In the "Global Mercantilism" scenario, the energy industry faces new rules and continuous reconfiguration of markets. In the "Sustainable World" scenario, it faces sharp increases in the value of clean fuels and processes relative to dirty ones and in the cost of its operation, as well as a substantial restructuring of the industry. The purpose of the scenarios is to recognize signals of change, making it possible to respond quickly and appropriately.

Lent, Tony, and Richard Wells. 1992. "Corporate Environmental Management: Study Shows Shift from Compliance to Strategy." *Total Quality Environmental Management* 1:4.

Article outlines how the environment is becoming a strategic issue for companies, drawing on data-based questionnaire responses from 41 Fortune 500 companies, designed by Lent and Wells of Abt Associates.

Lovins, Amory. 1994. "Supercars: The Next Industrial Revolution." In *EcoTech Conference Proceedings, 1994.* Snowmass, CO: Rocky Mountain Institute.

Review of the way in which long-term environmental trends are reshaping the auto industry's response to car design, drawing on Lovins' extensive involvement with key energy and auto industry players through the Rocky Mountain Institute.

Lynn, F., and C. Chess. 1994. "Community Advisory Panels Within the Chemical Industry: Antecedents and Issues." Greening of Industry Network special issue. *Business Strategy and the Environment* 3:2.

This paper examines the emerging role of community advisory panels in the interpretation of the Responsible Care Program by the U.S. Chemical Manufacturers Association. It explores the way these panels are established and advises chemical companies on local environmental concerns.

Management Institute for Environment and Business (with U.S. EPA). 1994. *The Competitive Implications of Environmental Regulations: A Study of Six Industries.* Washington, DC: MEB.

Study of the relationship between country regulations and company/ industry competitiveness, undertaken in collaboration with Michael Porter and Claus van der Linde. Detailed analysis of six industries from paints and coatings through pulp and paper. Emphasis on understanding regulatory impacts on technology development and competitive implications. Forms analytical foundations of forthcoming article by Porter and van der Linde to follow up on Porter's original *Scientific American* article (see Porter 1991).

McKinsey and Company. 1991. *The Corporate Response to the Environmental Challenge: Summary Report.* Amsterdam: McKinsey and Company.

Review of questionnaire findings from McKinsey's survey of over 400 senior executives spanning six industry sectors across the globe. Investigates executives' recognition and understanding of the environmental challenge, their readiness to act, and the kind of partnerships they seek to build in the broader policy arena.

Morgan, G. 1986. *Images of Organizations*. London: Sage Publications.

This text draws on metaphorical analysis to provide depth and understanding to perspectives of organizations. Valuable insight into the interaction of business and the environment is provided by the notion of autopoeisis and its relationship to egocentric and systematic wisdom.

Porter, Michael. 1991. "America's Green Strategy." *Scientific American.* 24 (4): 168.

Porter provides a preliminary viewpoint on the relationship between the stringency of a country's environmental regulations and its impact on the competitiveness of its industries and nation. He argues that stronger regulations result in long-term sources of competitive advantage.

Roome, N. 1992. "Developing Environmental Management Strategies." *Business Strategy and the Environment* 1 (1): 11–24.

This paper considers alternative strategic positions for companies responding to environmental issues. It distinguishes these positions in terms of their characteristics and the changes required to achieve each of these options—for example, marginal changes to incorporate environmental tools and techniques; structural change to integrate environmental management systems; and fundamental change to develop values that support excellence in environmental and commercial performance.

Roome, N. 1995. *The Environmental Agenda—Promoting Sustainable Practice Through Higher Education Curricula: Management and Business.* London: Pluto Press.

This monograph considers the changes in higher education curricula needed to progress toward more sustainable practices. The monograph focuses on the management and business curriculum. However, the monograph is part of a broader series of publications which consider change across the range of higher education curricula, including management, engineering, science, humanities, as well as adult and continuing education. It advocates education that is more systemic, interdisciplinary, and values-based than current practice.

Roome. N. 1994. "Business Strategy, R&D, and Environmental Imperatives." *R&D Management* 24 (1): 65–82.

This paper outlines connections between the strategic planning of firms and the strategic importance of environmental issues in research and development. It identifies the importance of matching learning networks, involving many different stakeholders, with learning techniques that enable the environmental impacts of new technologies to be assessed.

Schmidheiny, S. 1992. *Changing Course.* Cambridge, MA: MIT Press.

This text was prepared by the author and the Business Council for Sustainable Development as a contribution to the debate about sustainable development at the Earth Summit. It contains chapters that rehearse the issues for business deriving from sustainable development. It then reviews a series of case studies of practical steps taken toward sustainable development by business.

Schwartz, Peter. 1991. *The Art of the Long View.* 1st ed. New York: Currency/Doubleday.

Review of scenario planning techniques originally developed by the Royal Dutch Shell Group and subsequently applied by Schwartz with several companies and government organizations. Informed by case experience, Schwartz offers a broad conception of practical "how to" approaches for developing scenario planning.

Senge, P. 1992. "Systems Thinking and Organizational Learning: Acting Locally and Thinking Globally in the Organization of the Future." *European Journal of Operational Research* 59 (1): 137–150.

Senge's paper examines the notion of the learning organization and the need for managers to become systems thinkers. Collaborative action research is seen as the structural mechanism that will enable systems thinking and learning to be translated into implementation.

Sethi, S. 1975. "Dimensions of Corporate Social Responsibility." *California Management Review* 17 (3): 58–64.

Sethi's paper reviews the reasons that propel a company to move beyond compliance with its legal obligations to the environment. From this review, he creates a typology of forms of corporate social responsibility.

Shrivastava, P. 1992. "Corporate Self-Greenewal: Strategic Responses to Environmentalism." *Business Strategy and the Environment* 1 (3): 9–21.

This paper emphasizes the interdependence of economic and ecological systems and the need to enter a process of organizational transformation based on those interdependencies. It suggests three strategic options for firms—managing business portfolios, managing risks and liabilities, and organizational restructuring.

Simmons, P., and B. Wynne. 1993. "Responsible Care: Trust, Credibility, and Environmental Management." In *Environmental Strategies for Industry.* K. Fischer and J. Schot (eds.). Washington, DC: Island Press.

> This analysis examines the way the U.K. Chemical Industry Association is developing the responsible care program in an effort to regain social trust and to advance the credibility of the industry.

Smart, Bruce, and World Resources Institute. 1992. *Beyond Compliance: A New Industry View of the Environment.* Washington, DC: World Resources Institute.

> Review of management challenges in moving "beyond compliance" in a strongly case-oriented format. Brief mention of Shell's scenario planning initiatives.

Stead, W.E., and J.G. Stead. 1992. *Management for a Small Planet: Strategic Decision Making and the Environment.* London: Sage Publications.

> This book takes a broad perspective on established management and strategic paradigms. It brings together a range of ideas concerning the way we think about organizations, the goals and values of managers, and the needs of the earth. It offers a vision of the ingredients of strategies for sustainability and then moves into a debate about possibilities for achieving sustainability through total quality management.

Steger, Ulrich. 1993. "The Greening of the Boardroom: How German Companies Are Dealing with Environmental Issues." In *Environmental Strategies for Industry.* K. Fischer and J. Schot (eds.). Washington, DC: Island Press.

> This chapter reports the results of a study of German companies, and it places their strategic positions on environmental management in a framework that relates market opportunities to environmental risks.

Stern, Alissa. 1991. "The Case of the Environmental Impasse." *Harvard Business Review* (May–June): 14–29.

> Stern investigates the relationship between an unnamed paper company's strategic decision regarding a new investment in tropical rainforest operations and their dialogue with a variety of environmental stakeholders. Reviews the interdependencies between these processes.

Includes commentaries and critiques from leading "experts" on the company's approach.

Stokke, P., *et al.* 1992. "Visioning (and Preparing for) the Future: The Introduction of Scenario-Based Planning in StatOil." *Technological Forecasting and Social Change* 40: 73–86.

This paper examines the development and use of scenario-based forecasting techniques as applied by the energy company StatOil.

Trist, E. 1983. "Referent Organizations and the Development of Interorganizational Domains." *Human Relations* 36 (3): 269–284.

A seminal work on organizational responses to turbulent environments and the need for interorganizational structures to help dampen that turbulence.

Walley, Noah, and Bradley Whitehead. 1994. "It's Not Easy Being Green." *Harvard Business Review* (May-June): 46–52. See also 12 responses in "The Challenge of Going Green," *Harvard Business Review* (July-August): 37–50.

The authors, McKinsey consultants, question the win-win strategy as cheap environmental rhetoric. They argue that real economic costs are attached to reaching the ambitious goals now set in environmental policy and that companies are not necessarily better off when they are leaders in the environmental field. Thus, it is argued that the shareholder value of company strategies should be placed before environmental emission-reduction targets. The article drew many responses in the subsequent issue of *Harvard Business Review.* The combination of the Walley and Whitehead article and the subsequent discussion provides a broad array of pros and cons of a more advanced environmental awareness for management.

Winsemius, Peter, and Ulrich Guntram. 1992. "Responding to the Environmental Challenge." *Business Horizons* (March-April).

Provides a conceptual framework to outline companies' responses to the environment across several stages of policy development. Provides a parallel framework for government environmental policies, again using a series of development "stages" that closely tracks the corporate responses. Suggests that company and government policy making are interdependent only to the degree to which they can progress through these "stages" in parallel. Basis for early McKinsey European environmental practice.

UNEP. 1994. "Company Environmental Reporting: A Measure of Progress of Business and Industry Toward Sustainable Development." In *United Environment Program—Industry and Environment*. Technical Report No. 24. Paris: United Nations Environment Programme.

This report reviews over 100 company environmental reports from around the globe. It provides an in-depth view of current standards and practices, concluding that few if any companies can yet claim to be sustainable as measured by their self-reported performance.

Vandermerwe, Sandra, and Michael D. Oliff. 1990. "Customers Drive Corporations Green." *Long-Range Planning* 23 (6): 10–16.

This article regards green customer pressures as important for directly and indirectly forcing change in business attitudes toward the environment. It examines trends such as the threat of "green products" from niche markets overtaking existing product positions, and increased acceptance of recycling and recycled goods. The necessary adjustments of doing business are related to marketing, advertising, and human resource management.

Chapter 2

Organization and Human Resource Management for Environmental Management

Ulrich Steger

Introduction

This essay emphasizes the need to integrate human resource management (HRM) and organizational aspects into environmental management in corporations. It explains how existing concepts and tools enable management to accomplish this task. The starting point is the need to apply concepts from organizational learning and organizational development and integrate environmental criteria into these processes. Compared to other areas covered in this bibliography the need to integrate environmental criteria, instead of just adding them to existing structures, is more encompassing because HRM and organizational structure are core elements of the building of corporate actions. There is no reason to build a separate environmental organization or create specialized HRM tracks for environmental management. The literature introduced in this essay is rather broad-ranging and goes beyond the boundaries of environmental management. The Anglo-Saxon debate on environmental management has neglected some important issues. Some aspects of the topic with which we deal here are, however, part of the generic debate on organizational learning and change (Mitroff 1994). In contrast, the HRM and organizational aspects play a key role in the German debate on environmental management (Meffert and Kirchgeorg 1993; Kreikebaum *et al.* 1994).

The Sustainable Corporation: The Paradigm of Integrated Environmental Management

In nearly all industrialized Western countries, three stages can be differentiated in the development of environmental policy (Serageldin 1993).

- In the late 1960s and early 1970s, environmental policy was focused on heavy polluters like power stations, refineries, and chemical plants, imposing "end-of-pipe" technology (EOP) in order to achieve emission reductions.

- In the 1980s, environmental policy was extended to nearly all branches of industry. This period can be characterized by the tightening of environmental standards and the introduction of waste management plans. All these measures, however, were still undertaken within a regulatory framework, based on the "command-and-control" approach, implying heavy use of EOP technology.

- Since the late 1980s, a new economic paradigm has emerged, that of sustainable development. It shifts the focus of environmental management from control to prevention, from EOP to clean technology, in order to achieve a decoupling between economic development and the use of nonrenewable resources and related pollution in a process of continuous improvement.

Additionally it can be argued that companies move along the different phases described, but in different ways. Moreover, according to Hunt and Auster (1990), these phases have implications for the development of environmental management as well as selectively chosen management attitudes. Hunt and Auster describe environmental management positions as beginner, fire fighter, concerned citizen, pragmatist, and pro-activist.

Innovation-Oriented Environmental Management

With regard to corporate requirements, this development basically implies a shift from compliance to an innovation-oriented approach to environmental management (Greening and Gray 1994). Like globalization or the introduction of new technologies, these changes in environmental policy demand an organizational learning and development process in a corporation. In such a process, new skills and qualifications are introduced and organizational structures and proceedings are changed in order to integrate environmental aspects into all functions and at all levels of the corporation (Habel 1993). Moreover, the organizational learning process includes changes

- in the corporate systems of basic values and objectives, the corporate culture, the way risks are perceived and opportunities are evaluated (Dierkes *et al.* 1993);

- in strategy formulation, to respond to emerging demands or a changing regulatory framework (Coyle *et al.* 1992);

- in the investment policy and decision making for technology options, with a preference for clean technology (Steger 1993);

- toward R&D policy for product development with criteria such as recyclability, energy conservation, and durability;

- in the operational implementation at the shop floor (Greening *et al.* 1994); and

- toward a complementary information-and-control system that collects relevant ecological information beyond its monetary bias and transfers it into operational criteria for decision making (Blundell *et al.* 1990).

The answer to the question of how this process of corporate evolution is organized and what skills and requirements are needed is very simple. All ideas are similar to other kinds of corporate development, such as globalization or changing technology, as will be shown in the following discussion.

One important factor in this development is the convergence of environmental management and the requirements of modern organizational management concepts (see Steger 1993 for more detail). In both cases you need flat hierarchies and a delegation of responsibilities, more cross-functional cooperation along the whole value chain of the corporation, and further, an open communication system with a free flow of information, rapid application of new technology, and a sense of responsibility for a larger community of stakeholders.

Traditional, hierarchical-functional, Tayloristic concepts of management turned out to be a greater impediment for integrated environmental management than concepts of lean management (Kreikebaum *et al.* 1994). Although this conclusion is difficult to prove empirically and is challenged in the literature, the main argument for it is the management of complexity. The management of complex systems like corporations requires a large organizational complexity in order to cope with the increased interaction and variables to be considered, which sometimes appear to be in conflict.

The concepts of organizational learning and development, which deal to a large extent with the management of complexity, can therefore be easily applied to sustainability, along with the integration of environmental criteria. (For an overview of the state of the art, see Argyris 1990; Dierkes *et al.* 1993; Habel 1993; and Sachmann 1991.) The appropriate responses to issues of resistance to change; incentives and pressure for a different organizational, as well as individual, behavior; uncertainty; conflicting interests and goals; and the arguments between reformers and status-quo defenders are identical within the relevant areas of corporate evolution. (The only exception might be that in some countries environmental issues are still ideologically controversial, which may lead to a learning blockade.)

The following description of organization and HRM as part of an integrated environmental management approach should be interpreted in this context.

Organization for Environmental Management

Environmental protection as an across-the-board task requires an analysis of the company as a whole in order that the potential for reducing costs and/or the environment-related strengths of the company can be recognized.

Applying Porter's Value Chain

The value chain developed by Michael Porter has proved to be a suitable instrument for this purpose (Porter 1986). For analyzing the corporation as a whole, Porter has redefined the instrument of the value chain. It represents a method of systematically analyzing and structuring all corporate activity and its relationships as a source of possible competitive advantages. The latter can be based either on cost advantages or on the possibility of differentiating the product of the corporation positively compared with its competitors—for example, through high product quality. Thus the relative strengths and weaknesses of a company can be determined.

The value chain can also be applied to environmental problems, and it must be extended to the complete life cycle of a product (Steger 1994). The value chain demonstrates the cross-functional organization needed for successful environmental management.

Figure 2-1 shows all relevant activities for the environmental management of the complete product life cycle within the framework of a value chain. Such a value chain

- allows transformation of the creation process of a product or service into individual activities and identification of strengths and weaknesses of the corporation, in environmental terms, in relation to its competitors;

- enables these to be traced back to their points of origin so that precise measures can be worked out in order to systematically eliminate faults or to build up strengths;

- provides for development of knowledge of environment-related value-creation potential, allowing a corporation to position itself strategically in the environmental area and to achieve clearer differentiation in comparison to its competitor; and

- provides measures that can be checked for appropriateness and consistency. Individual measures can quickly lose their benefit or even become counter-productive when they are not regarded as a part of a whole series of activities covering the complete value chain.

The value chain reflects the very important fact that every single activity at every level of the product life cycle is concerned with envi-

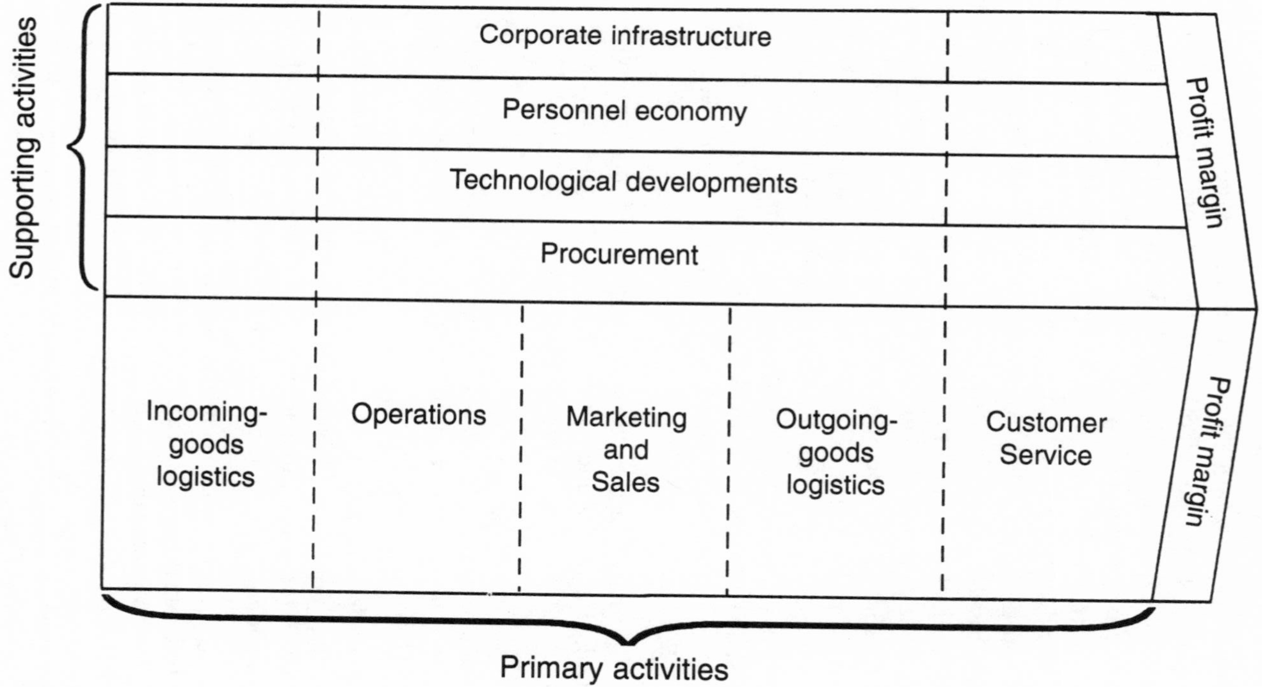

Figure 2-1
Model of a Value Chain

Source: M.E. Porter, *Competitive Advantage* (Frankfurt am Main and New York: The Free Press, 1986), 62.

ronmental questions. Thus environmental protection affects all corporate functions and has to be integrated into the individual task areas as a "natural" part in order to be effective. It implies organizational consequences with regard to structure and the routines arising out of them, to the creation of special positions, and to the employees themselves (Hastam 1991).

As the value chain indicates, the organization of integrated environmental management starts at the *beginning* of the pipe—the purchasing policy of the company. This means first of all that the employees are aware of environmental risks and motivated not to allow entrance of hazardous substances. This can be organized, for example, with checklists for purchasing criteria that include environmental issues or by sending questionnaires out to suppliers asking for specific information on environmental risks. In a second step, a closer cooperation with the supplier has to be organized in order to develop new input materials that substitute for hazardous materials in the production or recyclable parts for the product (Wagner 1992).

Environmental Management in Production

Environmental protection has to be integrated into production since the most visible environmental problems arise in this area. Environmental protection can be integrated in three terms (Karch 1992):

1. In a production concept including a strong focus on efficiency that avoids the waste of resources and materials and includes a permanent improvement process. In such a process, new know-how and proposals of the customers can be used to correct defects of products and processes. Thus an environmentally clean production can be achieved in a gradual but permanent process.

2. In a system assuring high quality of products and manufacturing processes. Both quality and environmental protection are not to be controlled but are integrated functional tasks. It is essential that environmental protection represents a further dimension of the multidimensional term "quality." It can often be regarded as an additional utility to the customer, as is the case when a product has to be durable and easily repaired or adapted, which extends the life cycle and reduces operational costs.

3. In an effective waste treatment and recycling system. Such a system includes the avoidance of waste, implying that environmental protection has already been considered in the design of the production process, the reuse of certain resources, and the recycling of products and materials. Therefore, separation and collection facilities have to be established.

Marketing

Environmental protection plays an increasingly key role in the marketing of products and services. Marketers were the first to acknowledge the importance of environmental aspects for the customer's buying decision. Thus environmental questions influence decisions on the basis of strategy, distribution, and communication of environmental advantages. Moreover, different forms of eco-sponsoring have been developed (Meffert and Kirchgeorg 1993).

Product Life Cycle

The development of a take-back or disposal system concludes the life cycle and enables the company to forge a convincing policy of environmental protection. The offer of a take-back of products after use by the consumer implies a total change of the character of a product: It becomes a service for which the corporation takes the total liability and guarantees its environmentally friendly production, use, distribution, and recycling or treatment (Steger 1994).

Besides the necessary upgrading of the environmental aspects of a product in a permanent improvement process, it becomes increasingly important to optimize the total product life cycle. That implies, however, that environmental aspects have to be considered in the R&D stage of the life cycle. The R&D process has to be changed from a science-based process to a target-group-based process. Weak signals have to be collected and transformed to allow for evaluation of the actual trends of the development in the environmental sector. These signals must be considered for ecological product differentiation with regard to environmentally friendly use and disposal (Blundell *et al.* 1990). Therefore interdisciplinary project groups have to be set up to allow for a more objective evaluation.

To ensure that environmental aspects are included in the decision-making process, a suitable information system has to be established. The main task of such a system is to provide the necessary information for decisions (Davis 1992). Therefore it should comprise the use of instruments that provide for recognition of weak signals or other instruments like life cycle analysis. A target-based information system including such instruments implies the use of quality and decision-making criteria (Shillito 1991).

Integrating Environmental Issues

A fundamental condition for the organization of environmental management of the product life cycle is the integration of environmental aspects into the goals, values, and culture of the corporation. The ability of a corporation to learn and to adapt to a changed environment is based on these goals. Empirical studies (Meffert and Kirchgeorg 1993) have demonstrated that

- Decentralized organizations have a structural advantage in managing environmental protection as an across-the-board task covering all functional areas (Argyris 1990). Such organizations are more skilled in coordinating matters horizontally since processes of reaching agreement form part of their daily tasks. However, this is not the case in strictly hierarchic and function-oriented corporations where managers see learning processes often as a sign of weakness or as mistakes. Creativity by subordinates and suggestions for solutions are perceived to be disruptive in such corporations.

- Flat hierarchies and open communication allow for a quick adaptation of individuals and the organization as a whole to new circumstances (Sietz 1994).

- The crucial question is the personal engagement of and the support given to the technical and management personnel entrusted with environmental tasks (Hastam 1991). The role of the "power promoter," which top management has to play in the environmental field, is one, if not the most important, organizational measure in environmental protection. As the "professional promoter" pushes environmental protection ahead with technical competence and zeal, she or he needs to be supported by the power promoter against

the lethargy of the organization. Only with such personal encouragement and visible examples of support from above will the
anchoring of environmental protection in the generic control level
be accepted and bolstered by the organization as a whole (Steger
1993a).

The culture, values, and goals of a corporation are the main factors influencing the organization of environmental management. An
additional factor for organizing environmental protection is that of
its overall compatibility with the existing organizational structures.
There is little sense in applying organizational rules to environmental protection that are different from those applied generally in the
corporation. Particularly with regard to integration, not just in terms
of content but also in terms of organization, it is clear that isolated
solutions should not be permitted for environmental protection. On
the other hand, organization for environmental protection should not
reinforce rigid and inefficient structures, but should help the organization to develop in an evolutionary manner (Steger 1993b).

Integrative Functions and Additive Functions

Taking these points into account, environmental protection can basically be organized in two different ways (Steger 1993a)—by integration into the existing organizational structure or as an additional
function. Supporting the former is the fact that environmental protection is an across-the-board task covering all functional areas of the
company. On the other hand, concentration on particular, additional
function posts (such as an environmental protection department)
would hinder the integration necessary, because the operative line-
managers would not feel individually responsible for environmental
protection. As a result, networked environmental protection activities
would not be worked out and developed (Sietz 1994). This would
reinforce the tendency to cure rather than to prevent environmental
problems and ensure that environmental protection remains a cost-
intensive additional task.

The fact that environmental protection tasks can only be subdi-
vided in part and require specific know-how and professionalism can,
however, be regarded as an argument for the functional-additive
organization (Kreikebaum *et al.* 1994). Furthermore, the environ-

mental activities in all areas have to be coordinated. Finally, self-monitoring of the corporation as a whole (for example, in the form of an environmental audit) requires a central post (Davis 1992). As can be seen from the above, both ways do not represent alternatives, but rather, the extreme positions at the ends of a continuum. Other factors influencing the decision on the form of organization of environmental management are more detailed in Steger (1993a):

- Legal requirements demanding additive organization for particular tasks (such as the environmental protection officer)

- The degree of exposure of the corporation in the area of environmental protection

- The state of development of environmental protection—for example, in early stages, it is easier to rely mainly on added functional posts. These posts, however, also have to promote the diffusion of environmental protection into the individual functional areas of the corporation. Thus the level of integration will gradually be increased.

There is, however, another way of solving the organizational problem of environmental management—by an overlaid organization. Environmental management can be separated into two types of tasks, routine and single tasks. For routine work, environmental management should be organized similar the company's normal structure, communication patterns, hierarchy, and so on. For single tasks, staff might be installed with an advisory function or as project groups or a project-matrix organization. In this way, it is assured that solutions are based on interdisciplinary decision processes. However, especially in the project-matrix organization, conflicts may occur concerning competencies or time schedules for co-workers (Greening and Gray 1994). Thus, a complete project organization within the company's normal organization bears many potential problems. Nevertheless, the advantages of this form, which can be seen in the change of members or the innovation support, are obvious (Steger 1993a).

Still, there is a possibility to combine both forms. For this, a steering committee should be installed where members of all departments with competence concerning power and know-how and with interest in eco-affairs will meet regularly. This committee selects environmental projects, determines group members, and is responsible for controlling and evaluation, for example. In short, this committee sets the margins and has to manage emerging conflicts. The project itself then will be performed by the project group. Routine work is integrated into the normal routine organization. That way, both requirements—being innovative as well as doing routine jobs—are fulfilled with this form of an overlaid organization.

To summarize, the author must admit that there is no clear best solution, but some sensible suggestions can be made. For tasks not connected with day-to-day business or general processes (such as collecting data, conducting eco-audits, or communicating with external groups), centralization tends to be the more suitable solution. Also, when implementing the subject for the first time, the functional-additive form corresponds better to typical problems such as overcoming the inertia of old structures, making employees sensitive to new ideas, or deciding when there is competition between two objectives—especially when the pressure to do something is nonexistent.

To conclude, beginning with centralization to start the process of diffusion with the help of someone with power promoting the project seems to be the best way. This is the base on which to build an integrated organization, where top management of course must promote both environmental activities and decentralization.

Human Resource Management in Integrated Environmental Management

The change in the organizational structure caused by globalization, introduction of new technologies, and environmental problems causes great challenges for the human resources of the company (Argyris 1990; Dierkes et al. 1993). Thus, human resource policy plays an increasingly important role in the management process. Empirical studies point to a great contrast between the existing goals of a company and the goals the company should pursue according to its younger management. Environmental issues are one area that companies should focus on much more than they do currently (Rosenstiel 1994). Human resource management demands and allows for an integration of environmental aspects in all its components.

Standards and Criteria

New standards for recruitment and selection of personnel, for both management and nonmanagement positions, become paramount. Employees will need the skills to perform in their present roles and the aptitude to develop those roles further (Karch 1992). They will need to be situation analyzers and decision makers, not automatons carrying out instructions. They will almost certainly need to be effective team members and team leaders, since so much of the activity of organizations requires teamwork. They will need to be people who are active learners, who relish change, who like experimentation, and who seek challenge and responsibility. People will be recruited and selected for their values as well as their abilities, for their preparedness to buy into visions of empowerment and shared responsibility. Managers and those selected for management advancement will need to be high on dimensions of caring, concern for the development of others, communications and listening skills, and team leadership skills (Karch 1992).

Environmental tasks represent a challenge for young people and thus an incentive to join a company. Therefore, criteria for the selection of personnel for the different environmental tasks have to be elaborated. Furthermore, job descriptions of every division should include information on the environmentally related tasks of the position (Rosenstiel 1994).

Creativity and Motivation

Integrated environmental management offers the opportunity to develop creativity and know-how and to increase the motivation of employees (Habel 1993). This is especially important with regard to the continuous improvement process and the improvement proposal system of a company. Many companies have extended their criteria for selection of improvement suggestions and have decentralized or reduced the decision-making process in order to motivate their employees and to achieve results similar to those of the Japanese Kaizen approach (Meffert and Kirchgeorg 1993). With regard to environmental improvement proposals, however, it is difficult to establish a monetary evaluation and reward system for avoidance of potential environmental risks. But these risks would have resulted in costs due to a probable accident if improvement measures were not taken. Some companies tried to solve this problem by paying an award for every improvement proposal with regard to environmental performance independently from its monetary effects (Rosenstiel 1994).

Another field where HRM should include environmental aspects is internal education and qualification (Karch 1992). Thus each member of the organization gets the opportunity to learn about the environmental activities of the corporation as a whole and to understand how his or her task is related to the overall policy (Hastam 1991). Furthermore not only can knowledge be taught but skills and attitudes can be developed. Such an education should be integrated in the training of apprentices as well as in the qualification of experienced stakeholders (Kreikebaum *et al.* 1994).

Finally, environmental protection can become a criterion of personal and professional evaluation. A problem arises, however, from the fact that this criterion cannot directly be measured by monetary indicators or quality standards. This problem of quantification is similar to judging the capability of a person to work in a team or to take responsibility (Shillito 1991). But all these criteria are essential for the development of young managers. As a first step, it is possible to evaluate the person, taking into account the number of improvement proposals, the support someone offers to the environmental protection officer, or the (voluntary) participation in qualification activities (Kieser and Wunderer 1994).

Environmental aspects should form part of the complete process of HRM: the recruitment, education, and evaluation of employees. With regard to qualification, however, it must be said that there is no pure environmental qualification that could meet the demands of integrated environmental management. On the contrary, such a managerial approach requires, in addition to an excellent specialization, key qualifications such as the ability to communicate with other specialists and to understand and structure new, complex problems in a short period of time (Steger 1994). Moreover, it is important to be able to make decisions allowing other people to understand and criticize them. Thus top management should use every environmental protection initiative to motivate and develop the personnel and to train young managers, especially in solving these complex problems. This implies that environmental protection is not just a question of knowing, but one of acting. It is important to change the attitude and the behavior of individuals and the whole organization toward this task. Excellent special knowledge and highly developed key qualifications are needed.

Barriers to the Development of a Sustainable Organization

The barriers to the organizational learning and development process toward an integrated environmental organization are as numerous as in other cases of innovation and organizational change. Out of the empirical research (with a certain German bias), the following issues seem pivotal:

- Lack of market or regulatory pressure to change processes and products and with them existing procedures and organizational patterns (Meffert and Kirchgeorg 1993)

- Monetary bias of the information system, reinforced by a corporate culture (which serves as a filter for information regarded as relevant), which encourages narrow, economistic, and short-term views on the changes in the markets and in the political framework (Sietz 1994)

- Uncertainty about the results of the new organizational structure, the cost of the transition, the change in power distribution, as well as the fear of a cultural revolution—a basic change in the company's identity and established relations inside and outside the company (Sachmann 1991)

- Concerns about the loss of well-regarded qualifications and know-how, fears whether one can adapt to the new requirements, and especially at the management level, whether one will be able to manage the increased complexity (Blundell *et al.* 1990)

- High personal identification with a structure (or product) one has helped to create and therefore a psychological rejection of any change (Dierkes *et al.* 1993)

- Difficulty in transforming a new vision or mission of a sustainable organization into a manageable process of corporate evolution, defining new operational goals, workable and more efficient processes and structures (Wagner 1992)

- Barriers from the organization itself—for example, when the structure is characterized by rigid hierarchies, resourcefulness and communication are impeded by lengthy information and decision-making processes (Steger 1994)

Open Research Questions

Open research questions can easily be derived from these obstacles to the transition toward a more sustainable corporation.

- What are the relevant features of corporate culture for promoting environmental responsiveness and the perception of ecological information?

- What are appropriate incentives or external leverages (for example, through the regulatory system) to accelerate organizational learning and to change toward a more integrated environmental approach?

- What are internal structures for promoting organizational learning and development in environmental issues?

- Is there a compelling requirement for an environmental organization in the company, or can the problems be managed by existing organizational concepts?

- What are appropriate management tools to handle the increased organizational complexity? This is especially interesting with regard to the combination of the environmentally empowered efforts of the employee with organizational priorities and focus.

- What is the interaction between environmental skills and qualifications on the one hand and organizational structure on the other? How does this interaction relate to organizational change?

- What is the role of trade unions, worker councils, and other stakeholders in the change to an integrated environmental organization?

Acknowledgments

I would like to thank Silke Brock, Evelyn Jakobs, and Thomas Teichler for their valuable and much appreciated help in the research for this essay.

Annotated Bibliography

Argyris, C. 1990. *Knowledge for Action: A Guide to Overcoming Barriers to Organizational Change.* San Francisco: Jossey-Bass.

This book may be regarded as the standard work for organizational learning. It covers the basic theory, the analysis of learning processes, and how to develop a larger learning capacity that allows the corporation to adapt more quickly to changing circumstances. The framework outlined can easily be applied to environmental issues, because from the structure, not necessarily the context, of the problems there is a strategic similarity with other learning issues, such as globalization or new technologies.

Blundell, W.R.C., J. Gandz, G.A. Peapples, I.D. Clark, J.E. Newall, D.H. Thain, D. Morton, J.R. McQueen, G. Relph, and J.M. Thompson. 1990. "Best Practices in Management." *Business Quarterly* 55: 69–120.

Several management topics are presented, including global competition, public administration, environmental responsibility, strategic management, management of technology, environmental management, industrial relations, information technology management, and training.

Coyle, S.W., R.S. Shirley, and B.D. Varchol. 1992. "CERCLA Integration with Site Operations—The Fernald Experience." *Government Reports Announcements* 6: 28–56.

A major transition in the Fernald Environmental Management Project (FEMP) site mission has occurred over the past few years. The production capabilities formerly provided by the FEMP are being transferred to private industry through a vendor qualification program. Environmental compliance and site clean-up are now the primary focus. In line with this program, the production of uranium products at the site was suspended in July 1989 to concentrate resources on the environmental mission. Formal termination of the FEMP production mission was accomplished on June 19, 1991. Environmental issues such as stored inventories of process residues, materials, and equipment are being addressed under the Comprehensive Environmental Response, Compensation, and Liability Act (CERCLA). The diversity of these hazards complicates the strategic planning for an integrated site clean-up program. This paper discusses the programmatic approach being implemented to ensure activities such as waste management, site utility and support services, health and safety programs, and Resource Conservation and Recovery Act (RCRA) programs are being integrated with CERCLA.

Davis, L. 1992. "How to Automate EPA Reports: Environmental Management 2000 Reporting Software from Software 2000 Inc." *Datamation* 38: 57–59.

Software 2000 Inc. produces Environmental Management 2000, an environmental regulation reporting software that runs on the IBM AS/400 and is compatible with IBM's System Application Architecture. Environmental Management 2000 helps managers meet requirements for reporting to the Occupational Safety and Health Administration and the Environmental Protection Agency. Environmental Management 2000 integrates with other Software 2000 products, such as Human Resources 2000 and Distribution Management 2000. The core of the modular Environmental Management 2000 system is Substance Master 2000, a database on hazardous materials. Modules include Hazardous Materials 2000, for compiling reports on the handling of hazardous materials and toxic substances; Industrial Health 200; Employee Safety Training, which tracks safety courses; and Industrial Hygiene and Sampling, which tracks readings taken by monitoring devices worn by employees. Prices for Environmental Management 2000 range from $25,000 to $100,000, depending on configuration.

Dierkes, M., L.V. Rosenstiel, and U. Steger (eds.). 1993. *Unternehmenskultur—Konzepte aus Ökonomie Psychologie und Ethnologie* (Corporate culture—conceptions from economy, psychology, and ethics/ethnology). Frankfurt am Main: Campus Verlag.

This book takes an interdisciplinary view (psychology, sociology, economics) at the function of corporate culture in creating meaning for the organization, providing a lens through which the world is perceived and which selects the relevance of information as a basis for decision making. It covers a comprehensive overview of the relevant literature, a delphi panel, and an elaboration of the limits of corporate culture to organizational learning.

Friedman, Frank B. 1992. "The Changing Role of the Environmental Manager." *Business Horizons* (March-April): 25–28.

The author makes a plea for integration of environmental management in all levels of management. Firms that make no effort to manage environmental affairs will manage poorly and incur great costs. Therefore, managers in the 1990s must cope with environmental issues now, because the costs of disregarding these issues are simply too high to ignore.

Greening, D.W., and B. Gray. 1994. "Testing a Model of Organizational Response to Social and Political Issues." *Academy of Management Journal* 37: 467–499.

The authors have developed and tested a conceptual model for explaining variability in the organizational structures of firms to help them identify, analyze, and respond to their social and political environments. Institutional and resource dependence theories offer plausible explanations for these structural differences. They tested both, finding that those explanations are distinct but complementary. Issues management is both an institutional response and a strategic adaptation to external pressures. But contrary to their predictions, each theory provided only a partial explanation by accounting for particular responses. Institutional constraints, especially in the United States, appeared to limit managerial discretion over corporate social responses. The authors propose a new contingency model of corporate social performance based on these findings.

Habel, M.J. 1993. "The Dynamics of Organizational Culture." *The Academy of Management Review* 18 (4): 657–693.

Corporate culture is changed primarily through intended and unintended learning processes. Top management efforts are only one of the many movers. The relevant factors—interaction with different segments of stakeholders and the structural conditions that shape the development of corporate culture—are analyzed in depth.

Hastam, C. 1991. *Environment Audit—A Complete Guide to Undertaking an Environmental Audit for Your Business.* London: Mercury-Books.

This manual allows for systematic checking on the adequacy of environmental management efforts within an organization and helps to identify targets for action. Each section deals with a specific aspect of the management of environmental affairs: policy and resources, operations, products, waste, emissions and discharges, energy, transport, people and tasks, land and premises, change, emergencies and special cases, and monitoring of feedback. In addition, each section contains guidance notes and checklists for the identification of environmental problems within enterprises.

Hunt, Christopher B., and Ellen R. Auster. 1990. "Proactive Environmental Management: Avoiding the Toxic Trap." *Sloan Management Review* (Winter): 7–18.

This article argues that firms need to be more aware of environmental problems. The current problematic nature of environmental issues leads corporations to neglect and undermanage such issues. The analysis centers around a description of managing environmental issues in five stages of environmental management program development. These phases are characterized in the following terms: (1) beginner, (2) fire fighter, (3) concerned citizen, (4) pragmatist, and (5) pro-activist. The authors make a case for environmental management as necessary for the long term and as a moral and business duty to protect long-term business interests—at the same time as protecting customers and the environment.

Karch, K.M. 1992. "Getting Organizational Buy-in for Benchmarking: Environmental Management at Weyerhaeuser." *National Productivity Review* 12: 13–23.

Environmental management at Weyerhaeuser Co. was the target of a benchmarking effort for improvement. At the time of the effort, literature and studies in benchmarking were unavailable, and Weyerhaeuser had to develop its own system. They formulated a plan designed to achieve performance improvement in competition with others. The key issues in the process were leadership, education, teamwork, benchmark functions and variables, support, company visits, and acquisition of independent data. This was the basis for restructuring of Weyerhaeuser's environmental policies.

Kieser, A., and R. Wunderer. 1994. *Handworterbuch der Führung.* Stuttgart: Haupt Verlag.

This handbook gives a general overview of all aspects of leadership in corporations, including the environmental dimension.

Kreikebaum, H., E. Seidel, and H.K. Zabel (eds.). 1994. *Unternehmenserfolg durch Umweltschutz* (Being a successful company by doing pollution reduction). Wiesbaden: Gabler Verlag.

This book opens with an overview of the general features and political, educational, and theoretical frameworks of successful environmental management. This is followed by a more specific discussion of functional implementation and corporate environmental management issues. A short overview of relevant case studies of successful environmental management is provided.

Meffert, H., and M. Kirchgeorg. 1993. *Marketorientiertes Umweltmanagement: Grundlagen und Fallstudien* (Market-oriented management: Basics and case studies) 2. Auflage, Stuttgart: C.E. Poeschel Verlag.

This book presents an excellent overview of how companies might behave and develop when facing environmental challenges. A theoretical presentation is supported by case studies. The relationships between economy, ecology, and environmental issues in economic research are presented. Further discussion concentrates on strategic questions of marketing and implementation of ecologic aspects as planned change of organizations. Case studies concerning environmental marketing in different markets like consumer goods, investment goods, and so on are presented and discussed.

Mitroff, Ian. 1994. "Crisis Management and Environmentalism." *California Management Review* (Winter): 101–113.

Mitroff argues that a series of issues that have developed over the last few decades can be analyzed together because of what they demand in terms of organizational capacity and management strategy. Mitroff identifies six of these issues as crisis management, issues management, total quality management, environmentalism, globalism, and ethics. These six areas are argued to be an essential part of all employees' jobs: no specialized departments should be set up. The functions are interrelated in that they provide input to the other functions as well as needing the output from them. It is argued that these six functions should be managed as one integrated system.

Norgaard, Richard B. 1988. "Sustainable Development: A Co-Evolutionary View." *Futures* (December): 606–620.

According to the author, it is possible to organize the challenges of sustainable development around three themes. First, modernization has been unsustainable because it has been supported by the use of hydrocarbon fuels and chemicals that are limited in availability and are damaging the environment. Second, political consensus and bureaucratic mobilization will be more difficult because we no longer believe that development is almost inevitable through the application of Western science. Third, we are shifting from a mechanical to a co-evolutionary understanding of systems, which helps explain why development has been unsustainable and what we must do to attain sustainability.

Pearson, Christine M., and Ian I. Mitroff. 1993. "From Crisis Prone to Crises Prepared: A Framework for Crisis Management." *Academy of Management Executive* 7 (1): 48–59.

This article discusses the manner in which organizations are prone to producing their own crises. The idea is to explain the chains of events and structures that have led to such disasters as Bhopal and the *Exxon Valdez* oil spill. Types of crises are identified, and the phases in which a crisis may develop are described. An important aspect described is the need to be aware of systems effects and the role of stakeholders in a potential crisis. It is argued that executives in organizations need to learn and adapt their organizations continuously to avoid crises and deal with them adequately when they occur. Crisis management is an ongoing process of thinking creatively about the unthinkable.

Porter, M. 1986. *Competitive Advantage: Creating and Sustaining Superior Performance.* New York: The Free Press.

This book is about how a firm can create and sustain a competitive advantage. It reflects the belief that the failure of many firms' strategies stems from an inability to translate a broad competitive strategy in the specific action steps required to gain competitive advantage. The concepts in the book aim to build a bridge between strategy formulation and implementation, rather than treating the two subjects separately.

Rosenstiel, L. 1994. *Führungsnachwuchs im Unternehmen, Wertkonflikte zwischen Individuum und Organisation.* (Management succession, value conflicts between the individual and the organization). München: Beck Verlag.

Regarding the current situation on the labor market, even young academics have difficulty in finding adequate jobs after finishing their studies. The book deals with the question of whether there are specific characteristic features or not which improve someone's chances on the labor market; and how the first experiences, both positive and negative, influence someone's attitudes.

Sachmann, S. 1991. *Cultural Knowledge in Organizations: Exploring the Collective Mind.* Newbury Park, CA: Sage Publications.

Coping with environmental issues through an integrated approach and working toward a "sustainable" company means changing corporate values as well as developing new goals and structures. Therefore, to practice successful environmental management, a basic understanding of how organizations learn and evolve must be gained by practitioners and researchers alike. The cited literature delivers a state-of-the-art survey on this topic and can be easily applied to environmental questions.

Schulz, Erica, and Werner Schulz. 1993. "Environmental Controlling within Companies, Part I" (in German: Betriebliches Umweltcontrolling, Teil I). *Umwelt Wirtschafts Forum* 3 (September): 19–24.

———. 1994. "Environmental Controlling within Companies, Part II" (in German: Betriebliches Umweltcontrolling, Teil II). *Umwelt Wirtschafts Forum* 4 (January): 9–14

Today nearly every company acts within the "stress frame" of ecological and economic objectives. Companies face threats, but also opportunities. Well-known "eco-losers" are producers of asbestos materials and CFCs. On the other hand, companies that are active in the fields of eco-friendly products and technologies become "eco-winners." The authors describe in Part I how to apply operational and strategic controlling to environmental matters within companies' risk–profit management. In Part II they show two important aspects of environmental controlling: (a) "costs of environmental protection in a firm" and (b) "strategic environmental controlling."

Serageldin, I. 1993. "Making Development Sustainable." *Finance-Development* 30: 6–11.

The 1992 Earth Summit, held in Rio de Janeiro, roused the conscience of the world to the urgency of achieving "environmentally sustainable development," defined as "meeting the needs of the present generation without compromising the needs of future generations." However, any effort to achieve this goal will fail if it does not integrate the viewpoints of three disciplines: economics, ecology, and sociology. The contributions of economists are important since their methods seek to maximize human welfare within the constraints of existing capital stock and technologies. The views of ecologists should also be considered because they focus on preserving the integrity of ecological subsystems essential to the stability of the global ecosystem. The perspective of sociologists is likewise essential given the importance of social factors in the development process.

Shillito, David. 1991. "Environmental Protection." *Chemical Engineering* 499: 14–28.

This article explains the managerial philosophy behind BS 5570 (British Standard), which heavily influenced the design of the European Eco-Audit Guideline, especially in standardization of processes and compliance with regulations. Along with corporate environmental policy, the requirements of the standard include definition and documentation of an inventory of releases, wastes, and energy and raw materials usage; inventory of legislative and regulatory requirements; assessment of environmental effects; formation of objectives and targets; environmental management plans; management manual, documentation, and records; internal environmental audits, an audit plan, reports, and follow-ups; specific requirements for control, verification, and testing; personnel factors of awareness, training, and qualifications. The standard is intended for use by all types of organizations. (However, experience so far indicates that small and medium-sized firms have difficulties in applying the standard.)

Sietz, Manfred (ed.). 1994. *Umweltbewußtes Management* (Environmental management) 2. Auflage vollständig neu bearbeitet. Taunusstein: Blottner Verlag.

This text focuses on changes of corporate structure in relation to patterns of communication and the external world. Information systems are discussed in terms of how they can serve for risk-reduction strategies. A very valuable guide for practitioners that delivers a "hands-on" approach with checklists and practical recommendations for implementing environmental management, especially concerning eco-auditing schemes.

Steger, Ulrich (ed.). 1993a. *Handbuch des Umweltmanagements—Anforderungs und Leistungsprofile von Unternehmen und Gesellschaft* (Handbook of environmental management—Profiles of requirement and performance concerning companies and society). Wiesbaden: Gabler Verlag.

This book examines the environmental problem from the corporate point of view, as well as society's. Requirements and responsibilities of these interest groups are discussed in detail. Chapters treat organization of environmental issues from different points of view. An introduction to ecologic problems in general and their interdisciplinary character is provided. The book concentrates on the political and market framework that companies have to face. A detailed map of significant components that are prerequisite for successful environmental management is developed. Examples of environmental management practiced within the German corporate world are used to support the author's conclusions.

Steger, Ulrich. 1993b. *Umweltmanagement—Erfahrungen und Instrumente einer umweltorientierten Unternehmensstrategie* (Environmental management—Experience and tools for an environmentally oriented strategy) 2. Auflage, Wiesbaden: Gabler Verlag.

In this publication, the reader will find an overview of all essential aspects of environmental management—from the first step of implementation to requirements of integration and strategic development. The author details the surroundings and frameworks of environmental management from diverse points of view. He then concentrates on strategic and normative questions concerning environmental management. Tools of strategic management are also presented.

Steger, Ulrich. 1994. "Umweltorientiertes Management des gesamten Produktlebenszyklus" (Environmental management across the whole product life cycle). Schmalenbach-Gesellschaft Deutsche Gesellschaft für Betriebswirtschaft (The German Association for Management Science) (eds.). Unternehmensführung und externe Rahmenbedingungen Kongress Dokumentation, 47. Stuttgart: Verlagsguppe Handelsblaht.

This document contains the keynote speeches and research papers presented at the 47th annual conference of the German Society for Business Administration. Of the papers examining environmental issues, many focus on marketing and information, management of and across the whole product life cycle, logistics, eco-auditing, and perspectives for further development of the regulatory framework.

Wagner, Gerd Rainer. 1992. *Ökonomische Risiken und Umweltschutz* (Economic risks and pollution reduction). München: Vahlen Verlag.

This book discusses the integration of risk reduction strategies and environmental issues. Especially interesting are an essay written by Ursula Hansen about the ethical aspects of risk and one written by Herwig Hulpke on management of conflicts.

Chapter 3

Strategic Cooperation and Life Cycle Analysis

Julie L. Hass
Peter Groenewegen

Introduction

A number of different governments' environmental agencies have recently started to influence businesses in a new manner. These government initiatives are forcing companies to look beyond their immediate boundaries and to encompass a wider perspective. Businesses are having to find mechanisms for responding to these initiatives. The concept of interorganizational cooperation and the methodology and tools of life cycle analysis are some of the mechanisms that businesses are developing in response to these government initiatives.

One example of a government initiative that forces businesses to look beyond their immediate boundaries is the requirement of the Dutch Environmental Policy Plan, which calls for proactive action by business to help close materials cycles (NEPP 1989). In a number of other European countries, with Germany as one of the leaders (Hopfenbeck 1993; Responsibility for the Future 1994), the emergence of the waste crisis has been a major factor in the passing of stringent regulations toward waste producers. These regulations essentially hold the producers responsible for their product waste. There is uncertainty, however, as to whether there are positive or negative environmental and economic outcomes as a result of these technology-forcing regulations (Brisson 1994).

One response by business to these governmental actions is to use a life cycle management approach toward products and in the design process. Adopting a life cycle management approach helps businesses to broaden their perspective and to look more systematically and holistically at products over their entire lifetime and not consider only the product manufacturing processes (the major focus of TQM and eco-efficiency approaches). Life cycle management forces companies to consider the entire spectrum, including product design, production, use, disposal, recycling, and/or reuse. There have been a number of initiatives to develop life cycle analysis methodologies and some moves toward codification (Chynoweth and Roberts 1992).

To encourage life cycle thinking specifically in design processes, a number of environmental agencies have initiated programs to help stimulate industry to establish green design projects (EPA 1993b). In addition to the various governmental interventions, industry itself is rising to the challenge and is increasingly thinking beyond narrow company interests to include other parts of the production chain as well as the wider community (Schmidheiny 1992).

In this climate, more systematic, "cradle-to-grave" types of approaches toward reducing environmental effects of business operations are becoming popular. Two distinct components of these approaches can be identified. The first component involves different types of cooperative efforts among companies related to environmental issues. The second component involves specific managerial instruments (life cycle management) and environmental information tools (life cycle analysis), which are required to determine the environmental effects over a product's entire life cycle. The integration of these two components into a single formulation is attempted in the development of concepts such as green design (EPA 1993b) and industrial ecosystems (Allenby and Richards 1994):

In this chapter, the discussion and references will focus on three major areas involving businesses and environmental issues:

1. Interorganization cooperation and network formation

2. Life cycle analysis (LCA), management, and "green" design tools

3. Linking life cycle analysis to interorganizational cooperation

In conclusion, there will be a brief discussion of the research needs and potential theoretical frameworks applicable to this area.

Cooperation and Network Formation

Interorganizational cooperation and environmental management standards have increasingly been proposed as the way forward for industry to reduce its burden on the physical environment (Schmidheiny 1992). These cooperative efforts can take a variety of forms, including industrywide initiatives such as the development of codes of conduct and standards for environmental management as well as more company-specific initiatives involving product channels and cooperation with nonindustrial partners. Two perspectives are being expressed: One involves a focused, often commercially linked perspective that includes both suppliers and customers within the supply channel, and the other involves a wider, heterogeneous network perspective that often includes noncommercial entities. The more focused, commercially linked perspective has been investigated in a number of studies. This research has focused on describing the changes that occur in production channels when more cooperative types of relationships develop.

Two studies propose managerial mechanisms aimed at improving interfirm cooperation. The first study introduces the concept of "product stewardship" from research done in the chemical industry (Dillon and Baram 1993). The second study, based on work in the wood preservatives, printing inks, cosmetics, and carpeting industries, proposes the idea of "environmental co-makership" (Cramer and Schot 1993). The Dutch government has also developed a managerial tool, known as "integrated chain management," to help in the implementation of their policies (NEPP 1989).

A third study, which focuses on the white goods industry, provides a theoretical discussion of interfirm cooperation with some empirical evidence (Roome and Hinnels 1993). The automobile industry has also begun to be analyzed using a wider network perspective. One study focuses on the integration of new entities, such as waste treatment organizations, into the automobile production system (Groenewegen and den Hond 1993; den Hond and Groenewegen 1993).

It has been argued that the interactions between (1) the networks that are focused and company specific and (2) the wider, more heterogeneous networks need to be assessed. For example, in a discussion of evolution of environmental cooperation on technology development in the chemical industry, a distinction is made between the technology networks, the environmental networks, and the production-oriented networks (Groenewegen and Vergragt 1991). A typology of wide network cooperations around the R&D function has been proposed by Winn and Roome (1993). Mitroff (1994) discusses the connections between crisis management and "environmentalism," which he considers a key function of business, from a managerial and systems approach. He links a number of different management functions together to indicate how they can complement each other and concludes that the best environmentally prepared organizations are often the best at being crisis prepared.

An even wider network perspective can be helpful when considering the contingent nature of firm behavior. Increasingly, a stakeholder approach is used. In this approach, firms consider their situation with respect to a variety of different groups such as workers, government regulators, communities close to production facilities, consumers, green pressure groups, and the public at large. A number of firms have found that increasing the dialogue with external stakeholder groups can help to reduce adversarial positions taken toward the company and that this dialogue process can also add valuable information and perspectives into the decision-making processes of the firm's managers. Schot (1992) proposes a stakeholder framework for analysis. He argues that companies should be regarded as coalitions within the firm boundaries, but that environmental coalitions extend across boundaries and pose a challenge to the credibility of the firm.

Other approaches are being suggested. For an in-depth discussion of cooperation between business and the public, see Chapter 4, "Industry Relationships with Communities: Business as Usual?" by Caron Chess and Frances Lynn.

Life Cycle Analysis, Management, and "Green" Design Tools

The field of life cycle assessment is developing rapidly both in terms of the methodology and in terms of its integration into emerging management tools. The terminology related to this field can be confusing, since a number of terms and abbreviations are used and interpreted in a variety of ways. Three key terms are eco-balances, life cycle assessment, and life cycle analysis (LCA) (Guinee *et al.* 1993a and 1993b). Two different yet related approaches are being taken. One approach is focusing primarily on the development of LCA methodologies and the other is focused on the integration of these LCA calculation processes into managerial tools. For comprehensive, technical, and managerial European source information, refer to the *LCA Sourcebook* (SustainAbility and SPOLD 1993).

The technical LCA tools are rapidly developing in a number of contexts, including work being performed by governments, industries, universities, and nongovernmental organizations. A number of helpful references for this material include Blumenfeld *et al.* (1991); Chynoweth and Roberts (1992); EPA (1993a, 1993b); Fouhy (1993); Guinee *et al.* (1993a, 1993b); and Rubik and Baumgartner (1992). A note about this growing set of literature: Although eco-balance is a fairly well defined component of the environmental management approaches used in many German companies, unfortunately most of the literature in this area is not particularly accessible to non-German readers.

In addition, analytical tools such as industrial metabolism, which use descriptions based on systems analysis to describe material flows through the economy, should be mentioned in this context (Ayres 1989; Allenby and Richards 1994).

The integration of the LCA methodologies into decision-support tools that managers can use is developing concurrently. The information that the technically oriented LCA calculations provide needs to be used by managers, but this linkage is problematic. While the LCA tools have applications in product labeling, including qualifying for different green label schemes and applications focusing on product comparisons, the methods also receive considerable criticism with regard to their applicability to decision-making processes at higher levels in companies. Since the LCA methodology involves such a broad and comprehensive inventory of environmental effects, it paradoxically provides too narrow a methodological focus to aid broader corporate decision making (Kooijman 1993). One example of the managerial decision-making frameworks is the Dutch chemical industry's three-phase decision-support tool using a concept called "integrated substance chain management." This tool was developed to provide a mechanism for consensus building within substance chains, and it includes both technical and more subjective information (VNCI 1991; Winsemius and Hahn 1992).

For more general managerial-related issues, Charlton and Howell (1993), Gray et al. (1993), Klassen (1993), Kooijman (1993), and Oakley (1993) provide a number of perspectives related to the use of LCA information.

Broadening the design process to include LCA information and to also consider product development, manufacturing, use, disposal, recycling, and/or reuse is being incorporated into the concept of green design. This approach is being supported by a number of governments—for example, the United States (EPA 1993b), the United Kingdom (Fairclough et al. 1993), and Germany (Responsibility 1994). Green design frameworks broaden the product design and development focus from a purely commercial focus to a product life cycle focus, which will hopefully provide a more informed basis for design. By initially designing products and processes using a life cycle perspective, pollution prevention becomes an inherent component in the process rather than an afterthought.

Life Cycle Analysis and Cooperation

In principle all these methodological tools may be significant for cooperation within industry; however, specific connections between these methodologies and the resultant interorganizational cooperation are only just beginning to develop. Strategic partnerships and other supply-channel interactions are slowly evolving.

One area in which LCA methodologies are starting to influence business decisions is in the purchasing of materials and in the screening of suppliers. A number of companies have used life cycle analyses to determine where the largest environmental impact is being made in the production of certain products. Once these major environmental impacts have been identified, some large companies have begun to require supplier information and audits concerning the manufacturing processes of the products being purchased. They are also ranking and selecting suppliers with respect to the supplier's environmental management and performance. Companies like BT, Scott Ltd. (Charter 1993), B&Q (Knight 1992), The Body Shop, IBM UK Ltd. (Taylor and Welford 1993), and Boots The Chemist have started to qualify and rank suppliers based on environmental criteria. Guidelines are also beginning to be developed by industry groups that will help purchasing departments know how to integrate environmental criteria into their purchasing practices (BiE 1992).

Although the outcome of methodological discussions will not necessarily assist in creating cooperation among different actors in the wider networks (companies, government agencies, and consumers) to ameliorate environmental problems, the methods do assist in improving the awareness of the relevant environmental impacts along different steps of the production chain. The emphasis given to the environmental improvement of products and processes might lead to improved mutual understanding and might also provide a rational and/or sufficing basis for interorganizational cooperation. The outcome of the methodological developments and of the discussions concerning the role of life cycle methodologies in decision-making processes could potentially influence the rationale and the shape of interorganizational cooperation involving environmental issues.

Research and Management Questions

Strategic cooperation and life cycle analysis are rapidly developing and are providing holistic approaches toward environmental management with developments occurring both with respect to the technical analysis tools and the managerial decision-support frameworks. These are active areas of current research; but looking to the future, there are a number of areas where additional research could provide insights, especially with a multidisciplinary perspective.

There are many issues surrounding the LCA tools—both technical and practical ones. There are debates concerning the use of LCA frameworks; it could be expected that work related to LCA will continue, especially as more and more information concerning products and processing inputs at various points in the manufacturing process becomes available through the establishment of LCA databases. With regard to the research focused on LCA tools and frameworks, much more attention is paid to rational methods of decision making and the technical tools, and very little focus is directed toward understanding the economic–political processes in which these tools are used.

As cooperation increases, especially among companies, a greater understanding of how LCA information is used in these situations could be of interest. In the literature, the actual form of coalitions is not well differentiated. It appears that these cooperations are expected either to simply fit into existing patterns seamlessly or that information exchange is supposed to be without costs. Neither of these situations is likely; therefore, the characterization of interorganizational relationships based on environmental criteria or motivations could be useful, since many cooperative ventures are conceptually elegant but practically infeasible. By researching both failures and successes of different types of ventures, the concepts of "product stewardship" and "environmental co-makership" could be more fully developed.

As supply channels become increasingly more integrated, supplier selection and de-selection with respect to environmental issues could also be of interest (Drumwright 1994). Trying to determine where the significant environmental impacts of products occur over a product's life cycle can depend heavily on the production processes of companies along the supply chain. The implications of their environmental management practices with respect to supplier status could become increasingly more important as environmental criteria become integrated into the supplier selection process.

Considering this topic from a more academic perspective, some theoretical frameworks or perspectives that may provide a basis for informing future research include systems thinking, networks, supply channel integration, organizational linkages, stakeholder analysis, social responsibility, environmental accounting and reporting, and strategic partnerships. In addition, the lack of contributions from an industrial economics perspective is particularly striking. Such studies could induce some realism into the current optimism. It also would allow for the assessment of technological consequences as well as competitive positions resulting from attempts to cooperate on environmental grounds. LCA and strategic cooperation related to the environment are rapidly developing fields that will continue to provide fertile ground for a wide range of research from perspectives including technical, managerial, organizational, and policy-oriented.

Annotated Bibliography

Allenby, Braden R., and Deanna J. Richards. 1994. *The Greening of Industrial Ecosystems*. Washington, DC: National Academy Press.

This book contains a collection of chapters that delineate the concept of industrial ecology. The approaches presented vary widely in their applicability to the subject of this chapter. Some of its contributions focus on the materials cycle while others deal with regulation and voluntary cooperation.

Ayres, Robert. 1989. "Industrial Metabolism." In *Technology and Environment*. Jesse H. Ausubel and Hedy E. Sladovich (eds.). Washington, DC: National Academy Press.

This essay can be regarded as the paradigmatic piece for the industrial ecology approach. Ayres argues that a change in the manner in which industry deals with materials and energy input and waste should be based on understanding the processes internal to the industrial ecosystem. The latter is roughly defined as the system of material flows and transformations.

Baram, Michael S., Patricia S. Dillon, and Betsy Ruffle. 1990. *Managing Chemical Risks: Corporate Responses to SARA Title III*. Medford, MA: The Center for Environmental Management, Tufts University.

This report examines compliance with and corporate response to the Emergency Planning and Community Right-to-Know Act (SARA Title III). The study directs attention to activities of companies that go beyond what is required by law and current standards for environmental performance. It focuses on accident prevention, emissions reduction, emergency response planning and risks communication, and public out-reach. The study is limited to case studies of eight firms producing or using a variety of chemicals. These cases were chosen to cover different environmental risks and life cycle characteristics. The study shows that SARA Title III had wide-ranging impacts both within companies and through the whole life cycle.

BiE (Business in the Environment). 1992. *Buying into the Environment: Guide-lines for Integrating the Environment into Purchasing and Supply.* London: BiE (8 Stratton Street, London W1X 5FD, UK).

As businesses become more integrated in supply channels, the relation-ships between buyers and suppliers can become a powerful lever to influence companies with respect to environmental issues. This publica-tion was developed by Business in the Environment in close cooperation with the Chartered Institute of Purchasing and Supply and a number of U.K. businesses. It is a practical guide that outlines seven principles for how businesses can incorporate environmental issues into their pur-chasing policies.

Blumenfeld, Karen, Ralph Earle III, and Jonathan B. Shopley. 1991. "Identifying Strategic Environmental Opportunities: A Life Cycle Approach." *Prism* (Third Quarter): 45–57.

This essay presents a systematic framework that links stages in strategy analysis to business; environmental analysis tools are presented. The four steps in the framework, called the Strategic Environmental Assess-ment Process, outline a procedure that companies can go through in developing strategic environmental initiatives. This model goes beyond just identifying four general analysis steps; it also identifies a number of tools to use at each step in the analysis process. According to this scheme, life cycle assessments are useful at Step 2 in the overall analysis process.

Step 1. Identifying key environmental issues.
         Tools: Issues analysis, regulatory monitoring, public policy research, customer research.

Step 2. Examining the environmental profiles of products or services.
         Tools: Life cycle assessments.

Step 3. Identifying competitive opportunities.
         Tools: Industry analysis, competitor analysis.

Step 4. Developing and implementing strategies.
Tools: Environmental value chain, environmental impact matrix.

Brisson, Inger. 1994. "Recycling Policies in Europe: Effective Responses to the Looming Waste Crisis?" *European Environment* 4 (3): 13–17.

This article discusses the recycling policies of four European countries: Germany, Austria, France, and the United Kingdom, examining the effectiveness of various government measures in the struggle to reduce waste. It is argued that measures such as the German take-back rules, which force industry to attend to life cycle management, might not be the environmentally most efficient manner for solving the waste crisis.

Charlton, Carol, and Belinda Howell. 1993. "Life Cycle Assessment: A Tool for Solving Environmental Problems?" *European Environment* 2 (2): 2–5.

Discusses the use of life cycle analysis in society and the main areas of application for product evaluation, product comparison, and evaluation of environmental politics.

Charter, Martin. 1993. "Scott Limited: Measuring Environmental Performance." *Greener Management International* (Issue 1) (January): 51–58.

Charter describes how Scott Ltd. has developed a supplier audit that has helped to identify suppliers which are not performing at an acceptable environmental level. It is reported that the ranking of suppliers has led to improved environmental performance and has helped Scott Ltd. to reduce the environmental impact of a number of its products. The power of the large purchaser is shown to be an effective method of forcing positive environmental changes through the supply chain.

Chynoweth, Emma, and Michael Roberts. 1992. "Green Pressures Force PVC to Take LCA Lead in Europe: Standard Methods Evolve for Ecobalances." *Chemical Week* 151 (20): 41–42.

Because of the focus on chlorine and dioxin by legislators, environmentalists, and industry, LCA of polyvinyl chloride (PVC) are being performed by a number of organizations. It was expected that the LCA information on PVC would introduce rationality into the debate surrounding PVC. However, since there is no generally accepted approach to LCA methodologies the debates continue and have even expanded to include discussions about the LCA methodologies themselves. Also included in this article are descriptions of a number of European and U.S. companies and organizations involved in developing LCA tools and methodologies and the efforts toward defining a generally accepted or even standardized LCA methodology.

Cramer, Jacqueline, and Johan Schot. 1993. "Environmental Comaker-ship Among Firms as a Cornerstone in the Striving for Sustainable Development." In *Environmental Strategies for Industry: International Perspectives on Research Needs and Policy Implications*. K. Fischer and J. Schot (eds.) 311–328. Washington, DC: Island Press.

Focuses on environmental information exchange among companies and on the setting of environmental requirements for suppliers. These two ideas are the main components of what Schot has proposed as "environmental co-makership" (see also Schot 1992). Two Dutch studies are described that present empirical data on willingness to exchange environmental information and information concerning companies' preparedness to work together with suppliers on environmental standards for products and production methods. From the empirical studies, the authors conclude that the current situation cannot yet be characterized as one in which environmental co-makership exists, but they envision this concept as taking on importance in the future with respect to designing sustainable business strategies.

Dillon, Patricia S., and Michael S. Baram. 1993. "Forces Shaping the Development and Use of Product Stewardship in the Private Sector." In *Environmental Strategies for Industry: International Perspectives on Research Needs and Policy Implications*. K. Fischer and J. Schot (eds.) 329–324. Washington, DC: Island Press.

Product stewardship is considered to be systematic company efforts to reduce product risks overall or in significant segments of the product life cycle. Voluntary efforts to increase the exchange of environmental and safety information along the product chain in the chemical industry are discussed. A significant effort is found within industry itself, due to external forces and market considerations, which develops an integration of environmental information into its dealings with customers, suppliers, and the public at large. It is recommended that governments should stimulate such developments without regulating too strongly or too quickly.

den Hond, Frank, and Peter Groenewegen. 1993. "Solving the Automobile Shredder Waste Problem: Cooperation Among Firms in the Automotive Industry." In *Environmental Strategies for Industry: International Perspectives on Research Needs and Policy Implications.* K. Fischer and J. Schot (eds.) 343–368. Washington, DC: Island Press.

The problem of automobile shredder waste is described and discussed in terms of the network structure of the automotive industry. Automobile manufacturers are not anxious to be connected with car dismantling or shredding companies since these waste handlers' practices are often viewed as being environmentally and/or legally questionable. Stricter legislation concerning waste disposal will require a better understanding and further development of the interorganizational linkages between the manufacturers and the disposal companies. A number of approaches being pursued by European car manufacturers are described and then classified into different types of strategy. The authors note that automobile recycling is very much in a developmental stage.

Drumwright, Minette E. 1994. "Socially Responsible Organizational Buying: Environmental Concern as a Noneconomic Buying Criterion." *Journal of Marketing* 58 (July): 1-19.

Drumwright's multiple–case study research has identified four types of organizational contexts for socially responsible buying (SRB) through the analysis of 35 different buying processes. The author addresses how and why SRB comes about in organizations. Two important factors are identified with respect to successful SRB initiatives: the presence of a skillful policy entrepreneur and the organizational context. A "Vendor Guide to SRB" is presented to help companies identify what type of SRB they are encountering from their industrial customers, and suggestions are made for vendor strategies to deal with each of the four types of SRB. The main contribution of this study is its perspective: It is using an industrial buying perspective and not a consumer behavior perspective with respect to a noneconomic buying criterion.

EPA. 1993a. *Life Cycle Assessment: Inventory Guidelines and Principles.* EPA/600/R-92/245, February 1993. Cincinnati, OH: U.S. Environmental Protection Agency.

EPA contracted with Battelle and Franklin Associates to document a procedure for conducting a life cycle assessment in order to set guidelines for its use. LCA is viewed as an objective technical tool that can be used to evaluate environmental consequences of a product, production process, package, or activity across its entire life cycle. The methodology consists of three complementary components: (1) inventory analysis, (2) impact analysis, and (3) improvement analysis. This is a comprehensive document that provides a good understanding of LCA.

EPA. 1993b. *Life Cycle Design Guidance Manual, Environmental Requirements, and the Product System.* EPA/600/SR-92/226, April 1993. Cincinnati, Ohio: U.S. Environmental Protection Agency.

Environmental objectives for design are considered to promote sustainable resource management and ensure environmental quality for future generations. The life cycle is outlined and related to design criteria derived from environmental problems. Design options cover a broad area, going beyond the more efficient use of materials to areas such as distribution, packaging, improved management practices, and tools for environmental analysis and accounting.

Fairclough, Sir John, Bob Whelan, and Jonathan Williams. 1993. "The Business of Green Design." *Greener Management International* (April): 14–20.

Provides a basic, overall description of green design concepts and how LCA can be used to provide a more informed basis of design. Makes the point that the emphasis on LCA has been product assessment, focusing heavily on consumer products and packaging, and advocates a wider use of LCA in product design of all types, not just consumer goods.

Fairtlough, Gerard. 1994. "Organizing for Innovation: Compartments, Competences, and Networks." *Long Range Planning* 27 (3): 88–97.

The author of this article argues that we are entering a "new industries" phase of development. Government and business planning, marked by short-termism during the last decade, should now take a long-term view and should concentrate on supporting innovation. The organization of innovation can best be done, according to the author, by encouraging the formation of networks of innovation and by developing and applying novel sets of concepts to innovation. The article introduces two of such sets: first, the distinction between firm-specific and profession-specific competences, and second, concepts centered on a department of a few hundred people, with the right kinds of boundaries and internal communications.

Fouhy, Ken. 1993. "Life Cycle Analysis Sets New Priorities." *Chemical Engineering* 100 (7): 30–34.

Describes a number of examples of how life cycle analyses have been used by businesses to help them improve their operations, including product formulation changes, production changes, energy savings, and waste disposal improvements. Covers the use and development of LCA for business and briefly describes a number of information and database sources.

Frosch, Robert A., and Nicholas E. Gallopoulos. 1989. "Strategies for Manufacturing." *Scientific American* 261(3) (September): 94–102.

Argues that technology development should be geared toward the development of industrial ecosystems. The ideal ecosystem should be one in which the use of energy and materials is optimized and where every product and manufacturing process has an economically viable role. This is a management and technology-oriented discussion that overlaps with Allenby and Richards (1994) and Ayres (1989).

Gray, Rob, with Jan Bebbington and Diane Walters. 1993. *Accounting for the Environment: The Greening of Accountancy,* part 2. London: Paul Chapman Publishing Ltd.

This book devotes one chapter to a brief, nontechnical introduction to life cycle analysis methodology and its role in business operations. In addition to being a good, overall introduction, an important connection is made between LCA and the role of accountants. Gray maintains a cautious perspective toward the numbers generated from an LCA process and concludes that the principal benefit from LCA lies in the process of undertaking the exercise rather than in believing the numeric results.

Groenewegen, Peter, and Philip Vergragt. 1991. "Environmental Issues as Threats and Opportunities in Technological Innovation." *Technology Analysis and Strategic Management* 4 (1): 43–55.

Discussion of the relevant changes required to integrate environmental considerations in company policy, especially technology strategy. The article is based on a preliminary study of five chemical companies in the Netherlands and the United States. The study argues that an essential condition for technology strategy that incorporates environmental considerations is the integration of R&D, environmental safety and health, and strategy networks within the firm.

Groenewegen, Peter, and Frank den Hond. 1993. "Product Waste in the Automobile Industry: Technology and Environmental Management." *Business Strategy and the Environment* 2 (1): 1–12.

Groenewegen and den Hond discuss the problem of automobile shredder waste as an example of how companies are responding to environmental issues. The problems of waste disposal are becoming very important to car manufacturers and no longer are a situation for only the car dismantling or shredding companies. A network model of the industry is presented.

Guinee, J.B., R. Heijungs, H. Udo de Haes, and G. Huppes. 1993a. "Quantitative Life Cycle Assessment of Products 1: Goal Definition and Inventory." *Journal of Cleaner Production* 1 (1): 3–13.

————. 1993b. "Quantitative Life Cycle Assessment of Products 2: Classification, Valuation, and Improvement Analysis." *Journal of Cleaner Production* 1 (2): 81–91.

In these two publications, a standard procedure for conducting LCA is described. Five separate methodological steps are discussed: (1) goal definition, (2) creating a materials inventory, (3) classification of impacts, (4) valuation of impacts, and (5) improvement analysis. The authors derive their method from the work done for the Dutch government on LCA methodology. LCA concepts, procedures are explained and some examples are given.

Hopfenbeck, Waldemar. 1993. *The Green Management Revolution: Lessons in Environmental Excellence.* English-language edition. New York and London: Prentice Hall.

The primary contribution of this reference is access to the German literature and thinking that would not normally be accessible to an English-reading audience. A number of the perspectives presented by Hopfenbeck take a slightly different approach to several topics than those presented in U.K. and U.S. publications, providing a better understanding of some of the thinking and developments in Germany. A number of chapters are relevant to interorganization cooperation, both from practical and theoretical perspectives. One chapter of particular interest focuses specifically on the role of the retailer and poses the question of whether retailers are pushers or blockers with respect to positive environmental change.

Klassen, Robert D. 1993. "The Integration of Environmental Issues into Manufacturing: Toward an Interactive Open-Systems Model." *Production and Inventory Management Journal* 34 (1) (First Quarter): 82–88.

Klassen attempts to develop an open-systems model for a manufacturing firm to provide a framework for understanding how the firm's external and internal systems, which are related to environmental management, are structured and interact with each other. In Klassen's model, the external system is composed of three interacting units. One unit is "government agencies," the second unit is composed of the "manufacturing firm and its competitors," and the third unit is composed of "customers and third parties." This external system then also interacts with the internal system of the manufacturing firm. How these two systems interact and influence each other can be used as a framework for understanding how environmental issues can be integrated in an interorganizational context.

Knight, Alan. 1992. "Corporate Response: Greener Retail and Supplier Audits, B&Q." In *Greener Marketing.* M. Charter (ed.) 303–305. Sheffield, England: Greenleaf Publishing.

One of Britain's largest D-I-Y (do-it-yourself/home improvement) retailers, B&Q PLC, has used an LCA approach to develop a supplier audit that has helped to reduce the overall environmental impact that B&Q brings into its own operations. Because B&Q is such a large retailer, they have used their influential position to require their major suppliers to create and implement environmental policies and undergo environmental assessments as a condition of the purchase agreement. This is a good example of how LCA tools and framework have been used within a business' purchasing department. It is also an example of how environmental issues are influencing businesses that are connected by value chain relationships.

Kooijman, Jan M. 1993. "Environmental Assessment of Packaging: Sense and Sensibility." *Environmental Management* 17 (5): 575–586.

Looking at food production as a case, Kooijman argues that the products should not be assessed in isolated chains, but that a system

approach involving packagers, food producers, and the needs of consumers should be the starting point. The argument is that too narrow a
focus on, for instance, the need to reduce the volume of packaging
material overlooks the potential of other environmental impacts such as
energy needed to produce food and the energy wasted by throwing
away food leftovers and spoilage. This clearly points to a need for broad
cooperation on methods to assess environmental improvements.

Mahoney, Joseph T., and J. Rajendran Pandian. 1992. "The Resource-
based View within the Conversation of Strategic Management." *Strategic
Management Journal* 13 (5): 363–380.

Presents the emerging framework of the resource-based view of the
firm and places this into the more traditional perspectives on management. Provides a bridge into a number of theoretical frameworks and
literature.

Mitroff, Ian I. 1994. "Crisis Management and Environmentalism: A Natural Fit." *California Management Review* 36 (2) (Winter): 101–113.

Mitroff presents the integration of actions in four dimensions: type of
crisis (underlying order or structure of crisis); phases (unfolding of the
crisis and relevant mechanisms); system (organizational and technical
variables); and stakeholders (large and complex number of individuals);
and distinguishes crisis-prepared from crisis-prone organizations. He
concludes that the best environmentally prepared organizations are
often the best crisis-prepared organizations.

Tweede Kamer. 1989. *NEPP (National Environmental Policy Plan)*, The
Hague: Staatsuitgeverij.

The Dutch environmental policy plan contains three main objectives:
(1) closing of substance cycles in raw materials, the production process–waste chain; (2) saving energy along with increasing efficiency and
using renewable energy sources; and (3) extending the use of substances
in the economic cycle. The plan has had a stimulating impact on the
strategic thinking of branches of industry in the Netherlands, notably
the energy and chemical sectors (see also VNCI 1991).

Oakley, Brian T. 1993. "Total Quality Product Design—How to Integrate
Environmental Criteria into the Product Realization Process." *Total Quality Environmental Management* 2 (3) (Spring): 309–321.

Design for the environment (DfE) promotes a holistic approach to the design of products so that environmental benefits achieved at one point of the product's life cycle do not result in a very high environmental price at another stage. By taking a systematic view of the total life cycle of a product, including raw material extraction and processing, manufacturing, consumer use/reuse and maintenance, and product retirement, environmental compatibility can be designed into the product and packaging. Oakley presents a succinct description of DfE and related concepts like design for recyclability, design for remanufacture, and design for disposal.

Responsibility for the Future: Options for Sustainable Management of Substance Chains and Material Flows, interim report. 1994. 12th German Bundestag's Enquete Commission on the Protection of Humanity and the Environment—Assessment Criteria and Prospects for Environmentally Sound Product Cycles in Industrial Society. Translated by W. Fehlberg and M. Ulloa-Fehlberg. Bonn: Economica Verlag GmbH.

This interim report, which has been translated into English, presents the assessment approaches for substance cycles and material flows that the Enquete Commission will use as a basis for designing further analysis instruments. The report contains useful background material and references to German government documentation and public discussion meetings, describes different approaches to materials control policy, but focuses on the methodology and implementation of life cycle analyses. Cadmium, benzene, HFC 134a and other CFC substitutes, and textiles/clothing are discussed in detail.

Roome, Nigel. 1994. "Business Strategy, R&D Management, and Environmental Imperatives." *R&D Management* 24 (1) 65–82.

R&D practice is an essential element of sustainable forms of business. Elements dealt with are technological networks, development of more systemic views of products and processes, and thinking through the consequences that these developments have for R&D management.

Roome, Nigel, and Mark Hinnells. 1993. "Environmental Factors in the Management of New Product Development: Theoretical Framework and Some Empirical Evidence from the White Goods Industry." *Business Strategy and the Environment* 2 (2): 12–27.

Roome and Hinnells examine the development of products in the white goods industry. Their assessment acknowledges the role of the supply chain in improving environmental performance. Identifying and acknowledging linkages along the production and use channels by taking a systems approach is advocated for environmental improvement.

Rubik, F., and T. Baumgartner. 1992. *Evaluation of Eco-Balances.* SAST (Strategic Assessment in Science and Technology) Project No. 7, Technological Innovation in the Plastics Industry and Its Influence on the Environmental Problems of Plastic Waste. Commission of the European Communities. Brussels: EUR.

Contains a critical evaluation of the current practice of life cycle analysis. The method is compared to other available methods for ecological evaluation of economic activities such as environmental impact assessment. They make a distinction between methods that list the impacts of products in disaggregated form and those methods that aim at aggregation of impacts in a multi- or single-score impact value. The former is closely related to the industrial metabolism approach and systems analysis.

Schmidheiny, Stephan, with the Business Council for Sustainable Development. 1992. *Changing Course: A Global Business Perspective on Development and the Environment.* Cambridge, MA and London: MIT Press.

Changing Course is a excellent introduction into an entire range of topics related to businesses and the natural environment. It provides not only a description of topics but also provides several chapters describing specific business examples to illustrate the topics covered in the earlier chapters. A main focus of this book is industrial ecology. Life cycle analysis is considered in the chapter describing innovation processes as well as in the case study chapter focusing on managing cleaner products.

Schmidt-Bleek, Friedrich. (1993) *Wieviel Umwelt braucht der Mensch?: MIPS, das Mass fuer oekologisches Wirtschaften.* Berlin: Birkhaeuser.

Contains a discussion of the necessity to reduce the overall environmental burden of society. It bases itself on similar systems thinking as contained in the concept of industrial metabolism. MIPS stands for material intensity per service unit. The concept is developed to show that analysis of the systematic linkages of material flows in society should be the basis to search for optimal solutions. The approach, while ecologically pessimistic, is technology oriented. Its analysis is related to systems thinking and life cycle analysis.

Schot, Johan. 1992. "Credibility and Markets as Greening Forces for the Chemical Industry." *Business Strategy and the Environment* 1 (1) (Spring): 35–44.

Based on research in eight multinational chemical companies, Schot investigates how credibility and markets are shaping the strategic responses of these companies. The concept of "environmental co-makership" is conceived and defined as the interaction between companies in terms of information exchange and demands to be met by suppliers. Five different types of strategies are identified: dependent, defensive, offensive, innovative, and niche.

SustainAbility Ltd. and SPOLD (Society for the Promotion of Life Cycle Development). 1993. *The LCA Sourcebook—A European Business Guide to Life Cycle Assessment.* London: Business in the Environment. (Available from SustainAbility Ltd., The People's Hall, 91–97 Freston Road, London W11 4BD, UK)

This reference book briefly describes sources of information about LCA and organizations involved in using or developing this methodology. European-based literature, consultants, university research groups, and businesses are all included in this comprehensive sourcebook.

Taylor, Geoff, and Richard Welford. 1993. "An Integrated Systems Approach to Environmental Management: A Case Study of IBM UK." *Business Strategy and the Environment,* 2 (3): 1–11.

IBM has developed a review of its suppliers in attempting to reduce the overall environmental impact of its products. When responses of suppliers were insufficient, in IBM's opinion, they were removed from supplier lists. However, recently the company has begun to work more closely with its suppliers to develop environmentally sound technology. One of the problems addressed in the paper is the interaction between major companies and their competitors with regard to environmental performance.

Thayer, Ann M. 1992. "Pollution Reduction." *C&E News* 70 (46) (November 16): 22–52.

Thayer discusses LCA in the wider context of pollution reduction and prevention and suggests that LCA will be used to shape many corporate decisions. She also describes green design and product stewardship in the chemical industry.

VNCI (Association of the Dutch Chemical Industry). 1991. *Integrated Substance Chain Management*. Leidschendam, the Netherlands: VNCI.

The concept of "integrated substance chain management" has been developed as a decision-support tool. The substance chain is visualized as a loop diagram assisting decision makers to consider not only production, usage, and recycling, but also leakages, amounts of raw materials, and amounts of substance regenerated for reuse. There are three phases: Phase I, Generate Options; Phase II, Prioritize Options; and Phase III, Plan Actions. The methodology is initially based on LCA types of calculations, but it broadens to incorporate more subjective factors in the later stages of the assessment process. The methodology is tested using three case studies: HCF22 (refrigerant), dichloromethane, and polycarbonate.

Welford, Richard. 1993. "Breaking the Link Between Quality and the Environment: Auditing for Sustainability and Life Cycle Assessment." *Business Strategy and the Environment* 2 (4): 25–33.

The adoption of new management principles for industry is essential in order to work toward sustainable development. It requires a change in the thinking of both industry and governments. The focus should be on integrating the responsible and proactive approach of business supported by government regulation. Life cycle thinking should be utilized and expanded to include the position of workers in the third world.

Winn, Sarah F., and Nigel J. Roome. 1993. "R&D Management Responses to the Environment: Current Theory and Implications to Practice and Research." *R&D Management* 23 (2): 147–160.

The relation between R&D management and the environment is still evolving. It is proposed that research should elucidate the relations further in a number of directions: technology paths, quality schemes, systems approach, and environmental product attributes.

Winsemius, Pieter, and Walter Hahn. 1992. "Environmental Option Assessment." *The Columbia Journal of World Business* 27 (3) 4 (Fall and Winter): 248–266.

Environmental option assessment is another name for the decision support tool developed by McKinsey & Co. in conjunction with VNCI, the

Association of the Dutch Chemical Industry (see VNCI 1991 for the original report). Winsemius and Hahn provide the core of the methodology with the example of PVC window frames as an illustration of how the methodology can be used.

Chapter 4

Industry Relationships with Communities: Business as Usual?

Caron Chess
Frances Lynn

Introduction

In the United States and Canada closer relationships between corporations and communities have resulted from necessity. Industry frustration with the siting of facilities, protracted litigation, and government regulations have led some companies to change their "business-as-usual" practices. In particular, the Chemical Manufacturers Association's Responsible Care Program has sought to overcome a crisis of public confidence by encouraging member companies to reach out to communities. The European Council of Chemical Manufacturers' Federations developed a similar initiative: CICERO (Communication Between the Chemical Industry and the Community on Emergency Response Organization).

This chapter explores the relationships between corporations and communities concerning potential environmental hazards, particularly near production facilities. Focusing primarily on the chemical industry, we describe several forms these relationships have taken, including mediations, community advisory committees, and good neighbor agreements. We explore their genesis, provide examples, discuss implications, and suggest further avenues of research. Our chapter is based primarily on experiences and research from the United States and touches only briefly on corporate development of "green" products, conservation efforts or collaboration between communities and corporations on legislative issues. The citations and the annotated references that follow were selected because they are (1) seminal works, (2) reviews or overviews of the subject, (3) edited volumes that provide a range of perspectives, or (4) represent a divergent perspective.

Antecedents to Corporate Relationships with Communities

In the United States corporate attempts to build relationships with citizens have developed within the context of government agencies' attempts at public participation. Modern forms of public participation emerged with the social programs (such as urban planning and the war on poverty) of the 1960s. However, many of these efforts were seen by some researchers as a charade that manipulated citizens rather than empowered them (Arnstein1969).

Environmental agencies also have a tradition of public participation, but their record is mixed. In many cases, procedural democracy has not been achieved (Fiorino 1989). Agencies are facing policy dilemmas because their competence with technical issues has outstripped their consideration of democratic processes.

Agencies have been pushed to the mediation table to resolve conflicts over regulations, land use, siting of facilities, and other problems (Bingham 1986). Although most mediations are sparked by polarized positions that the parties themselves cannot resolve, the mediation process can improve relationships between government agencies and other groups at the table. In fact, some mediations have developed primarily to improve communication or transfer information (Bingham 1986).

However, mediation is most likely to be successful when all parties feel their interests are best served by the process. Some of the warring parties might prefer litigation because they see greater strength in their legal arguments than in their bargaining position (Bingham 1986; Crowfoot and Wondolleck 1990). Increasingly, agencies are trying a variety of other collaborative techniques that involve corporate and interest group representation, including regulatory negotiations, policy dialogues, and public-private partnerships (Gray 1989; Long and Arnold 1994).

Because agencies are recognizing that citizen participation may help avoid environmental gridlock, citizen advisory committees (CACs) are proliferating at all levels of government. However, a review of CACs concluded that the impacts of CACs on policy are highly contingent on the motivations of the agencies involved (Lynn and Busenberg 1995). Agencies' decisions regarding selection of members, access to information, and extent of independence may influence the effectiveness of CACs. Some CACs have been formed solely to fulfill legal mandates or to persuade citizens to legitimate agency positions, while others have had significant policy impacts.

There have also been more-ambitious attempts to integrate citizen input into decisions that affect both corporations and communities. For example, the U.S. Environmental Protection Agency (EPA) mounted a major communications effort in Tacoma, Washington, when it became clear that a regulatory standard for arsenic would have tremendous implications for the community. The community was deeply divided about the fate of an arsenic-emitting copper smelter, which was both a major polluter and a significant contributor to the area's economy. EPA initiated an ambitious series of workshops and meetings to provide citizens with scientific information and to solicit input about an appropriate arsenic standard. This effort, which was ended prematurely by the plant's demise, was nonetheless deemed a "qualified success" by EPA's then administrator (Krimsky and Plough 1988).

Thus, environmental agencies have demonstrated both the promise and problems of developing relationships with citizens. These efforts provide a backdrop for understanding the history of corporate efforts.

History of Corporate Efforts

Pressures from community concern, environmental activism, and government regulation forced corporations to provide information about technological risks to the public. In Europe the explosion in Seveso, Italy, in 1976 led the European Community (EC) to issue the Directive on the Major Accident Hazards of Certain Industrial Accidents, more commonly known as the Seveso Directive, which specifies in detail the information that must be generated about major hazards in the EC (Kasperson and Stallen 1991; Gow and Otway 1990). The 1986 Sandoz warehouse fire and subsequent contamination of the Rhine was another wake-up call for the European chemical industry (Durkee 1989).

The 1984 tragedy in Bhopal (Jasanoff 1988; Shrivastava 1992) is also considered a turning point for relationships between the chemical industry and outside publics. In the United States, fear and distrust limited corporations' ability to operate. Truck routings, plant expansions, and other formerly routine operations became more difficult in communities which, after Bhopal, no longer saw plants as good neighbors.

Bhopal provided the impetus for the U.S. Congress to enact federal right-to-know legislation in 1986. The Emergency Planning and Community Right-to-Know Act (EPCRA) requires many manufacturers to provide information to government agencies about emissions. These data are then available to citizens.

Corporations realized that reporting significant releases of toxic chemicals to land, water, and air was likely to further erode public confidence. As a result, some manufacturers made pledges to reduce emissions. Many also initiated communication with citizens who had previously been treated with indifference or worse. Other corporations changed their environmental practices but did not change their relationships with surrounding communities (Baram et al. 1992).

In the wake of Bhopal, the Chemical Manufacturers Association (CMA) pushed its members to develop relationships with communities. CMA's Responsible Care Program encouraged proactive communication (Ann Green Comunications 1994) and the development of community advisory panels, which by 1994 numbered more than 200 (Reisch 1994). CMA also sponsored a series of workshops on risk communication to help manufacturers cope with releasing environmental data. The U.K. Chemical Industries Association launched a program based on six guiding principles, including a commitment to make information relevant to health, safety, and the environment available to the public (Simmons and Wynne 1993).

From Risk Perception to Risk Communication

There is limited research on the relationships between industry and communities, in part because little communication took place until recently. The research that exists has evolved largely from literatures examining individual and societal responses to technological risk. In the early 1970s, the nuclear power industry turned to research psychologists to "fix" what the industry saw as public irrationality. Those pioneering studies (for example, Slovic *et al.* 1980) suggested that lay people's perception of risk is different and much richer than that of experts who measure technological risk in terms of expected annual mortality. Thus, lay people may agree with experts' very low estimates of annual mortality for a risk such as a chemical plant, but communities might refuse to accept a new plant because of the potential for catastrophe or because the risk does not benefit them directly.

Perception of risk is also shaped by a variety of social forces. Kasperson and colleagues have suggested that the impact of a technological incident may be amplified through societal institutions (Kasperson *et al.*1988). Thus, one accident, such as the one in Bhopal, may cause ripple effects throughout the world.

Researchers have also explored why societies are averse to certain risks while they ignore others (Krimsky and Golding 1992; Kasperson and Stallen 1991). Research suggests that people of different ethnicities may view risks differently due to their experiences, beliefs, and shared cultural values (Vaughan 1995).

People may also care more about how decisions are made about a risk, and the resulting fairness of those decisions, than about the risk itself. Probabilities, and even consequences of risks, may not concern people as much as procedural justice (how decisions are made) and distributive justice (how resources are allocated) (Vaughan 1995). For example, the United States' environmental justice movement was launched by studies suggesting that low-income communities and communities of color are disproportionally burdened by environmental hazards (Bryant and Mohai 1992).

Researchers have pointed out that experts' perceptions are also influenced by a variety of factors that can cause them to be overly confident about their data, to develop narrow definitions of problems, and to overlook important information (Freudenburg 1988).

The chemical industry realized that labeling people as irrational would not help build public confidence. As the CMA pointed out in 1988, "Plant managers are understandably concerned about the public's distrust of the chemical industry. However, it is important for you not to dismiss the distrust as irrational."

Risk Communication

There is a consensus that risk communication must consist of dialogues between communities and industries rather than monologues by industry (National Research Council 1989). But there is increasing evidence that tinkering with words is not sufficient to send a risk message (Fessenden-Raden, Fitchen, and Heath 1987); that knowledge does not necessarily change beliefs (Johnson 1993); that information alone may not be sufficient for effective action (Simmons and Wynne 1993; Hadden 1989; Jasanoff 1988); and that the use of third-party intermediaries may be necessary to provide evidence that an accepted set of rules is being followed (Simmons and Wynne 1993). Questions have also been raised about the ethics of risk communication when the motivations of the source of the information are different than the needs of recipients (Morgan and Lave 1990).

Increasing attention is being paid to how controversies are resolved rather than to how information is transmitted. For example, empirical research has suggested that siting noxious facilities may be more acceptable with public involvement (Kunreuther et al. 1993) and that trust in facilities may increase with community oversight (Slovic 1993). Similarly, public relations theorists see one-way communication aimed at changing citizens' behavior as less useful than two-way, symmetrical communication that may result in changes of both the corporations and the citizens (Grunig et al. 1992).

Examples of Relationships

Local Emergency Planning Committees

The U.S. federal right-to-know law mandated the formation of local emergency planning committees (LEPCs) to develop emergency response plans. The legislation, which required LEPCs to include representatives from a range of organizations, provided a context for communities and corporations to work together. However, case studies of LEPCs in four communities found that formal citizen participation was limited and that citizens were passive recipients of information (Rest *et al.* 1991). These LEPCs were also reluctant to take on responsibilities for communicating information to communities.

A survey of LEPCs across the country indicated that LEPCs with a higher percentage of community representatives are more involved in hazard reduction and proactive hazard communication than those without community groups (Kartez 1993). The presence in the LEPC district of a facility that is committed to the CMA's voluntary outreach program is also strongly associated with LEPC support for corporate hazard reduction. Although the jury is still out, it seems that some LEPCs have forged closer ties between industry and communities, but others do not have meaningful citizen involvement.

Citizen Advisory Panels

The information on corporate-sponsored CAPs is limited, but suggests that they vary considerably; some have significant impact on plants' environmental management and others focus merely on building personal relationships. As with government CACs, there are questions about the extent to which corporations want input from communities—and whether industry will respond to such input (Lynn and Chess 1994).

Preliminary evidence suggests the track record is mixed (Reisch 1994). Some CAPs have exploded and members have resigned due to conflicts about suitable issues for CAP discussion. However, other CAPs have influenced corporate clean-ups, increased corporate purchases from local suppliers, examined right-to-know information in depth, and demanded better warning systems (Reisch 1994).

Good Neighbor Agreements

While CMA has urged corporations to form CAPs, some environmental groups have urged grassroots groups to negotiate good neighbor agreements designed to give community representatives the right to negotiate directly with companies (Lewis 1992). To date, dozens of agreements have been signed that stipulate actions companies must take. For example, the Rhone Poulenc facility in Manchester, Texas, pays for an environmental and safety audit, including hazard assessments and dispersion modeling, by an expert of the community's choice. The company also agreed to fund a community-conducted health study, off-site monitoring, and community participation in water sampling (Lynn and Chess 1994).

Mediation

Mediation often involves at least three parties: government, industry, and public interest groups. An early example resulted from an explosion in 1977 at Rollins Environmental Services, a hazardous waste treatment facility in New Jersey. The local fire departments had difficulty fighting the fire due to lack of information about toxics handled at the site. Residents against Rollins called for a shutdown of the facility and, at the urging of the New Jersey Office of Dispute Resolution, entered into negotiations, which also involved government agencies. The end result was that Rollins was allowed to reopen based on agreements reached with agencies, the community group, and Rollins (Bingham 1986).

Collaborative Efforts

Consumer pressure has led some companies to change their product lines and packaging (Kleiner 1991). McDonald's is the best-known example. McDonald's use of styrofoam and other packaging triggered a deluge of letters from school children concerned about the environmental impacts. A national campaign coordinated by an environmental group also resulted in local citizen groups protesting at McDonald's restaurants around the country. Ultimately, McDonald's and a more moderate environmental organization, the Environmental Defense Fund, collaborated on the development of alternative packaging and other approaches to waste reduction (EDF-McDonald's Corporation Waste Reduction Task Force 1991).

Innovative Approaches to Building Relationships

In the fall of 1988, Sybron Chemicals, a small specialty manufacturer with headquarters and a plant in Birmingham, New Jersey, released 40 pounds of ethyl acrylate into the air (Chess *et al.* 1992). As a result of the stench and the failure of the plant to provide clear information, the fire department evacuated 60 people at 2:00 A.M. After the incident, elected officials pressured for change, the New Jersey Department of Environmental Protection investigated the plant, and some in the community called for a shutdown of the plant. Sybron, which previously treated the community with self-described "benign neglect," embarked on a crash course in community relations. One of the company's most high-profile responses was the development of a telecommunications system that both alerts neighbors in the event of an emergency and promotes routine communication between the community and plant operators. Anyone who has a concern can call a well-publicized number 24 hours a day and hear a message about the status of plant operations or leave a message. Plant supervisors update recorded messages on plant operations, return calls, and respond to concerns. Community reports of odors have helped the plant track operational problems.

The plant's most innovative step was developing an odor identification (ID) team, composed of neighborhood residents who were provided with training and meteorological equipment. The members help the company literally sniff out odors, determine (based on wind direction) whether the odor came from Sybron or other sources, and serve as sources of information for their neighbors with concerns. Thus, Sybron's partnership with members of the odor ID team not only improved communication but also improved environmental management.

Conclusion

These corporate-community relationships evolved out of conflict. Yet, there is no doubt that the rhetoric is less furious than 20 years ago, when most corporations either ignored communities or actively resisted requests for information. Communities and corporations are talking, and in an increasing number of cases, the tone is conversational rather than adversarial. Some conversations result from fragile truces in ongoing battles between industry and communities. But, given the history of industry-community relationships, truce may be an essential prelude to building relationships.

However, the problems that haunt government agencies' public participation efforts are also problems for industry-community relationships. For example, some environmental activists have accused companies of being more interested in lulling communities to sleep than in providing them with meaningful information or soliciting their input (Reisch 1994).

Building industry-community relationships is an experiment without documentation due to the dearth of academic research or meaningful evaluation by any of the parties. Much information is anecdotal, based on reports in trade journals or citizen newsletters. Significantly more research is needed to examine the motivation of companies entering into such relationships, the relative efficacy of various mechanisms of community involvement, the organizational factors sustaining the endeavors, and the impacts on both the company and the community.

Acknowledgments

This review was funded by the New Jersey Institute of Technology's Hazardous Substance Management Research Center, the New Jersey Agricultural Experiment Station, and the University of North Carolina. We appreciate the assistance of our colleagues Michael Greenberg, Nevin Cohen, and George Busenberg, who have contributed to our understanding of industry-community relationships. Linda Hooper and Victoria Cluck also provided assistance.

Annotated Bibliography

Ann Green Communications. 1994. *CMA Community Advisory Panel Handbook*. Washington, DC: Chemical Manufacturers Association.

This guide contains suggestions about developing and maintaining community advisory panels. The handbook, designed to be useful to plant managers and CAP members, suggests approaches for determining membership, designing meetings, and revitalizing CAPs. Also included are brief case studies and samples of by-laws and minutes. Although the manual does not critique different methods, it provides basic, down-to-earth suggestions that should be helpful to anyone considering development of a CAP.

Arnstein, Sherry. 1969. "A Ladder of Citizen Participation." *AIP Journal* (July): 216–224.

This early article on citizen participation explicitly discusses the power dynamics between citizens and agencies that ask for citizen input. Arnstein provides a typology of citizen participation on an eight-rung ladder, according to the power granted to communities: manipulation, therapy, informing, consultation, placation, partnership, delegated power, and citizen control. Federal social programs are used as examples of this typology. Arnstein argues that agencies sometimes manipulate "have-nots" to think they have power when, in fact, they have none.

Baram, Michael S., Patricia Dillon, and Betsy Ruffle. 1992. *Managing Chemical Risks: Corporate Response to SARA Title III*. Boca Raton, FL: Lewis Publishers.

This study describes the voluntary initiatives of eight companies in response to the United States' federal right-to-know law. Accident prevention, emissions reduction, emergency response planning, and public outreach are examined. The study concludes that although companies undertook environmental initiatives, their relationships with communities were limited; and that if right to know does not embody "a right to understand the . . . meaning of information," then the law is falling short of its intent. The authors also suggest that the promise of local emergency planning committees has not been realized.

Bingham, Gail. 1986. *Resolving Environmental Disputes: A Decade of Experience*. Washington, DC: The Conservation Foundation.

This book is based on an examination of 161 environmental dispute resolution cases over a decade. Corporations were involved in 34 percent of the site-specific cases studied. The book includes a discussion of the history of environmental dispute resolution, evaluation techniques, factors that contribute to reaching a successful resolution, and a comparison of voluntary dispute resolution with litigation. Bingham concludes that environmental disputes are so varied that no one dispute-resolution process is likely to be successful in all situations. She found more success in mediation of site-specific disputes than in policy dialogues or negotiations. The most significant factor in the success of an agreement was the participation of organization representatives with the authority to implement the decisions.

Bryant, Bunyan, and Paul Mohai (eds.). 1992. *Race and the Incidence of Environmental Hazards: A Time for Discourse.* Boulder, CO: Westview Press.

This volume includes chapters by many scholars who are conducting research about the extent to which environmental contamination falls disproportionally on low-income communities and communities of color. Case studies, empirical research, and suggestions for remedying inequality are included. The impacts of hazardous waste, consumption of toxic fish, occupational hazards, pesticide exposure, and uranium mining are discussed.

Carley, Michael, and Ian Christie. 1992. *Managing Sustainable Development.* London: Earthscan.

This book examines the managerial and organizational dimension of sustainable development. It analyzes the challenges posed by environmental problems to political culture and organizational structure in industrial societies and identifies the roots of ecological problems in our economic and social systems. Action-centered networks are discussed as solutions. Most networks that are discussed consist of bottom-up local initiatives and innovative management approaches that link business, government, and voluntary organizations in problem solving. Four cases are analyzed more extensively, at the local level: the Groundwork Trusts in Britain, regional watershed management initiatives in a number of African countries, a state-level project in California, and the planning process of the Dutch National Environmental Policy Plan.

Chess, Caron, Alex Saville, Michael Greenberg, and Michal Tamuz. 1992. "The Organizational Links Between Risk Communication and Risk Management: The Case of Sybron Chemicals Inc." *Risk Analysis* 12 (3): 431–438.

This article explores the internal organizational factors that were associated with one company's effort to increase credibility. After a crisis of public confidence, Sybron chemicals initiated a community relations program that resulted in complex links between risk communication and risk management. For example, the company's risk management efforts were influenced by communication with plant neighbors. The authors suggest that a number of internal factors may have sustained Sybron's efforts, including diffraction of responsibility for communication rather than delegation of these responsibilities entirely to public relations staff. Effective internal communications, especially mechanisms to transmit bad news, were also associated with Sybron's efforts..

Crowfoot, James E., and Julia M. Wondolleck (eds). 1990. *Environmental Disputes: Community Involvement in Conflict Resolution.* Washington, DC: Island Press.

This edited volume describes the experiences of citizen groups involved in environmental dispute resolution. Environmental dispute resolution is defined as direct and voluntary interaction among the parties involved, leading to mutual agreements or consensus decisions. The authors present seven case studies of citizen groups that have used environmental dispute resolution to manage conflict over environmental issues, including national forest management, agricultural policy, water resources planning, and groundwater legislation. The authors suggest why some attempts were less successful than others.

Durkee, Linda C. 1989. "Risk Communication and the Rhine River." *International Environment Reporter.* 12 (10): Part II.

Two years after the Sandoz spill into the Rhine, Durkee spent two months interviewing representatives of government, industry, public interest groups, academia, and the press. She concluded that in countries such as France and the Netherlands, where data have been more accessible, there appeared to be less likelihood of intense public reaction to disclosure of specific data. However, in a country such as Germany, where data were withheld, reactions were greater.

Fessenden-Raden, June, Janet M. Fitchen, and Jenifer S. Heath. 1987. "Providing Risk Information in Communities: Factors Influencing What Is Heard and Accepted." *Science, Technology, and Human Values* 12: 94–101.

This article is based on case studies of public response to chemical contamination of the drinking water of more than a dozen nonmetropolitan communities. The researchers found that people perceive the message and the messenger as closely related. If the messenger is distrusted, the message may also be distrusted, no matter how technically accurate it may be. Additionally, the initial response of government officials to the contamination was found to strongly affect the subsequent dynamics between residents and government. Officials that elicited more trust were forthcoming, open, and honest.

Fiorino, Daniel J. 1989. "Environmental Risk and Democratic Process: A Critical Review." *Columbia Journal of Environmental Law* 14: 501–547.

This extensive review of the literature explores how democratic institutions can reconcile technical expertise with the concept of Jeffersonian democracy. Fiorino suggests that the consideration of how to involve the public in environmental policy decisions lags behind agencies' technical expertise. As a result, the United States is facing a "participatory dilemma." He traces the history of public participation in environmental policy and concludes that the public is placed in a reactive posture and that there is rarely "sharing of power." He proposes the elements of a participatory ideal in which lay people are seen as citizens, not subjects; design of institutions allows for direct participation of "amateurs"; participatory mechanisms include "face-to-face" discussions over time; and mechanisms put citizens on a "basis of equality" with environmental experts.

Freudenburg, William R. 1988. "Perceived Risk, Real Risk: Social Science and the Art of Probabilistic Risk Assessment." *Science* 242: 44–49.

The author suggests that the dichotomy between "real" and "perceived" risk is less valid than often assumed. The author includes descriptions of cases in which expert judgment has failed due to experts' overconfidence in their estimates of technological risks. Risk estimates fail to take into account human factors. Thus, improving risk estimates may require involving social science expertise.

Gow, H.B.F., and Harry Otway. 1990. *Communicating with the Public About Major Accident Hazards.* The Netherlands: Elsevier Applied Sciences.

This volume includes papers from a conference held in Varese, Italy, in 1989. The papers, which were presented by representatives of the organizations involved in the implementation of the Seveso Directive, highlight the history of European Community regulations relating to hazardous industrial operations and the right of the public to information. Numerous cases of corporate implementation of the directive as well as academic evaluations are included.

Gray, Barbara. 1989. *Collaborating: Finding Common Ground for Multiparty Problems.* San Francisco: Jossey Bass.

Gray draws on organizational theory to describe a variety of collaborative strategies for business, government, labor, and communities. She includes a matrix that links motivations and expected outcomes to the selection of the design of the collaboration. She uses this theoretical framework to examine two case studies: one involving urban renewal and another the National Coal Policy Project. The book also provides pointers on how to overcome obstacles to collaboration.

Grunig, James E., with David Dozier, William Ehling, Larissa Grunig, Fred Repper, and Jon White (eds.). 1992. *Excellence in Public Relations and Communication Management.* Hillsdale, NJ: Lawrence Erlbaum.

This volume reviews the public relations literature, including both theoretical perspectives and empirical research. Public relations has earned a negative reputation, according to Grunig and his colleagues, in part because public relations has been defined largely by narrow self-interest. Grunig in his opening chapter posits an "idealistic social role" for public relations as a "mechanism by which organizations and publics interact in a pluralistic system to manage their independence and conflict." The authors contrast this perspective with the ways in which public relations has been practiced. They also consider organizational issues related to public relations theory and practice including effective planning of communications, characteristics of excellent public relations departments, organizational roles of public relations practitioners, and evaluation of public relations efforts.

Hadden, Susan. 1989. *A Citizen's Right to Know.* Boulder, CO: Westview Press.

This volume traces the history of right-to-know from its roots in the labor movement to federal legislation granting the community a right to know. Hadden suggests that providing information can encourage risk reduction by industry and empowerment of citizens. Hadden feels that right-to-know laws open the door to the operations of industry and government and foster social trust that reduces the resources spent on adversarial proceedings. The book contains a detailed discussion of the strengths and limitations of right-to-know data and proposes improvements.

Hance, Billie Jo, Caron Chess, and Peter Sandman. 1990. *Industry Risk Communication Manual.* Boca Raton, FL: Lewis Publishers.

This manual provides how-to guidance for industrial managers seeking to communicate with a fearful public. Efforts of leading risk-communication professionals are described. Checklists for action are also included. The manual extrapolates from both experience and the limited number of empirical studies and as such should be seen as containing well-informed guidance rather than conclusions based on extensive empirical research.

Jasanoff, Sheila. 1988. "The Bhopal Disaster and the Right to Know." *Social Science Medicine* 27 (10) 1113–1123.

Based on a description of events prior to the Bhopal tragedy, the author looks at three concerns central to right-to-know policies: Who has the right to receive the hazard information? What information should be disclosed? What knowledge would prevent disasters such as Bhopal? Lessons learned from Bhopal suggest that knowledge must be tied to the ability to act preventively. The author suggests that hazard information should be available to developing countries before the siting of potentially hazardous facilities.

Johnson, Branden. 1993. "Advancing Understanding of Knowledge's Role in Lay Risk Perception." *Risk: Issues in Health and Safety* 4 (3) (Summer): 189–212.

The article categorizes current research on lay risk perception into three categories: grasp of facts, hueristics, and conceptual frameworks. Johnson concludes that all three types of studies focus too heavily on probability, facts, and uncertainty, as opposed to cultural influences on risk. He also points out that experts seem to be most upset about lay "ignorance" of hazards for which expert knowledge is most uncertain. He suggests that researchers pay more attention to the daily contexts in which knowledge becomes real for people.

Kartez, Jack. 1993. "LEPC Roles in Toxic Hazard Reduction: Implementing Title III's Unwritten Goals." Final Report under EPA Grant R81730-03-0. Washington, DC: U.S. Environmental Protection Agency.

In 1989 and 1992 surveys of local emergency planning committees (LEPCs) were conducted in 42 states to explore whether LEPCs supported actions to reduce toxic hazards. The participation of neighborhood groups was the most important factor in explaining LEPC support for hazard reduction goals. The presence in the LEPC district of a facility committed to the Chemical Manufacturing Association's (CMA's) voluntary outreach programs was also strongly associated with support for private industry hazard reduction. The study also found that LEPCs in areas with industrial firms committed to communication are undertaking active risk communication with the public.

Kasperson, R.E., and P.J.M. Stallen (eds.). 1991. *Communicating Health and Safety Risks to the Public: International Dimensions.* Dordrecht, the Netherlands: Reidel.

This comprehensive volume examines risk communication practices in both Europe and the United States. Included are chapters describing the implementation of the Seveso Amendment in various EC countries, information provision in the Netherlands, and the requirements for risk communication under various laws in the United States. Additional chapters probed the outcomes of research concerning communication about various risks, including contaminated soil and nuclear radiation. The role of the media and social dynamics are also assessed.

Kasperson, Roger E., Ortwin Renn, Halina Brown, Jacque Emel, Robert Goble, Jeanne X. Kasperson, Samuel Ratick, and Paul Slovic. 1988. "The Social Amplification of Risk: A Conceptual Framework." *Risk Analysis* 8 (2): 177–204.

This article proposes a theoretical basis for explaining why risk events that experts judge to be small often elicit strong public concerns and result in "substantial impacts on society and economy." The authors suggest that hazards interact with psychological, social, institutional, and cultural processes in ways that may amplify or attenuate public responses to risk. The analogy of dropping a stone into a pond illustrates the impacts of the social amplification of risk. The ripples first hit victims of the hazard event, then touched other institutions and, in more extreme cases, hit other parts of the industry or social arenas.

Kleiner, Art. 1991. "What Does It Mean to Be Green?" *Harvard Business Review* (July-August): 38–47.

This overview describes companies' attempts to improve environmental practices in response to outside pressures. The author discusses three questions by which to gauge corporate greenness: Is the product worthwhile? How much is disclosed? Where can pollution be prevented? He attempts to answer these questions with examples of industry improvements. He also notes the paradoxical pressures of the marketplace, which demand both easy-to-use, disposable products and green ones. He concludes that "The environmental movement is not at odds with corporate interests; it is at odds with the slow pace of inevitable corporate change."

Krimsky, Sheldon, and Dominic Golding (eds.). 1992. *Social Theories of Risk.* Westport, CT/London: Praeger.

This edited volume discusses the societal responses to risk as viewed by scholars with diverse perspectives. The overviews of psychometric research and cultural theory make this a useful reference for exploring the social aspects of technological risk. The articles raise major issues in the field, such as the roles of experts and various publics in making decisions about technological risk. Reviews of empirical research as well as theoretical perspectives are included.

Krimsky, Sheldon, and Alonzo Plough. 1988. *Environmental Hazards: Communicating Risk as a Social Process.* Westport, CT: Auburn House.

Detailed case studies of risk communication illustrate the authors' distinctions between technical and cultural perceptions of risk. The cases describe controversies over the pesticide EDB, the release of the biologically engineered "ice minus" bacteria, the government's response to naturally occurring radon, the impact of an arsenic standard on a controversial copper smelter in Tacoma, Washington, and the Nyanza Superfund site. Each of the case studies includes description of the context for the controversy; discussion of the interactions between government agencies, industry, and various publics; conclusions about the outcomes; and implications of the case. A final chapter provides a conceptual approach to bridging the gap between technical and cultural perspectives of risk.

Kunreuther, Howard, Kevin Fitzgerald, and Thomas Aarts. 1993. "Siting Noxious Facilities: A Test of the Facility Siting Credo." *Risk Analysis* 13 (4): 301–318.

This article describes an empirical test of the 1990 Facility Siting Credo, which is based on the premise that community involvement is more likely to lead to siting. Questionnaires probed 29 cases involving siting of hazardous waste facilities. The authors developed a ranking of the importance of various aspects of the Credo and concluded that three aspects need to be addressed: (1) finding ways to deal with the "different values and goals of the key stakeholders," (2) changing the "tendency to maintain the status-quo," and (3) dissolving "the mistrust that pervades siting issues."

Lewis, Sanford. 1992. *The Good Neighbor Handbook.* Acton, MA: The Good Neighbor Project (P.O. Box 79225, Waverly, MA 02179).

The manual is built around successful cases of industry signing binding agreements with communities concerning environmental issues. Lewis stresses the importance of independent audits or inspections by citizens of industry actions. These audits have, in some cases, resulted in industry saving money by adopting pollution-prevention measures. The manual also includes model contract language.

Long, Frederick, and Matthew Arnold. 1994. *The Power of Environmental Partnerships.* Washington, DC: The Management Institute for Environment and Business.

The authors analyze 12 studies of voluntary partnerships aimed at improving environmental protection related to issues such as ozone depletion, growth management planning, waterfowl protection, wastewater treatment, and pollution prevention. Factors seen as critical for creating successful partnerships are inclusivity, clear agendas, respect, and shared implementation and evaluation. The authors suggest a typology of partnerships ranging from those designed to diffuse a hostile situation to those that netted social, political, and financial gains.

Lynn, Frances, and George Busenberg. 1995. "Citizen Advisory Committees and Environmental Policy." *Risk Analysis* 15 (2): 147–162.

This article, which is included in the proceedings of a national symposium on risk communication held in June 1994, analyzes 14 empirical studies of citizen advisory committees (CACs), including case studies, large-scale surveys, and consultants' reports. The review shows that CACs may merely fulfill legal mandates or may lead to more formal, binding negotiations. The keys to successful participation of CACs are well-defined mandates, adequate resources, and neutrally facilitated processes.

Lynn, Frances, and Caron Chess. 1994. "Community Advisory Panels within the Chemical Industry." *Business Strategy and the Environment* 3 (2) (Summer): 92–99.

This article reviews the evidence to date about corporate community advisory panels (CAPs) and sets an agenda for future research. The article describes the diversity of CAPs including examples of those whose primary concern is to foster better communication between the company and the community and others that are more intimately involved in corporate decisions. The article is based on preliminary research for a multiyear study of CAPs.

McDonald's Corporation and the Environmental Defense Fund. 1991. *Waste Reduction Task Force: Executive Summary.* Washington, DC: Environmental Defense Fund

This report was written collectively by McDonald's waste reduction task force, which included representatives from both McDonald's and the Environmental Defense Fund. The report describes the origins and outcomes of this unusual collaboration to change the way the company handles wastes. The six-month process went beyond the original intent of suggesting options for reducing solid waste to produce a comprehensive waste-reduction policy. The summary highlights McDonald's plan of action, including source reduction, reuse, recycling, and composting. The changes McDonald's made to instill organizational commitment are briefly described.

Morgan, M. Granger, Baruch Fischhoff, Ann Bostrom, Lester Lave, and Cynthia Atman. 1992. "Communicating Risk to the Public: First, Learn What People Know and Believe." *Environmental Science and Technology* 26 (11): 2048–2056.

This article analyzes why some materials communicate risk information better than others. Using radon as an example, the authors explain the importance of understanding people's pre-existing "mental models" before conveying new information. Empirical research found that the differing structure of three radon brochures influenced readers' ability to respond to radon issues. The brochure that was structured to address lay people's mental models of radon was more likely to elicit appropriate responses to questions about solving radon-related problems. The authors suggest four steps to risk communication: (1) open-ended elicitation of people's beliefs about hazards, (2) structured questionnaires to determine the prevalence of beliefs, (3) development of communication based on what people need to know to make informed decisions, and (4) iterative testing of successive versions of those communications using open-ended, closed-form, and problem-solving instruments administered before, during, and after the receipt of messages.

Morgan, M. Granger, and Lester Lave. 1990. "Ethical Considerations in Risk Communication Practice and Research." *Risk Analysis* 10(3): 355–358.

The authors point out that the motivations of the sources of risk communication and the needs of recipients may differ, and that these differences raise ethical issues. The potential for ethical problems is greatest when sources have selfish or covert motivations or when recipients need to make decisions based on the information. Ethical problems are less likely to arise when the recipients are looking for general information rather than information on which to base their decisions. When communicators are overt about their motivations and the communication tools they are using, ethical conflicts are also less likely. In addition, societal consensus about issues, such as smoking, reduce the likelihood of ethical problems. The authors caution that risk communication research is providing results that can be used for both "overt and covert purposes" by sources of information.

National Research Council. 1989. *Improving Risk Communication*. Washington, DC: National Academy Press.

This seminal report stresses that improving risk communication is more than merely crafting better messages. The process of risk communication can be as important as the message. The volume includes an extensive appendix by Baruch Fischhoff, designed to aid the diagnosis of risk controversies and promote understanding of the psychological principles that influence risk communication.

Nelkin, Dorothy. 1992. *Controversy: Politics of Technical Decisions.* Newbury Park, CA: Sage Publications.

Cases of controversies point out the tensions among government agencies, corporations, and citizen groups. The descriptions of the etiology of disputes provide a basis for understanding the nature of conflicts over scientific and technical policies. Although many of the cases are less useful for appreciating how corporations become enmeshed in controversy, others deal specifically with corporate issues. Nelkin's introduction is a concise analysis of the struggles that take place when values clash over the roles of technology and science in society.

Reisch, Marc. 1994. "Chemical Industry Tries to Improve Its Community Relations." *Chemical and Engineering News* (February 28): 8–21.

This overview describes the history and current efforts of the Chemical Manufacturers Association to improve credibility with communities. In particular, the author examines citizen advisory panels' (CAPs') goals and impacts. He also explores how companies select members for CAPs and the different ways they deal with activists. He describes positive relationships and failed efforts, concluding that CAPs vary tremendously.

Rest, Kathleen, Sheldon Krimsky, and Alonzo Plough. 1991. *Risk Communication and Community Right-to-Know: A Four Community Study of SARA Title III.* Medford, MA: The Center for Environmental Management, Tufts University.

Interviews and surveys of members of local emergency planning committees (LEPCs) are the basis of a study concerning the responses of four communities to the federal right-to-know law enacted in 1986. The communities included Springfield, Massachusetts; Baytown, Texas; Texas City, Texas; and Newark, New Jersey. The authors found that LEPCs have focused largely on emergency planning and have not become involved in helping citizens understand emissions data. Differing perceptions of LEPC members from industry are discussed.

Shrivastava, Paul. 1992. *Bhopal: Anatomy of a Crisis.* London: Paul Chapman.

In this updated edition, Shrivastava gives a detailed history of the accident at Bhopal and examines the causes, the consequences, and the events since 1987. Using Bhopal as an example, he suggests new business and social policies that could help to prevent such a tragedy from occurring in the future.

Simmons, Peter, and Brian Wynne. 1993. "Responsible Care: Trust, Credibility, and Environmental Management." In *Environmental Strategies for Industry: International Perspectives on Research Needs and Policy Implications.* Kurt Fischer and Johan Schot (eds.) 201–226. Washington, DC: Island Press.

The authors examine the response of the Chemical Industries Association in the United Kingdom to a crisis of credibility and its attempt to regain public trust by establishing environmental performance standards for the chemical industry through its responsible care program. They conclude that the challenge for industry now is to exploit the opportunities for involving citizens in the policy process and for improving the capacity for social learning.

Slovic, Paul. 1987. "Perception of Risk." *Science* 236: 280–285.

This overview of risk perception research is useful for those unfamiliar with the field, focusing on the differences between lay and expert perceptions of risk. Slovic concludes that the public's concerns need to be taken seriously.

Slovic, Paul. 1993. "Perceived Risk, Trust, and Democracy." *Risk Analysis* 13 (6): 675–682.

Slovic suggests two trends in American society that have affected responses to risk: (1) an increase in fear of technological risks, due to a lack of "participatory democracy" and changes in technology; and (2) an increase in the contentiousness of risk assessment and risk management. He examines the development of these trends over the years and reviews the literature relevant to trust. He also discusses the results of an empirical study that asked respondents to consider situations that would increase or decrease trust in a nuclear power plant. This study concludes that trust is asymmetrical: easy to break, but hard to restore. The measure most likely to restore trust, according to respondents, empowers a citizen task force to shut down the facility in the event of problems.

Slovic, Paul, Baruch Fischhoff, and Sarah Lichtenstein. 1980. "Facts and Fears: Understanding Perceived Risk." In *Societal Risk Assessment: How Safe Is Safe Enough?* R.C. Schwing and W. Albes (eds.) 181–214. New York: Plenum.

This is a detailed review of early risk perception research, examining biases of lay people and experts when making judgments about risks. The authors conclude that risk judgments by both are "fallible," and they demonstrate that experts' opinions are not free of bias. They suggest that informing lay people more adequately might help reduce misunderstandings of technological risk.

Susskind, Lawrence, and Jeffrey Cruikshank. 1987. *Breaking the Impasse.* New York: Basic Books.

The book is intended for the lay person, but draws heavily on the research of the Public Disputes Program at MIT. The book includes discussion of assisted and unassisted negotiations and describes steps in the consensus-building process. The authors contend that decentralized initiatives for consensual dispute resolution are more effective for solving problems than centralized government regulation. The authors suggest that negotiated consensus building, which involves face-to-face interaction among stakeholder groups, is the best way to break impasses among government, citizens, and business.

Vaughan, Elaine. 1995. "The Significance of Socioeconomic and Ethnic Diversity for the Risk Communication Process." *Risk Analysis.* 15 (2): 169–180

Vaughan discusses how ethnicity and socioeconomic variables influence perception of risk. (This discussion is included in the proceedings of a national symposium on risk communication, June 1994.) The paradigm of the environmental justice movement, she argues, looks at risk through the lens of procedural justice (how decisions are made) and distributive justice (who benefits). The author notes the difficulties agencies have in reconciling this social justice paradigm with technical definitions of risk. She concludes that significant research is needed to determine how these frameworks can be accommodated.

Chapter 5

Environmental Performance Measurement

Peter James
Walter Wehrmeyer

Do not always say what you know, but always know what you are saying.
—*Mathias Claudius, 1740-1815*

Introduction

Environmental performance measurement (EPM) can be related to many parts of business conduct. Relevant aspects of this conduct include the relation between plant operations and energy use, waste produced, and emissions to air, water, and soil. Increasingly, the external demands for performance measures are focusing on an integration of the overall impacts of production, such as the source and environmental impact of incoming resources, transportation, and services. Thus, in the actual data needed for EPM, an enormous variety of information is covered. Because the field is moving rapidly, we focus here on the organizational aspects of EPM.

A number of forces are now driving organizations to measure their environmental performance (James and Bennett 1994). They include:

- The need to demonstrate progress toward organizational targets and to gain better data for environmental decision making (Business in the Environment 1992)

- The need to supply data on emissions, wastes, and other topics to regulators (Freedman and Jaggi 1986, 1988)

- Demands from environmental, community, and other external groups for quantified data about potentially hazardous emissions and wastes (Seidel 1988)

- The need to satisfy investors, debtors, and insurers that environmental problems will not threaten their financial interest in an organization (Lascelles 1993)

- Demands by customers for more information about the environmental performance of products and the processes used to create them (Wells *et al.* 1992)

- Requirements of environmental management standards such as the U.K. British Standard 7750 (BS7750) or the European Union Eco-Management and Audit Scheme (EMAS) (Gilbert 1993, 1994)

EPM is still in its early stages. Few companies are able to measure all environment-related parameters, and even fewer are able to determine the ultimate environmental impacts of their actions. Nonetheless, there is a burgeoning literature on the topic and its role in environmental management (see James and Bennett 1994 and Wehrmeyer 1994 for literature surveys).

Key Themes in Environmental Performance Measurement

Environmental performance measurement, like all forms of performance measurement, is concerned with the development and implementation of metrics to assess performance in environmentally significant areas of activity. Some of the most common EPM metrics— such as measures of energy efficiency and material utilization—have long been used for business reasons. One key theme is whether EPM activities should focus on metrics that have business as well as environmental significance or whether it should be driven primarily by environmental considerations (James and Bennett 1994; Wehrmeyer 1992).

A second, closely related, theme is whether EPM should be built on a holistic, quasi-scientific, "cradle-to-grave" consideration of an organization's environmental impacts or whether it should be driven by management considerations such as useability and simplicity of concept (Schreiner 1992). The German literature distinguishes these approaches as "eco-balancing" and "eco-controlling," respectively, and has generally focused on the former. Anglo-Saxon literature has generally been more practitioner-oriented and has therefore had a managerial eco-controlling orientation.

This is in turn related to a third theme, which is whether EPM should be concerned with driving organizations to a predetermined situation, such as sustainability, or whether limitations of data and methodology favor a more incremental and diverse approach in which EPM is used in organizationally specific ways to meet organizationally specific targets (Welford 1993).

A fourth theme is the extent to which EPM is an internally or externally focused activity. As discussed below, EPM to date has been shaped by the need to report performance data to external regulators, and some believe that all EPM data should be made available to external stakeholders. This position sees EPM as the equivalent of financial accounting, which is primarily concerned with reporting financial performance information to shareholders. However, much work is now focusing on the management accounting dimension of EPM—that is, development of metrics to support internal decision making (Bennett and James 1994; Chapter 6 references).

A final, emergent theme is the difference between EPM and environmental accounting. There have been extensive discussions of the general differences between performance measurement and accounting. Performance measurement gurus believe that traditional accounting has been overly concerned with financial performance measurement, collecting purely monetary information—particularly reporting to shareholders—for purposes that form only part of an organization's strategic concerns. They argue that measurement activities need to be driven much more by overall strategic objectives, which will require measurement of nonfinancial aspects of performance and a wider range of nonfinancial metrics (Eccles 1991). While there is no reason in principle why accountants cannot make this shift—and indeed academic management accountants have been at the forefront of the debate—in practice, nonfinancial performance measurement has been driven by relevant specialists (such as marketeers for customer-related measures).

As Chapter 6, "The Greening of Corporate Accounting," shows, some academic and practitioner accountants have applied these precepts to the environmental area and encouraged the collection and reporting of data about emissions, wastes, and other nonfinancial parameters. A number have also sought to translate these parameters into financial measures of their impact on the business (Bennett and James 1994; Chapter 6 references). However, in most companies the accounting function and accountants have not been central to EPM, which has been driven by environmental specialists. It seems likely that for the foreseeable future they—and related specialists—will be better placed to integrate the environmental, managerial, and strategic dimensions of EPM.

General Principles of Performance Measurement

Neely (1993) has identified three levels of analysis of performance measurement activities:

- individual performance measures
- the performance measurement system as an entity
- the relationship between the performance measurement system and the external environment

Individual Performance Measures

All companies and industries are different, and it is no surprise that a large number of performance measures have been developed. Practitioner discussions have grouped these into a small number of generic measures. Hodgkinson (1993) of Deloitte Touche Tohmatsu, for example, distinguishes facility/operational from management measures, while Business in the Environment (1992) identifies impact, risk, contributor, and external relations measures. Wells et al. (1992) distinguish between pressures of process improvement, environmental results, and customer satisfaction. In the academic literature, Azzone and Manzini (1994) identify five basic measures and James and Bennett (1994) identify 10.

Most EPM activity to date has focused on emission and, to a lesser extent, wastes of substances and efficiency of energy and materials utilization (Business in the Environment 1992; Hodgkinson 1993; Schreiner 1991). This is largely because regulators have required the collection of data in these areas. Indeed, the single biggest influence on EPM to date has probably been the U.S. Toxic Release Inventory (TRI) legislation, which requires public reporting of emissions of specified toxic chemicals to air, land, and water. This has not only given U.S. companies a useful means of measuring environmental progress—year-by-year reductions in TRI emissions—but has also facilitated comparisons between sites and companies (ENDS 1993).

However, the rise of pollution-prevention approaches to environmental management has provoked a debate about the value of TRI and other emissions measures. These require measurement of the emissions and wastes that are *avoided* as a result of waste minimization activities (Freeman *et al.* 1992). This is difficult both because it requires accurate knowledge of existing emissions and wastes and because reductions can be due to other factors such as reduced action volumes. Schulz and Schulz (1993) point out that measurement against potential should be attempted, but this creates difficulties because the goalposts are always moving. Many companies are using reduction of TRI emissions as a measure of pollution prevention; but Hearne and Aucott (1992) challenge this view, raising some general issues of EPM.

In recent years companies have sought to extend EPM by considering the risks (Shorthouse 1991), impacts (James and Bennett 1994), and financial implications (Bennett and James 1994; Schreiner 1991, 1992; Schulz and Schulz 1993) of environmental actions; the perceptions of customers and stakeholders (Wells *et al.* 1992); and the effectiveness of the environmental processes that ensure good environmental performance (Greenberg and Unger 1992). An example of the latter is the work of the U.S. Global Environmental Management Initiative (GEMI) (1992)—a consortium of large U.S. corporations— which has translated the 17 principles of the International Chamber of Commerce's Business Charter for Sustainable Development into a measurement template, the environmental self-assessment program (ESAP).

One developing area of measurement is the normalization of environmental measures—such as TRI emissions—to a measure of business activity, such as production or turnover. Normalized measures are important because they screen out macro fluctuations, such as varying levels of output, and allow critical operational relationships to be identified and managed. In an important study, Behmanesh, Roque, and Allen (1993) conclude that the precise choice of, business activity measure is not significant to industry rankings of environmental performance, although more work is needed to test the validity of this proposition.

The Performance Measurement System

Most discussion of performance measurement stresses the importance of deriving measures from an organization's strategic objectives (Neely 1993). However, the diversity of environmental issues, national circumstances, and individual organizational strategies makes it inevitable that EPM activities will be heavily influenced by contextual factors. The industry sector is likely to be the most significant contingent variable, as this will affect both the nature of the environmental impacts and the degree and nature of public concern. Other factors that might affect the measurement system are the political climate and legislation of the country, the size of the organization, and its management style and culture (Schreiner 1991).

In any performance measurement system there is a risk that attention can become focused on only a few measures at the cost of paying inadequate attention to others. Kaplan and Norton (1992) have therefore advocated the need for a "balanced scorecard" of financial and nonfinancial measures. The same potential conflict between individual measures can be discerned in the environmental area. The environmental balanced scorecard will therefore need to contain a variety of measures. The key question for each is the number and type of measure, given the need to strike a balance between comprehensiveness and simplicity.

Effective financial and operational performance measurement depends on sophisticated systems for collecting, collating, analyzing, and using relevant data. However Orlin, Swalwell, and Fitzgerald (1993) have argued that most existing environmental management information systems (EMIS) are fragmented and inflexible. A good example of this is Hallay (1990) who introduces a comprehensive environmental information system for physical (impact) measures, but has no measures to assess management systems. The underlying techniques for collecting data inputs to EMIS—such as life cycle analysis and material accounting systems—are also underdeveloped, as Charlton and Hovell (1992) rightly point out.

Relationship with the External Environment

In recent years, EPM has been driven by external reporting. The disclosure requirements of the TRI legislation have shaped the activities of many American companies, while both they and some European companies have seen reporting as an important means of achieving credibility with external stakeholders. However, while reporting is clearly useful and desirable for many companies, it can sometimes distract attention from the development of EPM for internal use. In particular, it may have led some companies to place less emphasis on customer and financial measures than would otherwise have been the case and would be perhaps desirable if environmental actions are to fully contribute to the achievement of strategic objectives (James and Bennett 1994).

One recurrent problem with environmental reporting, and indeed EPM, is lack of comparability of data. Organizations and their divisions are often measuring different things, in different ways, for different purposes. Comparisons therefore have to be against historical performance or with preset targets or benchmarks but cannot be between organizations. (Germany may be a partial exception, as EPM has had more academic inputs so that comparison has had a higher priority.) For some this is not a problem. They will not be interested in making external comparisons, either because of the difficulties of developing standardized measures or because they fear the results of such comparison. On the other hand, there are growing pressures for the development of comparative measures. Investors, insurers, and others see them as a means of reducing financial risks from poor environmental performance, environmentalists and regulators see them as a means of highlighting poor performers, and some companies themselves see them as a basis for benchmarking and continuous improvement.

One comparative system has already been established by the Investor Responsibility Research Center (1992), which calculates toxic emissions and violations per million dollars of turnover (sales) for Fortune 500 companies. The Council on Economic Priorities operates a similar, if more qualitative, scheme. Its data provided the basis for a *Fortune* magazine survey of 130 leading U.S. corporations (Rice 1993). This gave marks for performance in 20 areas (of different weighting) and identified 20 leaders, 10 most improved, and 10 laggards. Nikkei Research (1993) has conducted a similar exercise of Japanese companies.

Organizations are also beginning to undertake benchmarking studies of several aspects of environmental management. In the United States, AT&T and Intel undertook a qualitative benchmark of corporate pollution-prevention programs (Klafter 1992), which was followed up by a site-level study by the U.S. Business Roundtable (1993). The latter found that best practice sites had different approaches and used different metrics, but shared an emphasis on measuring key pollution prevention parameters and setting quantitative targets for them. James (1994b) summarizes the results of a U.K. event on the topic.

National Approaches to EPM

Much of the contemporary English-language literature on EPM is written by, and directed to, environmental practitioners. Two exceptionally useful practitioner reports are by the U.K. organization, Business in the Environment (1992), and the U.S. President's Commission on Environment Quality (1992). The latter discusses measurement within the context of total quality management (TQM). TQM places greater emphasis on the use of measurement to identify the root causes and costs of problems and to drive continuous improvement; it therefore supports pollution prevention and the desire to assess the financial costs and benefits of environmental action.

Much U.S. literature has been driven by a TQM approach, and key articles from two leading U.S. TQM-influenced journals, *Pollution Pre-*

vention Review and *Total Quality Environmental Management*, have been collected in Willig (1994). Leading U.S. multinationals have also established the Global Environmental Management Initiative (GEMI) as a center for TQM approaches to environment, and the proceedings of their annual conferences (1991, 1992, 1993, 1994) contain many papers on the topic of EPM.

Smart (1992) of the World Resources Institute also provides short case studies on measurement in a number of U.S. corporations. The study of Polaroid's innovative environmental accounting and reporting system (EARS) by Nash *et al.* in Willig (1994) is unusual in being a case study written by academics. Smart (1992) is a compilation of a number of American case studies, compiled under several headers, such as goals, measurement, and accountability. Wolfe and Howes (1993) also provide a thoughtful description of the process and outcomes of designing an EPM system for the Canadian utility Ontario Hydro. Another Canadian article uses Northern Telecom to illustrate general principles of EPM (Eckel *et al.* 1992). Fitzgerald (1992) and Peacock (1993) do the same for some U.S. companies. M. Charter provides a case study of the U.K. operations of Scott Paper and discusses implementation problems.[1] Nielson (1991) overviews experience in packaging measurement at Digital.

Much U.K. activity has also linked measurement to quality but has focused on the narrow topic of environmental management systems. As a result, there is considerable literature discussing EPM within the context of the British Standards Institute's standard for environmental management systems, BS7750. Examples are Wright and Kennedy (1994), who relate BS7750 to the quality concept, and Gilbert (1994) who compares EPM as represented in the BS7750 specification with that in the European Union eco-management and audit regulation. Hocking and Power's (1993) discussion of environmental measurement techniques is an exception, as is the practitioner handbook by Bragg, Knapp, and McLean (1993), based on their experience as consultants with Arthur D. Little.

Most literature on the application of TQM to the environment has been uncritical. However, Welford (1993) has been scathing of the

---

1. M. Charter, "Scott Limited: Measuring Environmental Performance," *Greener Management International* (January 1993) (1): 172–179.

narrowness of BS7750—which allows companies to set the targets to which measurement of progress is directed—and also argues that any quality approach is too incremental to deal with the challenge of sustainable development, which requires new measures of sustainability. James (1994a) makes a similar point.

German and Swiss organizations have been driven by exacting and extremely difficult regulatory requirements. This has created considerable German-language literature on both eco-balancing (scientific) and eco-controlling (managerial) approaches (Pfriem and Hallay 1992; Seidel 1988). However, as a generalization, German-speaking scholars have focused on holistic, scientifically based attempts to map the overall impacts of both processes and products and to integrate impact measures into the existing resource and materials accounting systems. Müller-Wenk (1978) outlines his pioneering system using coefficients for each pollutant, which then can be summarized to provide an overall EPM system. Wehrmeyer (1992) has adapted this approach to a study of U.K. paper companies. BUWAL (1991) provides standardized data about emissions, energy, and resource usage per kilogram of packaging material. ÖBU (1992) provides case studies of eco-balancing approaches in Swiss companies. However, Freese and Kloock (1989) and Schreiner (1992) have developed eco-controlling approaches based on translation of environmental parameters into financial metrics.

Future Challenges

EPM is in its early stages and it is therefore not surprising that its practice is currently fragmented. The challenge for researchers is to reduce this fragmentation by helping to clarify the purposes of EPM, to refine the tools and data resources that it calls on, and to assist in its integration with other areas of organizational activity.

One important research topic is to ascertain whether EPM influences behavior—for example, by comparing organizations with sophisticated EPM approaches with those where they are lacking. Such research might also identify key factors that influence the success of EPM, such as extensive involvement in the development of measures by those who must implement them. One danger is that emphasis on EPM directs attention to areas that can be measured and away from those that cannot, however important they may be. Is this actually happening? Indeed an important line of research will be to explore the extent to which EPM is an attempt by large corporations to "managerialize" and "rationalize" environmental concern and thereby marginalize an alternative approach that argues for more ethically, spiritually, and socially transforming approaches to the environmental challenge.

Within the present paradigm, a key theme is likely to be the bringing together of managerial (eco-controlling) and scientific (eco-balancing) approaches to EPM. Managers need better information on the relative importance of different environmental options, while the often complex scientific approaches need to become more consistent and better adapted to the practical needs of management (Baumgartner and Rubik 1993). The answer probably lies in the production, by internationally consensual methods, of standardized environmental data that organizations can use for their decision making. An important part of developing this will be studies of how managers actually use EPM data. Another will be the development of cost-effective environmental information systems and their integration with other management information systems.

One of the intellectually most challenging and most basic aspects of designing EPM systems concentrates on which environmental factors are to be taken into account. This challenge relates to the boundaries of the organization in environmental terms. Can methods be found to evaluate an organization's ultimate environmental impact, for example, on river basins or biodiversity? Should the remit of EPM be broadened in line with the sustainability debate to intergenerational and intragenerational (geographical and social) equity? Companies wishing to be seen as environmental leaders will have to pay more attention to impact measures generally and measures of sustainability in particular. This will probably require the development of an international institutional infrastructure to make operational the concept of sustainability (for example, to sustainable global, national, regional, and ultimately firm emissions of substances) so that it can be incorporated into an organization's individual EPM activities. James and Bennett (1994) develop a short, fictional scenario of such a situation.

The final and perhaps most important challenge is to develop standardized forms of EPM so that comparisons between sites, organizations, and industries can be made more easily. While diversity will make complete standardization impossible, the development of standardized financial performance measures from similarly unpromising circumstances over the last century means that it is perhaps not too fanciful to imagine that a combination of government action, initiatives by international standards and ratings organizations, and inter-firm cooperation will achieve this condition. Indeed Lascelles (1993) has discussed the possibility of an environmental equivalent of the bond-rating agencies, Moody's and Standard and Poor, issuing semi-objective ratings of environmental performance. The emergence of institutionalization and standardization is less fanciful when one important maxim of performance measurement is borne in mind: It is better to be approximately right than precisely wrong. Long-term consistency in measurement may be more important—and perhaps more easily achieved—than absolute accuracy.

Annotated Bibliography

Azzone, G., and R. Manzini. 1994. "Measuring Strategic Environmental Performance." *Business Strategy and the Environment* 3 (1) (Spring): 1–14.
Focuses on key measures for environmental management control. Divided into three sections, the essay first identifies five conceptual requirements for an EPM system—completeness, long-term orientation, external orientation, measurability, and cost. The second section identifies and discusses five generic measures, while a third section develops a model of parallel physical and financial environmental accounting systems.

Baumgartner, Thomas, and Frieder Rubik. 1993. "Evaluating Techniques for Eco-Balances and Life Cycle Assessment." *European Environment* 3 (3) (June): 18–23.
The authors report from a EU-funded study of 132 eco-balance stud-

ies. Although the studies are predominantly LCAs, their findings have implications for the development of eco-balances in general. The authors describe the substantial methodological and technical problems of integrating environmental effects into aggregate measures and conclude that there is some convergence on the methodological and procedural differences, but as yet it is too early to find a fully acceptable integration of approaches.

Behmanesh, N., J. Roque, and D. Allen. 1993. "An Analysis of Normalized Measures of Pollution Prevention." *Pollution Prevention Review* (Spring): 161–166.

Examines the sensitivity of normalized Toxic Release Inventory (TRI) emission measures against various measures of business activity. The business activities studied include total payroll of employees, wages, value added by manufacture, value of shipments, total number of employees, and number of production employees. The study concludes that the business outcomes are insensitive to the particular emission measures used.

Bennett, Martin, and Peter James. 1994. "Financial Dimensions of Environmental Performance: Developments in Environment-related Management Accounting." Paper prepared for British Accounting Association Annual Conference, Winchester, UK, October 29–30.

Literature survey, with cases, of financial measures of environmental performance.

Bragg, Sara, Philippa Knapp, and Ronald McLean. 1993. *Improving Environmental Performance: A Guide to a Proven and Effective Approach.* Letchworth/Herts, UK: Technical Communications.

Useful, if bald, practitioner-focused overview of key steps in improving environmental performance. The analysis is based on the author's experience with Arthur D. Little and short cases on B&Q, BAT, and Waste Management International. One chapter on EPM gives useful tips on avoiding pitfalls.

Business in the Environment. 1992. *A Measure of Commitment—Guidelines for Measuring Environmental Performance.* London: Business in the Environment (5 Cleveland Place, London, SW1V 6JJ, UK).

This is arguably the first English report condensing the efforts of companies' environmental performance measurements into a "how-to" manual. Differentiating between contributor, process, and overall impact measures, the report advocates an integrated model of performance management if not measurement.

Business Roundtable. 1993. *Facility Level Pollution Prevention Benchmarking Report.* Washington, DC: The Business Roundtable.

The most sophisticated environmental benchmarking exercise yet undertaken. A wealth of information on how to approach pollution prevention.

BUWAL. 1991. *Ökobilanz von Packstoffen 1990* (Eco-Balancing for Packaging Materials 1990) Schriftenreihe Umwelt #132 (Environment series No. 132). Bern: Bundesamt für Umwelt, Wald und Landschaft. (Bern: Swiss Federal Agency for Environmental Forestry and Landscape).

A technical and highly detailed analysis of the environmental impacts of packaging materials. The results are separated for glass, aluminum, paper, plastics, and tin; the presentation covers emissions and energy consumption data across the life cycle of these materials. Included is a sensitivity analysis for each packaging material. This analysis has been the basis for several LCA studies. The book is designed for use in determining environmental impact, but the data have initially been limited to Switzerland.

Charlton, Carol, and Belinda Hovell. 1992. "Life Cycle Assessment: A Tool for Solving Environmental Problems?" *European Environment* 2 (2): 2–5.

After a general introduction into life cycle assessment, the article outlines the methodological problems and the substantial technical difficulties of producing meaningful results from LCAs. They suggest that a gradual consensus on many of the assumptions made will facilitate the acceptability and hence usefulness of LCA.

Eccles, Robert. 1991. "The Performance Measurement Manifesto." *Harvard Business Review* (January-February): 131–137.

Performance measurers can be passionate! A call for all companies to move beyond financial performance and measure nonfinancial dimensions of their business, with discussions of key issues.

Eckel, Len, Kathryn Fisher, and Grant Russel. 1992. "Environmental Performance Measurement." *CMA Magazine* (March): 16–22.

Discusses EPM from general management accounting/performance measurement perspective, using Northern Telecom as case material.

ENDS. 1993. "Improving the Chemical Industry's Performance—Lessons from the U.S.A. and Netherlands." *ENDS Report* (August): 16–19.

Interesting comparison of approaches to environmental management and EPM between U.S. and European chemical industries, with discussion of the role of TRI legislation in shaping U.S. responses.

Fitzgerald, Chris. 1992. "Selecting Measures for Corporate Environmental Quality." *Total Quality Environmental Management* (Summer): 329–337. Reproduced in *Greener Management International* 1 (1) (January): 25–34.

Discusses EPM from TQM perspective, with short cases on AT&T, Intel, Sandoz, Niagara Mohawk, Green Environment, Xerox, 3M, and EPA initiatives.

Freedman, Martin, and Bikki Jaggi. 1986. "Pollution Performance of Firms from Pulp and Paper Industries." *Environmental Management* 10 (3): 359–365.

———. 1988. "Impact of Government Regulations on Pollution Performance of Pulp and Paper." *Environmental Management* 12 (8): 391–396.

In this early analysis of pollution performance, Freedman and Jaggi develop a pollution score of BOD, TSS, and pH and compare 13 of the largest U.S. paper firms. They attribute some degree of the large differences found between firms (1986) to the impact of government. The later study is a follow-up where the authors find some convergence on the emissions.

Freeman, Harry, Teresa Harten, Johny Springer, Mary Ann Curran, and Kenneth Stone. 1992. "Industrial Pollution Prevention: A Critical Review." *Journal of Air and Waste Management Association* 42 (5) (May): 618–665.

All you ever wanted to know about pollution prevention, with analysis of 472 sources. Discusses role of measurement in pollution prevention, which it describes as the "biggest issue facing the pollution prevention community."

Freese, E., and J. Kloock. 1989. "Internes Rechnungswesen und Organisation aus der Sicht des Umweltschutzes" (Internal accounting and administration from an environmental perspective) In *Betriebwirtschaftliche Forschung und Praxis* (Business administration research and practice) vol. 41, 1–29.

Freese and Kloock summarize the interface between cost and materials accounting and EPM. They focus more on the impact environmental issues have had on accounting than on ways in which environmental impacts of firms can be measured on a continuous basis.

Gilbert, Michael. 1993. *Achieving Environmental Management Standards. A Step-by-Step Guide to Meeting BS7750.* London: Pitman Publishing/Institute of Management.

————. 1994. "BS7750 and the Eco-Management and Audit Regulation." *Eco-Management and Audit* 1 (2): 6–10.

For better or worse, the British Standards Institute's Environmental Management Standard has already had a profound influence on the way environmental performance is assessed. The BS7750 specification lays out in detail what is expected of firms to obtain accreditation of their management systems, including setting of targets and measurement of progress. Gilbert (1993) has produced an easy and simple guide to BS7750 with a number of management practice ideas. Gilbert (1994) is a very informative comparison between the European Environmental Management and Audit Scheme, which were intended as complementary but at the moment appear to compete. He sees BS7750 as a stepping stone for EMAS.

Global Environmental Management Initiative. 1992. *Environmental Self-Assessment Program.* Washington, DC: Global Environmental Management Initiative (2000 L Street NW, Suite 710, Washington, DC 20036).

The often debated notion of sustainable development has been interpreted by the International Chamber of Commerce in its Business Charter for Sustainable Development. GEMI and Deloitte Touche Tohmatsu have operationalized this charter into a number of self-scored questions. Companies can thereby assess their current situation, track

their progress and—through Deloitte's centralized database—compare
their responses with others.

Greenberg, Richard, and Cynthia Unger. 1992. "Improving the Environmental Process." *Total Quality Environmental Management* (Spring): 269–276.

Analyzes nature of environmental processes and identifies eight key—
and measurable—inputs. These are people, equipment, methods, materials, physical setting, internal support and administrative functions,
external groups, and feedback.

Hallay, Hendrick (ed.). 1990. *Die Ökobilanz—Ein Betriebliches Informations system (Eco-balancing—A management information system)* Berlin: Institut für ökologische Wirtschaftsforschung (Berlin: Institute for Ecological Business Research.)

Hallay's report is based on a case study of a medium-sized packaging
firm in Germany that has introduced one eco-balancing approach into
their existing management information system. It describes the implementation history in some detail and thus provides excellent guidelines
for similar efforts in other firms.

Hearne, Shelley, and Michael Aucott. 1992. "Source Reduction: Why the
TRI Cannot Measure Pollution Prevention." *Pollution Prevention Review*
(Winter): 3–16.

Argues that tracking reductions in TRI emissions is not a good basis for
measuring pollution prevention. Advocates use of comprehensive material accounting systems as an alternative. This has already been adopted
in New Jersey.

Hocking, Roland, and Shaked Power. 1993. "Environmental Performance
Quality: Measurement and Improvement." *Business Strategy and the Environment* 2 (4) (Winter): 19–24.

Short paper outlining quality measurement techniques that can be used
in the environmental area. A concluding section discusses some of the
difficulties of EPM.

Hodgkinson, Simon. 1993. "Coming Clean: Measuring and Reporting on
Corporate Environmental Performance." Paper presented at the Greening
of Industry Network Conference, Boston, MA, November 14–16, 1993.
London: Deloitte Touche Tohmatsu.

Account of the European Green Table's study of EPM in the oil, petro-chemicals, and paper industries. One of the few surveys of how EPM is being used in practice.

Investor Responsibility Research Center. 1992. *Corporate Environmental Pro-files Directory.* Washington, DC: Investor Responsibility Research Center (1755 Massachusetts Ave., NW, Washington, DC 20036).

Invaluable source of information about the environmental performance of Fortune 500 companies.

James, Peter. 1994a. "Quality and the Environment: From Total Quality Management to Sustainable Quality Management." *Greener Management International* 6 (Spring): 62–71.

Describes points of connection between TQM and environmental man-agement—of which performance measurement is a central one—with mini–case studies of the application of TQM approaches to environ-ment at AT&T, Baxter Healthcare, and BP. Argues that TQM often fails and may need to be transcended to achieve the environmental improve-ments needed to achieve sustainability.

James, Peter. 1994b. *Environmental Benchmarking: Summary of Workshop Pro-ceedings.* Berkhamsted, UK: Ashridge Management Research Group.

Summary of presentations by Baxter Healthcare and Du Pont, plenary sessions, and small group discussions at a two-day workshop concerned with environmental benchmarking held in September 1994.

James, Peter, and Martin Bennett. 1994. *Environment-related Performance Mea-surement in Business.* Berkhamsted, UK: Ashridge Management Research Group.

An overview of the current status and possible future trends of EPM. Individual chapters discuss the drivers of EPM, generic categories of measurement, the business areas in which it can be applied, and the need for a strategic approach to the area. The report contains a num-ber of business examples.

Kaplan, Robert, and David Norton. 1992. "The Balanced Scorecard—Measures That Drive Performance." *Harvard Business Review* (January-February): 71–79.

Insightful discussion of the need for a balanced scorecard in generic performance measurement. The ideas can easily be applied to EPM.

Klafter, Brenda. 1992. "Pollution Prevention Benchmarking: AT&T and Intel Work Together with the Best." *Total Quality Environmental Management* (Autumn): 27–34.

Interesting account of the methodology of the two company's benchmarking study of corporate pollution-prevention programs.

Lascelles, David. 1993. *Rating Environmental Risk.* London: Center for the Study of Financial Innovation.

Short paper exploring the value and feasibility of standardized rating of the environmental performance and risks of companies.

Müller-Wenk, Ruedi. 1978. *Die Ökologische Buchhaltung. Ein Informations- und Steuerungs-instrument für umweltkonforme Unternehmenspolitik* (Ecological bookkeeping. An information and decision-support instrument for environmentally sensitive corporate policy). Frankfurt am Main: Campus Verlag.

With regard to integrated impact measures, this is a milestone. It is the first moderately successful model which, with some environmental justification, provides a mathematical way to combine different emission types into one framework. It does so by producing coefficients to standardize emissions into dimensionless figures, which then can be summarized across firms, units, or geographical areas.

Neely, Andy. 1993. *Performance Measurement System Design—A Process-based Approach.* Cambridge: University of Cambridge, Manufacturing Engineering Group.

Discussion and critique of existing approaches to performance measurement and development of a generic framework for implementing performance measures. Insightful discussion of key issues in any kind of performance measurement activity.

Nielsen, Larry. 1991. "Packaging Waste Management—A Key Element in Digital's Total Quality Program." *Total Quality Environmental Management* (Winter 1991/92): 167–174.

Discussion of how Digital used measurement of packaging volume, weight, and value to establish priorities for packaging-reduction programs and to monitor progress.

Nikkei Research. 1993. *Survey on the State of Corporate Responses to Global Environmental Issues.* Tokyo: Nikkei Research.

Interesting survey of Japanese companies, revealing that some are more advanced than many outsiders imagine. Respondents were asked to identify the most "environmentally advanced" companies in their sector. Hitachi and NEC emerged as the clear leaders.

ÖBU. 1992. *Ökobilanz für Unternehmen (Eco-balancing for business).* St. Gallen: ÖBU (Postfach 9, CH-9001 St. Gallen, Switzerland).

All you really need to know about eco-balancing and the organizational context in which it is likely to be successful. It includes practical cases from Baer Weichkäserei, Geberit, Jowa Teigwaren, the Schweizerischer Bankverein, Sika, and Walser AG, which have been analyzed and compared separately in the text.

Orlin, Judy, Peg Swalwell, and Chris Fitzgerald. 1993. "How to Integrate Information Strategy Planning with Environmental Management Information Systems." *Total Quality Environmental Management* (Winter 1993/94): 193–202.

The authors are all IT experts who criticize the present generation of environmental management information systems as fragmented, expensive, and too inflexible to deal with the rapidly changing demands of environmental management. They argue for a more strategic approach and emphasize the need to link EMIS with other corporate information systems.

Peacock, Marcus. 1993. "Developing Environmental Performance Measures." *Industrial Engineering* (September): 20–22.

This is a short, insightful discussion of EPM. The article identifies three key principles—measuring improvement, fairness, and a range of measures—and discusses four EPM tensions: simplicity versus complexity, qualitative versus quantitative, ends versus means, and conservation versus compliance.

Pfriem, Reinhard, and Hendric Hallay. 1992. "Öko-Controlling als Baustein einer innovativen Unternehmenspolitik" (Eco-controlling as part of innovative corporate policy). In *Handbuch des Umweltmanagements* (Handbook of environmental management), Ulrich Steger (ed.) München: Verlag C.H. Beck.

Pfriem and Hallay offer a general review of German "eco-controlling"—a concept that probably can best be described as an environmental management control system. Their contribution emphasizes the necessity of integrating this with overall management systems as a precondition for innovative and flexible organizations. The competitive advantages that may arise from this are stressed.

President's Commission on Environmental Quality. 1993. *Total Quality Management: A Framework for Pollution Prevention.* Washington, DC: President's Commission on Environmental Quality.

Practitioner report on how TQM principles and techniques can be applied to environmental management. Measurement is a key part of TQM. A series of case studies examines the metrics that were used to drive pollution prevention. Case companies are AT&T, Chevron, Dow, Du Pont, Ford, General Electric, International Paper, Merck, 3M, Procter and Gamble, and U.S. Generating Company. Interesting to note that three of these—Du Pont, General Electric, and International Paper— appear among the 10 worst performers in the *Fortune* survey (Rice 1993).

Rice, F. 1993. "Who Scores Best on the Environment?" *Fortune* 26 (July): 104–111.

Interesting and—for a news magazine—sophisticated attempt to rank 130 leading U.S. manufacturing companies on 20 dimensions of environmental performance. Some interesting names among the leaders and laggards.

Schreiner, Manfred. 1991. *Umweltmanagement in 22 Lektionen. Ein ökonomischer Weg in eine ökologische Gesellschaft,* 2nd ed. (Environmental management in 22 lessons: An economical way toward an ecological society). Wiesbaden: Gabler Verlag.

One of the first environmental management textbooks, Schreiner devotes two of his 22 lessons to evaluating the impact that existing accounting systems have on the environment and which measures exist to assess corporate environmental performance.

Schreiner, Manfred. 1992. "Betriebliches Rechungswesen bei umweltorientierter Unternehmensführung." (Management accounting under environmentally oriented corporate policy). In *Handbuch des Umweltmanagements* (Handbook of environmental management), Ulrich Steger, (ed.), 469–485. München: Verlag C.H. Beck.

Integrating environmental impacts into the management information system is a complex task. Schreiner (1992) provides the so-far most comprehensive general introduction to the subject by subsuming environmental effects as part of traditional cost accounting. He does so mainly by referencing how the various methods would have to be modified to better account for environmental impacts.

Schulz, Erika, and Werner Schulz. 1993. *Umweltcontrolling in der Praxis. Ein Ratgeber für Betriebe* (Environmental controlling in practice: A guide for business). München: Verlag Franz Vahlen.

Based on the German business administration tradition, Schulz shows in a practical and readable guide the efforts that have been made to integrate environmental cost and benefit estimates into the existing cost attribution grid of accounting and balancing. It includes an analysis of environmental cost-minimizing strategies for companies and a plethora of case studies, anecdotes, tips, and tricks.

Seidel, Eberhard. 1988. "Ökologisches Controlling" (Ecological controlling). In *Betriebswirtschaftslehre als Management und Führungslehre*, 2nd ed. (Business administration theory as a theory of management and leadership). R. Wunderer (ed.). 301–322, Stuttgart: C.E. Poeschel Verlag.

Seidel provides a critical yet very insightful overview into the German approach to environmental policy control and evaluation. He suggests eco-balancing as the first information system that may act as a database for process, product, and materials analyses, which then inform about the efficacy of policy.

Shorthouse, Barry. 1991. "Using Risk Analysis to Set Priorities for Pollution Prevention." *Pollution Prevention Review* (Winter 1990/91): 41–53.

A technical discussion of how risk assessment techniques can be applied to the environmental area.

Smart, Bruce (ed.). 1992. *Beyond Compliance.* New York: World Resources Institute.

> An optimistic book of case studies on environmental management by industry. The text includes a section on environmental performance measurement examples from S.C. Johnson Wax, Monsanto, AT&T, New England Electric System, Xerox, and Allied-Signal.

Wehrmeyer, Walter. 1992. "Ranking Corporate Environmental Performance in the Paper Industry." Paper presented to the First Annual Conference on Business and the Environment, Leicester, UK, September 1–2.

> This paper presents the results of a comparative study of environmental performance of several U.K. paper-manufacturing firms. The comparison is based on a modification and extension of the model proposed by Müller-Wenk (1978) and thus represents the first use of this eco-balancing approach in the English-speaking sphere. Some general conclusions about the use and usefulness of this method are included as well.

Wehrmeyer, Walter (ed.). 1994. *Environmental References in Business.* Sheffield: Greenleaf Publishing.

> A book of about 2000 selected references separated into a large number of environmental management categories. Designed for newcomers from practice and academia alike who want to find their way into the field.

Welford, Richard. 1993. "Breaking the Link Between Quality and the Environment: Auditing for Sustainability and Life Cycle Assessment." *Business Strategy and the Environment* 4 (Winter): 25–33.

> A former advocate of linking environmental management to quality systems now argues that a quality framework directs attention to incremental improvement and away from radical change in corporate culture and from activities necessary to make their activities compatible with sustainable development. He suggests that companies need to audit— and measure—their progress toward sustainability to achieve this shift.

Wells, Richard; Mark Hockman, Stephen Hochman, and Patricia O'Connell. 1992. "Measuring Environmental Success." *Total Quality Environmental Management* (Summer): 315–327.

> Identifies three generic measures of environmental success: environmental results measures (emissions and wastes), process improvement

measures (existence and efficacy of management systems), and customer satisfaction measures (perceptions of company's environmental
actions by buyers and stakeholders). Argues that the latter two can be as
important as the first and that customer measures are especially important because they link the environment to issues of competitive advantage. Uses Xerox as an example.

Wicke, Lutz, Hans-Dietrich Haasis, Franzjosef Schafhausen, and Werner
Schulz. 1992. *Betriebliche Umweltökonomie: Eine praxisorientierte Einführung*
(Corporate environmental economics: A practical introduction). Mün-
chen: Verlag Franz Vahlen.

Though primarily based on business economics, Wicke *et al.* provide
very detailed and comprehensive analyses of corporate environmental
information systems, which include a discussion of Müller-Wenk's
approach as well as the way in which such information systems can be
embedded in the existing MIS.

Willig, John (ed.). 1994. *Environmental TQM*, 2nd ed. New York: Executive
Enterprises.

A collection of general and company-specific articles from *Pollution Prevention* and *Total Quality Environmental Management* issues. Contains sections
on general principles of TQM, applications to environmental management and auditing, environmental benchmarking, and performance
measurement. Companies whose EPM activities are profiled include
Polaroid, Procter & Gamble, and Union Carbide. Together with the
President's Commission report, an excellent introduction to current
U.S. thinking and practice in the area.

Wolfe, Anita, and Helen Howes. 1993. "Measuring Environmental Performance: Theory and Practice at Ontario Hydro." *Total Quality Environmental Management* (Summer): 355–366.

Discusses three aspects of EPM at Ontario Hydro: identifying key environmental performance indicators, the development of usable measures, and the communication and use of the resulting data.

Wright, Michael, and Gary Kennedy. 1994. "Getting Value from BS7750:
Lessons Learnt from Quality Management." In *Eco-Management and Audit* 1
(2) (Spring): 14–16.

After the initial fashion of BS7750, the first experiences of implementing this standard are reported. Wright and Kennedy offer "do's and don'ts" and warn of the fallacy that following the requirements of BS7750 may cloud the direction of environmental management and performance measurement.

Chapter 6

The Greening of
Corporate Accounting

Mark Gijtenbeek
Johan Piet
Allen L. White

Introduction

Corporate environmentalism is a multidimensional concept. The firm seeking to position itself as an environmental leader must look with a critical eye both internally at its management systems and decision processes and externally at how it relates to a broad array of stakeholders, such as investors, environmentalists, customers, and the communities that host its facilities. The burgeoning level of regulatory and voluntary standards demands increasingly higher standards of practices from corporations worldwide. Corporate environmentalism has moved well past the point where simple technological improvements act as the sole measure of environmental excellence.

One critical though only lately recognized ingredient in the pathway toward environmental excellence is the firm's accounting system. Traditionally left to the financial accounting professional and geared almost exclusively toward external reporting to shareholders and regulators, corporate accounting systems increasingly are viewed as pivotal in driving managers toward greater environmental conscious-ness. For some firms, this recognition derives from internal pressures to control the rising environmental costs in day-to-day business oper-ations. For others, the pressures have come primarily from external sources such as U.S. Securities and Exchange liability disclosure requirements, emerging International Standards Organization's (ISOs) 207 standards on environmental management systems and auditing, or the European Community's EMAS standards. Whatever the source, it is increasingly evident to managers that in the environ-ment, as in other areas of business management, if "it doesn't get measured, it doesn't get managed."

Signs of change in the accounting profession are visible on many fronts and in both the North American and the European accounting communities. In the European Community's Fifth Action Program on the Environment, "getting the prices right" is viewed as a key underpinning of achieving sustainable development. "Getting the prices right" means measuring and ultimately pricing goods and ser-vices at their full social cost, including costs associated with "exter-nal" environmental impacts. The proposals require involvement of accounting professionals in two ways. First, the Fifth Action Program proposes a "redefinition of accounting concepts, rules, conventions, and methodology so as to ensure that the consumption and use of environmental resources are accounted for as part of the full costs of production and reflected in market process." Second, the program urges the disclosure of a company's environmental policies, pro-grams, expenditures, and risks in their annual reports to regulators and shareholders (FEE 1992).

In North America, similar pronouncements and standards are evi-dent. The chief executive officer of Dow Chemical has made "full cost accounting" a company objective, while recognizing that restruc-turing internal accounting systems is the first step toward achieving this long-range objective. Trade associations such as the American Petroleum Institute and the Global Environmental Management Ini-tiative (GEMI) have environmental accounting committees at work developing guidelines and case studies of improved corporate prac-tices. The Canadian Institute of Chartered Accountants (1993) has issued a study aimed at sensitizing accounting professionals to envi-ronmental issues within the firm. And the U.S. Environmental Protection Agency (U.S. EPA) (1994) has organized an action agenda to spur corporate, consulting, and academic accountants toward improved environmental accounting and capital budgeting practices.

These initiatives reflect an emerging awareness of the critically important yet largely unrealized role of the accountant and accounting information in incorporating environmental issues into both internal and external aspects of business management. Internally, accounting information plays an essential role in three activities in the firm (Todd 1994). The first activity is *decision support*—for example, decisions related to product mix, product pricing, product choice, make-or-buy decisions, and capital expenditures. The second activity is *monitoring*, tracking both routine "knowns"—such as production volume costs, sales, quality, and waste disposal costs—and nonroutine "unknowns"—such as contingencies and market shifts. The third activity is *control and motivation*, or information that informs the achievement of profit and quality targets, optimal use of the firm's assets, and new business development.

All three activities contribute to effective management, and all three depend in part on the steady compilation and flow of reliable environmental information. For example, decision support in relation to product pricing and product mix necessitates the allocation of environmental costs to products and processes in such a way that their true costs are fully apparent to managers. Monitoring waste disposal volume tells managers a great deal about production efficiencies and where to target improvement initiatives. Environmental information pertaining to waste disposal uncertainties and costs helps motivate managers to consider prudent risk-management practices.

In contrast to internal management activities, the role of environmental information in external matters is more familiar territory to the accounting community. This in large measure is due to the heavily external-focused function of accounting information in general—for example, income statements, balance sheets, debt-to-equity ratios, and other performance indicators, as well as reporting to government regulators as in the case of 10-K filings with the U.S. Securities and Exchange Commission. For external purposes, information generally is historical in nature, aggregated, and contains few uncertainties and contingencies. This may be compared to internal management information needs, which principally are served by disaggregated, future-

oriented, and contingent types of information to support management decision making. These characteristics, while applicable to
internal accounting information in general, especially characterize
environmental information.

Scanning the environmental accounting literature in the mid-
1990s reveals a burgeoning volume of material from scholars and
practitioners. Indeed, as the attached citations will attest, prior to
1990 the literature was extremely scant. [See, for example, General
Electric Corporation (1987) and Schulz (1989).] Beginning in the
early 1990s and driven by both internal pressures to rationalize corporate management systems while remaining competitive and external pressures for greater information disclosure, environmental
accounting moved into prominence. In the United States, liability
disclosure requirements are probably the single greatest impetus; in
Europe, a mix of green product labeling and voluntary environmental reporting has been a major force. Gray (1990) marks a turning
point in the evolution of green accounting. From the accounting and
auditing world many publications followed (DTTI 1993; FEE 1992;
EGT/ DTTI 1993; Gray et al. 1993; Grayson and Woolston 1994;
Owen 1992; Piet 1990, 1992, 1993; Scholtens 1992). We anticipate
that this flurry of activity will persist well into the 1990s and enter a
more operational phase as environmental accounting moves from the
textbook into corporate practice.

Much of the environmental accounting literature can be placed
within three principal topics: (1) environmental information systems,
(2) environmental costing, and (3) environmental reporting.

Environmental Information Systems

In the theory of management information, a distinction is made
between the terms "data" and "information." Data are raw facts
about the position of or activities within the company. They are the
ingredients for the production of management information. Information represents the increase in knowledge obtained by data users.
Managers need information to appraise and select options leading to
strategic decisions—what products to produce, in what volumes,
whether to use in-house or outside suppliers, and how to choose

among competing uses of capital. Information also provides the raw material on which internal and external reporting is based, and on which decisions are evaluated and reconsidered.

Information is necessary for management to control environmental decisions at the strategic level. Using the instruments of management information for controlling purposes, we can design relevant, effective, and reliable information about the environmental aspects of the business activities and the instruments to influence the results of these activities. Environmental performance indicators (EPIs) can help to show the results of efforts to improve the environmental performance.

Strategic environmental information starts with the assessment of the environmental issues of a specific firm, defined by both internal and external users of information. Stakeholder analysis covering both internal users (production engineers, product designers, purchasing staff, environmental staff) and external users (shareholders, environmentalists, host communities) is an essential step in designing an information system (Freedman 1993; Piet 1992; White 1994).

Evaluating investments in new processes or products may benefit from an "eco-rating method" to compare alternatives. The eco-rating method is limited to the sphere of management influence. Krozer (1992) draws the total life cycle of the product in this evaluation process. He uses an input-output matrix to represent the emissions during the life cycle of a product. Another eco-rating-like method is the "standard Dutch" life cycle approach by Wit *et al.* (1993), a model for selecting alternatives for environmental investments.

When all audiences are considered, it becomes clear that environmental information needs are decidedly diverse. Materials accounting, materials mass balances, raw materials purchases, energy use, and air and water emissions are all part of the information base that accountants must cultivate to adequately meet the diverse needs of these various audiences. This makes clear the critical role of rigorously developing data of a *physical* nature (kilograms, tons, gallons) to create a sound foundation for measuring *monetary* units (waste disposal costs, liability, licensing and permitting fees, profitability of pollution prevention investments). Piet (1990) and Scholtens (1992) describe measures that achieve reliable information. Environmental information in a broad sense is described by Bartolomeo (1993) and Schulz

(1989). The design of internal management information by environmental performance indicators is presented by DTTI (1993) by order
of the European Green Table.

Environmental Costs

Defining, compiling, analyzing, tracking, controlling, and reporting
cost information is the essence of the accountant's role in the firm. As
environmentalism has penetrated corporate management, however, it
has become clear that *environmental* costs present special and unique
challenges to traditional accounting practices.

Why is this the case? First, environmental costs are often probabilistic, or contingent, in nature. They may be incurred only if certain events arise, such as improper waste disposal by a disposal service vendor. In addition, potential political developments, such as
enactment of new air quality regulations, may dramatically affect
pollution control costs in the next decade. Dealing with these types of
probabilities is unfamiliar territory for most of the accounting profession.

Second, many environmental costs traditionally are left to overhead accounts, where they are indistinguishable from other general
administrative costs (Todd 1993, 1994). In times when environmental
costs represented a very small share of operating costs, this practice
had few material effects on management's ability to make the best
investment. In recent years, however, the situation has changed substantially. No longer are environmental costs trivial in the scheme of
the firm's cost structure. In their direct and indirect forms, these costs
may now compete with other standard cost items (energy, labor, raw
materials, capital) in the daily, monthly, or yearly operations of the
enterprise. Thus, it violates the basic principles of sound cost management to relegate environmental costs to overhead accounts
detached from the process and products responsible for their creation, or to link them to units of output, when in fact they are driven
by facility, product line, or plant-level drivers. The effects of such
practices are felt throughout the firm in the form of suboptimal pricing, product mix, investment, and other decisions.

These special characteristics of environmental costs may be illustrated in the context of capital budgeting for environmental projects oriented to pollution prevention or cleaner technology approaches (U.S. EPA 1990; White, Becker, and Goldstein 1991; White 1993a, 1993b.) Here, accountants face the challenge of bringing usable, consistent cost information to the project review and justification process in a way that permits such projects to be evaluated in an unbiased fashion vis-à-vis competing uses of capital.

Each year, the Organization for Economic Cooperation and Development (OECD) countries invest an estimated 1 to 2 percent of their Gross Domestic Product (GDP) in environmental protection. In all likelihood, this figure will increase during the 1990s. In the United States alone, an estimated 3.6 percent of GDP will be required to achieve ambient environmental standards by the year 2005. At the sectoral level, OECD industries invested approximately $100 billion in 1990 in environmental protection.

To date, the overwhelming fraction of these environmental investments have been of a compliance or "must-do" type, driven by national or state regulations. Not surprisingly, investments in environmental projects have mirrored the evolution of environmental regulations themselves. Such regulations have been largely "end-of-pipe" oriented, aimed at controlling the release of pollutants after their generation. This is the case with air-pollution control equipment such as scrubbers, filters, and precipitators; wastewater pretreatment and treatment systems; and private and commercial landfills for disposal of solid wastes. These control approaches represent one extreme of an environmental technology continuum. In the middle of this continuum are recycle and reuse technologies, with on-site and in-process recycle and reuse more akin to clean technology practices than off-site and out-of-process. At the other end of the continuum are approaches at the core of the clean technology "gene"—process changes, product redesign, and materials substitution that reduce or eliminate the generation of pollutants.

In practice, of course, boundaries along this technology continuum are blurry. Changes in current practices within a single process line, for example, may involve a mix of process changes and on-site recycling, combined with upgraded wastewater pretreatment prior to discharge to a publicly owned treatment facility. Nonetheless, as firms

move further upstream in production processes and along the technology continuum toward core forms of clean technology practices,
certain opportunities for capital budgeting and investment decision
making are identifiable.

First, upstream changes linked to clean production techniques by
definition create complex and disparate repercussions midstream and
downstream. Changing material inputs from more to less toxic substances, for example, necessitates careful consideration of how such
changes will affect equipment performance and product quality. In
the same vein, product redesign likely requires equipment modifica-
tions within a process line. Accompanying these technology adjustments will be a set of capital and operating costs and savings that
may be far-reaching, indirect, and not immediately evident. Thus, in
evaluating the profitability of such investments, compiling and analyzing operational and capital costs becomes that much more com-
plicated and prone to error and/or omission of potentially significant
cost items. Accurate costing quickly moves beyond the capabilities
and data sources of a single staff person, such as the environmental
engineer, the materials manager, the production engineer, or the
financial officer. Contributions from multiple, rather than single,
departments will be necessary to assemble such data.

Figure 6-1 presents a simple taxonomy of costs to highlight those
most prone to omission and/or underestimation as corporations
move to cleaner production strategies (White, Talbot, and Savage
1993). The inner rectangle represents costs that are conventionally
considered by firms in their various managerial accounting activities,
such as capital budgeting, control, pricing, or other functions. For
capital budgeting, for example, costs of upgrading air-pollution control include equipment, materials, utilities, site preparation, engineering and legal fees, depreciation, and operating and maintenance
over the expected life of the investment. These are part of normal
business operations and usually are tracked with reasonable reliabil-
ity, though not necessarily allocated correctly to processes and products.

The second rectangle, labeled "Less Tangible, Hidden, Indirect
Company Costs," extends the boundary of conventional costs in two
ways. First, costs that are real but unrecognized, or recognized but
not incorporated into decision making, are added to those contained
within the first rectangle. We refer to this as adjustments in cost

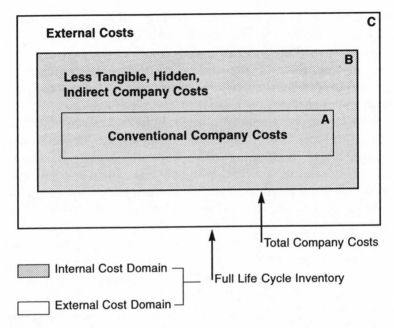

Figure 6-1
Costs for Cleaner Technologies
Source: Tellus Institute

inventory. Future liability for cleaning up property or groundwater, hazardous chemicals, or nuclear wastes may fall into this category. More subtle savings of clean technology practices also may elude the first rectangle and fall into the second: increased employee productivity from reduced exposure to workplace toxics, future value of sales of tradeable air pollution permits, market gains owing to improved corporate or product image, and reduced expenditures of staff time owing to improved community relations.

Misallocation of costs is a widespread phenomenon in manufacturing industries, and environmental costs are particularly prone to such misallocation. Insofar as this occurs, the information vital to support capital budgeting is lost to management. Lumping waste handling and storage, waste disposal, liability, licensing, permitting, training, and monitoring costs is common practice. The reason is twofold: (1) inertia—it's the way such costs have long been allocated; and (2) change is costly—reshaping accounting systems to disentangle such overhead costs is likely to take time and staff resources, and occasion temporary slowdown and confusion.

Further exacerbating the allocation problem is the inappropriate choice of cost "drivers." Even if overhead costs are identified and aligned with specific process or product lines, such costs are often miscalculated owing to their assumed correlation with one cost driver, namely, units of product produced. In fact, numerous other drivers may be operative—for example, set-ups, material movements, purchase orders, and inspections, which are *batch-level* activities; process engineering, product specifications, engineering change notices, and product enhancements, which are *product-sustaining* activities; and plant management, building and grounds activities, and heating and lighting, which are *facility-sustaining* activities. When environmental costs represent part of these subactivities, simply moving them out of overhead accounts is not enough. Optimally, they should be aligned with units of production, batches, product lines, or facilities—whichever is responsible for their creation in the first place.

Clean technologies are associated with certain contingent benefits that are difficult to predict and quantify. Avoided liability is the prime example of this situation. The firm examining a potential project aimed at eliminating a hazardous waste stream or emission may be motivated by a desire to eliminate certain risks of litigation linked to personal or property damages. However, such risks are probabilistic in nature—that is, they may materialize if and when an accident occurs or a claimant sues the firm for such damages. This could occur next week, next month, next year, or never. Thus, incorporating the future monetary benefits of such an investment into a project profitability analysis is problematic. The monetary benefits depend on if, when, and how much liability cost is avoided.

Clean technology profits may materialize well beyond the two-to-five-year time frame commonly applied in investment analyses. Though the savings of some practices—such as improved inventory control—may accrue in the short term, major and more costly changes to processes, materials, and products are likely to extend well beyond the two-to-five-year time period. Analytical methods that fail to capture this future stream of savings contain inherent biases against clean technology investments. In the competition for limited capital resources, such investments are likely to be rendered noncompetitive with more traditional pollution control projects and projects that are primarily driven by nonenvironmental objectives.

In short, the successful introduction of clean technologies hinges to a substantial degree on how effectively these projects compete in the capital budgeting process. Success, in turn, is closely coupled to how costs and savings are inventoried and allocated, how long investments take to show positive cash flows, and how effective profitability indicators capture future streams of savings. When conventional project-evaluation approaches fail to deal effectively with these issues, the prospects for adopting clean technologies are commensurately reduced. In this sense, accountants and accounting information are capable of distinguishing a firm from its competition in terms of environmental leadership and anticipatory investment practices.

While internal costs may be the immediate challenge for green accounting, the forces of regulation and public accountability are widening the internal costs to include additional items that today are squarely in the external cost domain. In other words, external costs of today may well be an internal cost tomorrow (Gray 1990; Gray et al. 1993; Krozer 1992; Milne 1991; Schulz 1992; White, Talbot, and Savage 1993).

Returning to Figure 6-1, beyond the second rectangle are external costs: those for which the firm is not accountable under current regulatory conditions and corporate policy. Because both regulations and corporate policy are subject to constant change, so too is the total company cost boundary. For example, a systemwide cap on greenhouse gas emissions or new regulations on air toxics that may be either certain or possible would lead to an outward shift of the total company cost boundary and a commensurate shrinkage in the external cost domain. Moreover, a firm committed to a corporatewide waste-reduction goal may cooperate voluntarily with a government program such as the U.S. EPA's "33-50" initiative,[1] and by so doing effectively push its total company cost frontier outward into the external cost zone. Whether voluntary or mandatory, it is certain that the

---

1. One of several voluntary initiatives launched by U.S. EPA since 1990 in which firms voluntarily agreed to reduce releases of 17 targeted chemicals by 33 percent in 1992 and by 50 percent by 1995.

external cost domain will contract over time. Corporations with a serious commitment to sustainable development will be at the forefront of this evolution. Accountants are in a position to facilitate this process by designing systems capable of handling external cost information.

Environmental Reporting

Parallel to attention directed at environmental cost has been the emergence of corporate environmental reporting in the form of either stand-alone documents or as part of traditional annual reports to shareholders. The latter has evolved because environmental performance, especially liabilities, are material to the financial condition of the firm and therefore must be disclosed to both regulators and shareholders. The Institute for Environmental Control Science's study, *Toward the Environmental Statement* (Piet 1993), explores how traditional instruments of financial reporting are applied to the environmental statement.

Ensuring that environmental liabilities are fully disclosed and appropriate provisions are made represents a major challenge for the accounting profession. The environmental statement can be designed using existing experience with and theory of financial statements. The audit of the environmental statement is analogous to a standard financial accounting audit, except that it focuses on systems and information. This activity can be performed by the normal financial auditor after a minimal orientation to the environmental issues facing companies (Piet 1993).

Beyond liability disclosure, present trends point to a near-term future when environmental reports move well beyond strictly financially relevant information to encompass a wide array of qualitative and quantitative indicators of management systems and performance. It is reasonable to predict that the stand-alone environmental report will emerge as a standard practice, at least among large, publicly traded firms.

Currently, no single definition, much less standard, exists for such reporting. Indeed, some firms are reluctant to use the term "report" to describe their communications activities, preferring the more neutral term "review." At this juncture, the distinction between environmental performance reporting and corporate communications is often blurred, and it is likely to remain so for some time.

Since 1989, each year has seen more companies publish an environmental report. Examples abound—Exxon Chemical Holland, EPON, NAM, Hoechst, BSO/Orgin, General Electric Plastics b.v., ARCO, Solvay, DSM, AKZO, Shell-Pernis, GE Plastics Europe, The Bodyshop, Norsk Hydro, Polaroid, Bristol-Myers Squibb, Merck, AT&T, Arco Chemical. Some companies are reporting in response to new regulations, others in response to emerging business requirements or changing public expectations. To a substantial degree, reporting environmental liabilities—for example, the U.S. Superfund and the Netherlands' soil pollution—is the forerunner of more detailed and encompassing environmental disclosure. Thus, while the format, content, and depth of reports vary widely, observers close to the issue seem to agree on one item—environmental reporting is here to stay (Gray 1990; Owen 1992).

With increasing numbers of reports available, the analysis of themes, trends, and best practices has been the focus of a number of assessments (Gray *et al.* 1993; Deloitte Touche Tohmatsu International 1993). From these studies have emerged two dimensions of reporting: (1) impetus—reporting may be prompted by either government mandate or voluntary action, including conformance to voluntary associations such as the International Chamber of Commerce; and (2) scale—reporting may be either at the site level, the firm level, or the sectoral level. The latter is exemplified by the U.S. Chemical Manufacturers Association report of sectorwide air, water, and solid pollutants and progress toward reducing them.

With respect to impetus, through the mid-1990s environmental reporting remains a voluntary practice, with the single but notable exception of liability information provided to regulators and stockholders as part of financial disclosure. A few companies (for example, Norsk Hydro, Monsanto, BSO/Orgin) have led the way with early, detailed, freestanding environmental reports. To date, no single method of reporting is evident, and opinions remain divided on where these new approaches will lead. The freestanding environmental report may be viewed either as a transitional stage toward mandatory disclosure or as the endpoint of a transition that will witness further refinement and standardization, but not regulation. DTTI (1993) argues that "a successful freestanding report can be seen as the 'jewel in the crown' of a company's environmental communications strategy." A report can be tailored to the needs of diverse audiences and therefore can appeal to employees, local communities, investors, or customers. The danger is that a report designed to appeal to everybody may end up serving nobody's real needs.

With voluntary reporting quickly becoming a standard practice, and with the anticipated release of new environmental management standards by the International Standards Organization (ISO) in 1996 or soon thereafter, voluntarism may well be replaced by a quasi-mandatory reporting. By the year 2000, it is entirely possible that outright regulations will follow this intermediate stage. The Netherlands, for example, has issued a draft act on environmental reporting.

With respect to scale, corporate reporting to date typically blends site-specific, anecdotal information (such as specific pollution-prevention "success stories") with more aggregated information describing corporate-level performance along both qualitative and quantitative lines. Choosing the right scale of reporting remains a formidable challenge to companies. Aggregated data generally provide little useful information to communities that seek to understand localized impacts of facility operations. These stakeholders find little value in consolidated data spanning multiple divisions, product lines, and often, dozens of specific production sites. On the other hand, disaggregated data on site-specific air, water, and solid pollution may be of little value to shareholders or regulators who seek a broader picture of corporate performance. For larger firms, including site-specific information is often viewed as creating an unwieldy document and, moreover, is rendered unnecessary since site-specific information is available through other sources to communities and other interested stakeholders.

Are there identifiable commonalities or themes among the burgeoning number of environmental reports currently published? In a survey of current reporting practices, DTTI (1993) identified a five-stage model of the evolution of environmental and sustainable development reporting. In the first stage, the company uses green glossies, newsletters, videos, and a short statement in the annual report. In the second stage, the firm produces a stand-alone environmental report, often linked to the first formal policy statement. The third stage consists of annual green reporting, linked to the environmental management system; the reporting becomes more qualitative than quantitative. In the fourth stage, the company provides full TRI-style performance data on an annual basis. The fifth and final stage consists of sustainable development reporting linking environmental, economic, and social aspects of corporate performance supported by indicators of sustainability. The concept of sustainable development is integrated, a situation that Gray refers to as "accounting for sustainability." DTTI identifies most reports as Stage 1 or Stage 2 documents; very few have reached Stage 3 or Stage 4.

Future Research Directions

Corporate environmental accounting means different things to different stakeholders. In its broadest sense, accounting serves a wide array of stakeholders within and outside the firm who need or desire information to track, assess, improve, and report environmental performance. Because users and uses of environmental information are so varied, and because no standards exist (in contrast to financial accounting), environmental accounting research opportunities are plentiful.

In Europe, both scholars and practitioners are seeking cooperation on research concerning environmental accounting and auditing through an initiative from the Limperg Institute in Amsterdam, the EMAA Research Contact Group. On its research agenda are the following topics: environmental issues at the macro-economic level; management, organization, and internal control; environmental accounting and environmental reporting; audit/verification of EMS and environmental reports; and contribution of the accountancy profession to environmental reporting and environmental auditing. The ICEAW report discusses the following areas for further research: accountability (corporate governance, environmental information in the capital markets, other users of information); corporate environmental disclosure; and the accountant's role in environmental reporting, management issues, fiscal instruments, and auditing.

In the United States, various activities are underway to document, develop, and test methods for improved environmental accounting practices. The Institute for Management Accountants (IMA), based on research with a few dozen firms, is developing guidelines to enhance the use of environmental information as an internal management tool. U.S. EPA, in collaboration with IMA and Tellus Institute, is sponsoring a national survey of current and best practices in cost accounting for capital budgeting of environmental projects. The World Resources Institute will publish in 1995 a report on environmental accounting practices, emphasizing cost allocation methods, in several large and small firms. The American Petroleum Institute and the Global Environmental Management Initiative (GEMI) have underway or have completed assessment of cost accounting methods as a key component of total quality management.

Activities such as these in Europe and the United States point to many opportunities for advancing environmental accounting from both an internal management and an external reporting perspective. Indeed, improved accounting methods are widely viewed as integral to the larger challenge of fostering corporate practices compatible with sustainable development. Managing for sustainability requires measurement of environmental costs both internal and external to the firm, and measurement of environmental costs requires improved systems for identifying, allocating, controlling, monitoring, and reporting environmental costs. By all indications, corporations are well aware of this challenge, spurred by pressures to both remain cost competitive and position themselves to meet emerging international standards.

To meet this challenge, researchers may usefully direct their efforts to answering questions such as the following:

- How can firms estimate external costs and use such information in business decision making while maintaining competitiveness with other firms who choose not to measure or report such costs?

- Should practices and standards of environmental accounting vary with the size of the enterprise?

- Should environmental reports be subject to auditing procedures, analogous to those that apply to financial reports?

- What indicators best provide a balanced, interpretable picture of corporate environmental performance?

- To what extent are mandatory, international environmental accounting standards both feasible and desirable?

- How can environmental accounting serve the broader objectives of measuring and reporting progress toward corporate environmental sustainability?

Annotated Bibliography

Bartolomeo, M. 1993. *The Eni Enrico Mattei Foundation Methodology for a Company's Environmental Balance Sheet—The First Implementation.* Milan: Fondazione Eni Enrico Mattei (FEEM).

A model for an environmental balance sheet is applied to an oil company in Italy, Agip Petroli. The balance sheet comprises three accounting sections: (1) physical accounts of inputs and their related economic value; (2) physical accounts of air emissions, water discharges, wastes, and noise; and (3) monetary values of environmental expenses to prevent, control, and eliminate the negative environmental effects of production and to protect natural resources. These three sections are linked to track the economic impact of pollution control on the company and to assess and manage consumption of raw materials. Furthermore, the report addresses environmental accounting in general and environmental performance indicators of two types: good management indicators and impact indicators.

Canadian Institute of Chartered Accountants. 1993. *Environmental Costs and Liabilities: Accounting and Financial Reporting Issues.* Toronto: Canadian Institute of Chartered Accountants.

A study group of the institute examines how public concern with environmental performance can be handled within the existing framework of corporate financial reporting. Two types of environmental costs are considered. First are costs associated with the prevention, abatement, or remediation of damages to the environment. These include costs that are expended directly for such purposes or, alternatively, that have such effects, but are principally targeted at other corporate objectives, such as new product development or cost-reducing process improvements. The second are costs in the form of penalties, fines, or legal settlements resulting from damages to third parties owing to environmental degradation. Specific topics include identification of costs of environmental measures and losses, capitalization versus expensing such costs, environmental liabilities, asset impairment (land or building contamination), and disclosure of present and future environmental costs.

The study group concludes that environmental costs are not easily accommodated in conventional financial statements for two principal reasons: (1) Financial statements report economic resources of the entity; environmental costs incurred, especially those in response to past environmental damages, may make no contribution to the economic resources of the firm. And (2) liabilities are normally viewed as obligations to other entities (including individuals and government) but not as obligations to society in general.

Cooper, R., and R.S. Kaplan. 1991. "Profit Priorities from Activity-Based Costing." *Harvard Business Review* (May-June): 130–135.

Two originators of the concept of activity-based costing (ABC) describe the principles and benefits of ABC, a concept integral to improved internal environmental accounting. ABC distinguishes between costs linked to unit-level activities versus those linked to batch-level, product-sustaining, and facility-sustaining activities. A traditional unit-cost perspective distorts managers' decisions by directing attention to the simplest and most obvious costs (such as direct labor, materials, machine time) at the expense of batch, product, and facility-driven costs (such as set-ups, process engineering, and plant management). When the latter are obscured or buried in overhead, signals to management are unclear and misleading regarding proper pricing, cost control, product mix, and other decisions, often with substantial penalties for the long-term viability of the enterprise.

Deloitte Touche Tohmatsu International. 1993. *Coming Clean: Corporate Environmental Reporting*. London: Deloitte Touche Tohmatsu International.

This report assesses the motives and views of over 70 companies that have produced freestanding environmental reports in Europe, North America, and Japan. It identifies the best practice in corporate environmental reporting, lists do's and don'ts, and provides 23 specific recommendations to help avoid the pitfalls associated with corporate environmental disclosure and maximization of opportunities created by the transition to more environmentally sustainable forms of economic development.

European Green Table/Deloitte Touche Tohmatsu International. 1993. *Environmental Performance Indicators* (handbook) London: Deloitte Touche Tohmatsu International.

This report is the first to describe a system of environmental performance indicators. This system is applied in the aluminum smelting industry, oil and gas exploration and production, oil refining, petrochemicals manufacturing, and paper manufacturing. Two sets of indicators are identified: management environmental performance, and facilities and operations environmental performance. The first set contains indicators on compliance, systems procedures and integration, integration with general business functions, and total quality management. The second set has indicators such as materials use, energy, air emissions, and release incidents.

Fagg, B., J.K. Smith, K.A. Weitz, and J.L. Warren. 1993. *Life Cycle Cost Assessment (LCCA): Preliminary Scoping Report*. Prepared for the U.S. Department of Energy, Office of Environmental Restoration and Waste Management. Research Triangle Park, NC: Research Triangle Institute.

LCCA is a key component of the second phase of the three-step LCA process: (1) inventory of emissions, (2) impact assessment, and (3) improvement analysis. This document was prepared as background material for a November 1993 workshop, organized by the U.S. EPA and U.S. Department of Energy (DOE), and focused on development of an LCCA model for DOE project evaluation. Topics include life cycle assessment framework, terms and concepts in LCCA, existing generic LCCA methodologies, and LCCA as a decision-support tool.

FEE (Federation des Experts Comptables Européens). 1992. *Environmental Accounting and Auditing: Survey of Current Activities and Developments*. Paris: FEE.

This report presents an overview of environmental accounting and auditing activities in Europe based on the responses to a FEE questionnaire on environmental accounting and auditing for all EC member states and all but one EFTA (European Free Trade Association) country. It discusses the current situation and future developments in both areas and the EC's Fifth Action Program on the Environment and the eco-management and audit scheme from an accounting and auditing point of view. Activities of national professional bodies, government, companies, and audit firms are discussed.

Freedman, M., and A.J. Stagliano. 1992. "European Unification, Accounting Harmonization, and Social Disclosures." *International Journal of Accounting* 27: 112–122.

While the European Community moves toward standards for corporate financial disclosure, companies continue to report social information in widely disparate ways. An analysis of 24 European firms' reports examines such information as community involvement, environmental protection, consumer relations, human resources, energy conservation, product safety, and occupational safety and health. Setting standards to achieve consistency, continuity, and comparability should occur immediately to ensure maximum value of future reports.

Freedman, M. 1993. "Accounting and the Reporting of Environmental Information." *Advances in Public Interest Accounting* 5: 31–43.

Accountants are in a unique position to measure, compile, and generate pollution data in tandem with more traditional cost-accounting and financial information. As early as 1972, identification of "social [nonmonetary] accounting" was identified as an appropriate function for the accounting profession. In the 1970s, reporting the financial consequences of industrial pollution (for example, future capital requirements and liabilities) became a requirement imposed by the U.S. Security and Exchange Commission. A case study of the pulp and paper industry demonstrates how publicly available data in marginally usable form can be transformed into understandable corporate pollution performance rankings of interest to investors, environmentalists, communities, and other stakeholders.

General Electric Corporation. 1987. *Financial Analysis of Waste Management Alternatives.* Fairfield, CT: General Electric Corporation.

One of the original attempts to examine the risks and hidden costs of waste generation, management, and disposal, and to suggest an approach to estimating the benefits of alternative approaches to reducing such costs. The report describes a methodology based on major risk factors in the waste stream (volume, toxicity), disposal technology (landfill, incineration), and historical prices for waste disposal services. The goal is to express such costs in the language of financial officers to help justify the case for projects that will avoid generation and management of hazardous wastes in the future.

Gray, R.H. 1990. *The Greening of Accountancy, the Profession After Pearce.* London: ACCA.

This monograph marks a turning point in accountants' efforts to build awareness of, skills in, and commitment to green accounting. The author indicates ways in which the normative models, put forward by accountants in the 1970s, may be operationalized without becoming dominated by the economist's market view of the world. Gray suggests an enhancement of a company's internal accounting and information systems to include data more directly concerned with avoiding environmental damage. A number of instruments are discussed. Gray furthermore discusses the external environmental reporting by organizations and sees merit in the pragmatic approach under development by the United Nations.

Gray, R., J. Bebbington, and D. Walters. 1993. *Accounting for the Environment.* London: Paul Chapman Publishing.

This book is a sequel to *The Greening of Accountancy.* Together, these books give an excellent description of the debate about environmental accounting and reporting. Of particular note are sections on accounting and controlling the cost of waste; energy; packaging and recycling; and investment, budgeting, and appraisal—with examples drawn from European firms. Most important, the book provides guidelines, ideas, and proposals for ways in which accounting may become more responsive to environmental needs.

Grayson, L., and H. Woolston. 1994. *Business and Environmental Accountability; An Overview and Guide to the Literature.* London: Technical Communications Ltd., The British Library.

This publication is a comprehensive and accessible guide to green accounting. Five chapters contain over 200 references, most of them annotated. Each section begins with a short introduction. The five chapters (1) the green challenge to business, (2) legislation and policy, (3) stewardship and accountability today, (4) stewardship and accountability tomorrow, and (5) the American experience. The volume is indexed by author, corporation, and subject matter.

Hafkamp, W.A. (ed.). 1991. *Kosten van milieumaatregelen, kostenberekeningsmeth-ode en toepassing in de beleidsvoorbereiding* (Cost of environmental measures, cost calculation, and application in policymaking). The Hague: Ministry of Housing, Physical Planning and Environment.

A three-tier method is presented for the calculation of the cost of envi-ronmental actions of companies. The method is applicable on the level of the individual company, business sector, and national economy. The method is based on a traditional economic perspective and accounts for the initial capital costs, the financing costs, operating costs, the savings or extra revenues generated, taxes, and subsidies.

Krozer, J. 1992. *Decision Model for Environmental Strategies of Corporations*, draft version. The Hague: Institute for Applied Environmental Economics.

The author presents a model to calculate a cost-effective environmental strategy. The model gives an indication of the environmental cost in the medium and long terms for companies and products with complex envi-ronmental implications. It uses an input-output matrix/mass balance approach to represent the emissions during the life cycle of a product. Measures are then selected to obtain a targeted emission reduction. Next, the total cost of the selected measures is calculated. By doing this for several strategies, an optimal strategy may be identified.

Macve, R., and A. Carey (eds.). 1992. *Business, Accountancy, and the Environ-ment: A Policy and Research Agenda*. London: Institute of Chartered Accoun-tants in England and Wales.

This report from the Environment Research Group of the ICAEW aims to give a fuller understanding of environmental issues from a financial perspective and to respond to the environmental challenges in the areas of corporate reporting, auditing, and management.

Milne, M.J. 1991. "Accounting, Environmental Resource Values, and Non-Market Valuation Techniques for Environmental Resources: A Review." *Accounting, Auditing, and Accountability Journal* 4 (3): 81–109.

The focus of this article is the measurement of nonmarket environ-mental effects. The formal decision analysis in traditional management accounting typically excludes a wide range of social costs that a firm may wish to consider. Different approaches to environmental resource decision making are discussed, along with different notions of environ-mental value, including use, option, and preservation values. Finally, the different methods suggested by economists to obtain monetary values for nonmarket resources—specifically the dose response, hedonic price, travel cost, and contingent valuation methods—are reviewed with reference to some implications for private decision makers and accountants.

Mogezomp, H.G., M.J. Diependaal, and P. Leroy. 1992. "Het milieukwaliteitskostenmodel" (Environmental quality cost model). *Milieu* 7 (1): 13–18.

A new tool for environmental management assesses the current environmental positioning of a company and investigates possible environmental improvements. The EQCM subdivides environmental costs of manufacturing plants into five categories: prevention, process-integrated, effect mitigation correction, internal failure, and external failure. The value of the different cost categories gives an indication of the quality of the corporate management on environmental issues. Improvements are based on reducing certain items in external failure costs. Limitations of the model and the results of a pilot study are also presented.

Owen, D. (ed.). 1992. *Green Reporting, Accountancy and the Challenge of the Nineties.* London: Chapman and Hall.

This edited volume provides an overview and suggestions for firms in preparing their major medium of communication: the company report. A variety of views on the future of green reporting is presented, including those of industry, trade unions, accounting professionals, green pressure groups, and investors. The current trends in green reporting are illustrated through a series of short case studies, highlighting the experience of companies in Western Europe.

Piet, J.L.P. 1990. "Administratieve organisatie van afvalstoffen in produktiebedrijven" (Internal accounting control of waste in industry). *Maandblad voor Accountancy en Bedrijfshuishoudkundes–Gravenhage* (June): 248–253.

This article discusses the controlling and handling of waste in industry through management information and the design of an internal control system. The material balance is only a minor part of the controlling system. Segregation of duties, description of the responsibilities, and instructions from the management are instruments that ensure tracking and monitoring of waste from the origin to disposal. The theory of internal control contributes to a well-designed environmental management system.

Piet, J.L.P. 1992. *Environmental Information Systems for Corporate Strategy, A Study in a Dutch Context.* Institute for Environmental Control Science (WIMM) Report 92/04–05. Amsterdam: WIMM.

This report describes the two phases of environmental policy formulation of a company—situation analysis and decision making—from the point of view of management accounting and accounting information. By means of a situation analysis and stakeholder approach, the available information channels can be opened. Structured information gathering will show limitations and opportunities in the future. To make environmentally sound decisions, existing techniques of management accounting and accounting information systems can be used to evaluate alternatives facing managers, a kind of eco-rating system. The environmental effects (including external costs or externalities) may be used to evaluate the environmental prices of raw materials and energy. The choice between processes can be made by showing environmental cost prices. The use of alternative products can be compared by using environmental consumption rate.

Piet, J.L.P. 1993. *Ontwikkeling van het milieuverslag* (Toward the environmental statement). Institute for Environmental Control Science (WIMM) Report 93/01. Amsterdam: WIMM.

The existing experience and theory of financial statements can inform the design of the environmental statement. The environmental statement reports to various stakeholders on the results of the environmental policy of a company. Existing environmental statements do not fulfill the information needs of stakeholders and do not reflect the performance of management with relation to company policy. The statement of the Dutch company BSO/Orgin exemplifies an improved approach. The audit of the environmental statement is comparable to an accounting audit based on systems and information. This can be performed by the financial auditor, provided he or she is properly oriented to the environmental issues of the firm.

Schaltegger, S., and A. Sturm. 1992. *Ökologieorientierte Entscheidungen in Unternehmen* (Ecology-oriented decisions in enterprises). Stuttgart/Bern: Verlag Paul Haupt.

Apart from a general introduction to the environmental issue and the discussion of several concepts (internalization of external cost, cost-effectivity methods, mass-balance, and so on), the essence of this book is a method that makes sure both economic and environmental issues are taken into account in a decision. The method can be used to assess processes, products, and investments. It can be represented by five modules. In module one all necessary environmental data is obtained. In module two the environmental side of the project is evaluated by determining the environmental damage of every alternative (SE). In modules three and four the same is done for the economic side of the project, leading to a contribution margin for every alternative (DB). In the fifth module the economic/environmental efficiency of every alternative is obtained through a maximization of +DB/+SE followed by an elimination of -DB/+SE. The result is a score for every alternative that can be used in the decision process.

Scholtens, A.M., and J.L.P. Piet. 1992. "Stoffenregistratie, een administratief-organisatorische beheersing van afvalstoffen binnen afvalinzamelende en -verwerkende bedrijven" (Registration of waste flows in companies: A contribution of internal administrative control to environmental management in waste collecting and treating companies). *Milieu* 1: 19–23.

The authors discuss the applicability of methods of accounting control to the control of waste flows. A well-developed management information system as part of environmental management systems can contribute to controlling the environmental problems of a company. Authors conclude from an experimental project involving three waste collection and treatment plants that an adequate system for the registration of waste flows may well add to a company's environmental control. A model for a proper administrative control system for waste treatment plants is proposed.

Schulz, W. 1989. "Betriebliche Umweltinformationssysteme" (Business environmental information systems). *Umwelt und Energie* (Environment and Energy) 6: 33–98.

Schultz presents an overview of several different business environmental information systems from the perspective of business accounting systems: the social report ("Sozialbilanzen"); ecological bookkeeping ("Ökologische Bilanzen"); environmental performance indicators ("Umweltkennziffern und einzelindikatoren"); mass- and energy balance ("Stoff-und Energiebilanzen"); and life cycle analysis ("Produktfolgeabschätzung und Produklinienanalyse"). Furthermore an analysis of the environmental information requirements of an enterprise is described and a checklist presented for the building and redesigning of an environmental information system.

Schulz, W. 1992. "Kosten der Umweltverschmutzung, keine rechenaufgabe fur unternehmen?" (Costs of pollution: Not an arithmetic problem for companies?). In *Umwelt und Energie: Handbuch fur die betriebliche Praxis* (Environment and energy: Handbook for business practice). Freiburg: Rudolf Haufe Verlag GmbH & Co.

In these two articles, the problem of internalizing external environmental costs is addressed. In the first article, the author discusses the transformation of external cost to business costs in the near future, supported by several examples from Germany. The second article focuses on profits associated with green practices. In the final part of this series, Schulz applies activity-based costing to environmental issues. He describes how activity-based costing can be used to calculate a comprehensive overview of the environmental costs of an enterprise, and how this can be used in corporate financial reporting.

Seidel, E. 1988. *Environmental Protection as a Challenge to the Enterprise.* (In English). Siegen, Germany: University of Siegen.

In two parts, the first theoretical and the second applied, this report argues for inclusion of environmental protection management in business management. The relationship between economic activity and ecology is explained in terms of contraproductivity, defensive costs, and failure of formal decision theory. Brief introductions are provided to ecological bookkeeping, ecological controllership, ecologically oriented marketing, and ecologically oriented culture management.

Slot, R.J. 1991. "Milieu en Financiën Binnen de Onderneming" (Environment and finance within an enterprise). Chapter 6 in *Milieumemorandum.* Utrecht: Moret Ernst & Young.

In this article the author proposes a method for environmental investment selection using the Dutch National Environmental Policy Plan as a frame of reference for prioritizing the several alternatives. An environmental score is calculated based on the environmental pressure of an alternative and the relevant priority according to Dutch policy. This score is used as a correction factor to traditional financial evaluation.

Surma, J.P., and A. Vendra. 1992. "Accounting for Environmental Costs: A Hazardous Subject." *Journal of Accountancy* (March): 51–55.

The accounting firm of Price Waterhouse in 1990 surveyed 125 firms regarding their management structure and accounting practices in relation to environmental issues. Some salient highlights are as follows: Fourteen percent had established a board of directors committee to oversee environmental matters. A wide range of practices exist regarding timing of accrual for clean-up costs of waste sites, as well as estimating the magnitude of such clean-ups. Post-remediation costs were not always included in establishing overall accruals. The overall impression left by these 125 firms is of a highly fluid, nonstandardized pattern of liability reporting and estimation for complying with the reporting requirements of the Securities and Exchange Commission.

Tellus Institute. 1992. *Tellus Institute / CSG Packaging Study: Assessing the Impacts of Production and Disposal of Packaging and Public Policy Measures to Alter Its Mix.* Prepared for the Council of State Governments, the U.S. Environmental Protection Agency, and the New Jersey Department of Environmental Protection and Energy. Tellus Study No. 89–024. Boston: Tellus Institute.

This voluminous study examines the life cycle impacts of paper, aluminum, glass, and plastics typically used in packaging material. Aside from a detailed emissions inventory, the study is one of the first to translate inventory data into monetized impact estimates based on a novel approach that combines relative health effects with the control costs of various emissions from production. Results are transformed into societal costs per unit of packaging—for example, per 12-ounce beverage container—to allow cross-material comparisons of actual packaging products in addition to unfinished materials (such as a ton of plastic or paper) comparisons.

Todd, R. 1993. "Basics of Managerial Accounting." In *Workshop Proceedings: Accounting and Capital Budgeting for Environmental Costs Workshop,* Dallas, December 5–7. EPA 742-R-94-002. Washington, DC: U.S. EPA, Office of Pollution Prevention and Toxics, May.

Management accounting plays a key role in decision support, monitoring, and control and motivation within the firm. Getting the right information flowing to decision makers in a timely fashion is essential to efficient operation of the enterprise. Accounting systems geared to external reporting are inadequate to meet these needs, especially in relation to environmental costs. To be useful, such costs must be disaggregated, prospective, and deal adequately with uncertainties, all of which apply especially to environmental costs within the firm.

Todd, R. 1994. "Zero-loss Environmental Accounting Systems." In *The Greening of Industrial Ecosystems*. B.R. Allenby and D.J. Richards (eds.). Washington, DC: National Academy Press.

A zero-loss accounting system effectively records and monitors the flows of all material inputs to a production system, and tracks the costs associated with such flows. Traditional accounting systems, geared primarily to financial reporting requirements, fail to provide such information to managers in a timely, disaggregated, and usable form relevant to key management decisions, such as product mix, retention, and pricing. Tracking environmental costs may be unwelcome by managers when a true accounting shows certain product lines less profitable than previously thought. An improved system will remove disincentives to gathering a comprehensive cost inventory and to properly allocating costs to production units and products. Such a system requires involvement of production engineers, environmental managers, procurement staff, and those responsible for functions in addition to accounting and financial staff.

U.S. Environmental Protection Agency. 1990. *Pollution Prevention Benefits Manual*. Report prepared for the Office of Solid Waste and Office Policy Planning and Evaluation by ICF Corporation. Washington, DC: U.S. EPA, October.

A four-tier approach to classifying project costs and savings comprises a hierarchical approach to estimating the benefits of pollution prevention projects. The four tiers are usual, hidden, liability, and less tangible. The first and second tiers are user-defined. Guidance on estimating liability and less-tangibles is structured around equations and default values, the latter of which may be adjusted according to site-specific information. This is one of the first attempts to systematically and quantitatively address uncertainties as contained in variables such as personal injury, economic loss, real property damage, and soil/waste/groundwater treatment.

U.S. Environmental Protection Agency. 1994. *Stakeholder's Action Agenda: A Report of the Workshop on Accounting and Capital Budgeting for Environmental Costs*, December 5–7, 1993. Proceedings of a workshop organized by Office of

Pollution Prevention and Toxics. EPA 742-R-94-003. Washington, DC: U.S. EPA, May.

As part of its Design for the Environment initiative, U.S. EPA is building an information and assistance program aimed at accounting and finance professionals to foster improved environmental accounting. The goal is to elevate awareness and skills of such professionals and to ensure that environmental costs are brought to bear on product, process, and management systems in relation to pollution prevention technologies. This document reports on the issues and action agendas for various stakeholder groups represented at the conference, including business staff (financial, accounting, environmental, and operations staff), accounting associations, small businesses, nonaccounting professionals, management consultants, academics, and government officials. Action agendas fall into four broad types of activities: (1) terms, concepts, and roles; (2) management incentives; (3) education, guidance, and outreach; and (4) analytic tools, methods, and systems.

White, A., M. Becker, and J. Goldstein. 1991. *Alternative Approaches for the Financial Evaluation of Industrial Pollution Prevention Investments.* Report prepared by Tellus Institute for the New Jersey Department of Environmental Protection, Division of Science and Research, November. Revised Executive Summary, June 1992. Boston: Tellus Institute.

Pollution-prevention project investment analyses often encounter biases owing to certain features of conventional profitability evaluation: (1) incomplete cost inventory; (2) failure to properly allocate environmental costs to specific products or processes; (3) use of time horizons that are too short to capture longer-term benefits of prevention investments; and (4) use of profitability indicators that do not capture the time value of money. This report examines how these shortcomings may be corrected by adoption of a total cost assessment (TCA) approach. Three case studies—paper manufacturing, metal fabrication, and fiber manufacturing facilities—demonstrate differing degrees of profitability change as TCA replaces conventional analytical approaches.

White, A. 1993a. "Accelerating Corporate Investment in Clean Technologies Through Enhanced Managerial Accounting Systems." Background paper prepared by Tellus Institute for the Organization for Economic Co-Operation and Development (OECD), Program on Technology and Environment, January (revised September 1993). Boston: Tellus Institute.

Accelerating clean technologies in the OECD community may be fostered through various approaches, including voluntary corporate environmental audits and annual reports, mandatory disclosure of use and releases of toxic materials, and pressure from nongovernmental organizations to adhere to codes of conduct and to report on environmental performance. The critical adjunct to these measures is the installation of management accounting systems that define, compile, analyze, and internally report environmental costs. Capital budgeting is the key beneficiary of such information, in addition to product pricing, product retention/mix decisions, and related tasks. Case studies drawn from the U.S. experience demonstrate the advantages of upgrading internal environmental cost-accounting systems. OECD can promote such approaches through development of analytical tools and training programs, assisting members to integrate accounting systems improvements into their respective regulations, establishing national standards and guidelines, and supporting a program of applied research.

White, A. 1993b. "Accounting for Pollution Prevention." *EPA Journal* 19 (3) (July-September): 23–25.

Among the many barriers to industrial pollution prevention, internal cost-accounting systems are one shared by both large and small firms. When costs are poorly articulated, prevention opportunities are obscured and/or unable to compete effectively for limited capital resources. Revamping such systems, however, can be costly and threatening to managers whose product lines may suddenly appear less profitable than had been thought. Two project examples from the pulp and paper industry using a total cost assessment approach demonstrate how improved accounting methods can substantially alter conventional company profitability analysis and potentially redirect resources toward or away from pollution prevention investments.

White, A., N. Talbot, and D. Savage. 1993. *Internal Cost Accounting; Concepts, Cases, and Recommendations for the New Ontario Hydro.* Report prepared by Tellus Institute for Ontario Hydro, Task Force on Sustainable Energy Development, Full Cost Accounting Team. Boston: Tellus Institute, November.

Ontario Hydro views its internal accounting system as a key supporting element of its top-to-bottom corporate restructuring. The company has initiated a process to track and report environmental costs, including both internal (compliance, testing, licensing, emissions controls, fees, penalties) and external (environmental and human health damages resulting from the company's operations). This report explores in preliminary fashion some of the definitional, organizational, and operational issues associated with introducing such an accounting system. Two case studies of potential capital projects—one related to coal-fired plants and a second related to a hydroelectric facility—illustrate some of the challenges of bringing improved environmental costing to the project justification process.

White, A. 1994. "Corporate Environmental Disclosure: What Do Stakeholders Want?" Paper presented at Workshop on Corporate Environmental Accounting and Disclosure, Environmental Law Institute, Washington, DC, June 1994.

Corporations committed to annual environmental reporting face a complex task in meeting the information needs of diverse stakeholders—investors, employees, host communities, environmentalists, and the public at large. While each has its own view of what the "right" information should look like, eight features of a corporate reporting system define those which, in general, will be most effective instruments of communication. These features are standardization, comprehensiveness, interpretability, specificity, accessibility, proactivity, verifiability, and accountability.

Wit, R., H. Taselaar, R. Heyungs, and G. Huppes. 1993. *REIM, LCA-based Ranking of Environmental Investments Model.* CML-Report 103. Leiden: Center of Environmental Science.

This report describes an innovative method for ranking environmental investments on the basis of their environmental cost-effectiveness. The environmental "return" is estimated on a cradle-to-grave basis using life cycle assessment. The traditional economic cost-benefit analysis is restructured according to a life cycle assessment approach.

Chapter 7

Clean Technologies

Kenneth Green
Alan Irwin

with contributions from
Paul Hooper, Andrew McMeekin, and Anthony Murphy

Introduction

It is now a commonplace that the best way to reduce the environmental impact of productive activity is through prevention. Such a notion is contained in the concept of clean technology, a term that implies the technological embodiment of a preventive approach to pollution control. By reducing waste at source, clean technologies would reduce levels of pollution, as well as lowering production costs, through more efficient use of raw materials and the recycling of waste streams. Thus, in contrast to the traditional view of pollution control technology—the end-of-pipe methods—clean technologies are expected to achieve both environmental *and* economic goals. In addition, the development and application of clean technologies can be seen as a central part of the longer-term solution to the creation of sustainable production, as opposed to end-of-pipe palliatives.

This chapter reviews recent literature on clean technologies. We set out some of the basic concepts of clean technology—including

related concepts like clean*er* technology, clean production, waste minimization, and source reduction—and discuss the differing ways in
which the concepts have been viewed. We review some of the policy
implications of supporting the introduction of clean technologies,
focusing on the incentives and barriers for introducing such technologies at the level of the firm.

The review and the list of annotated references that supplement
the chapter concentrate on what has been happening in developed
countries, especially Europe and the United States. The bibliography
also contains some references to the use of clean technologies in
developing countries (see UNEP 1993; Forester and Skinner 1992).

In writing this chapter we have not confined ourselves to the literature that specifically mentions clean technology or its synonyms.
The reorganization of production processes and the development of
new environmentally friendly products (as the notion of clean technology implies) require an understanding of the broader literature on
social choice of technologies—that is, the manner and extent to
which economic, political, and cultural factors influence the selection, development, and diffusion of technologies.

Clean Processes, Clean Products, or Clean Production?

The clean technology concept emerged from the expanding set of
strategies developed to cope with environmental problems over the
last 10 years. Many of these strategies have been directed primarily
toward solving existing problems. At worst, it has been necessary to
spend vast amounts of money on repairing damage that has been
inflicted on the environment, using remediation procedures. Another
reactive strategy has been the development of end-of-pipe equipment
that can be added to existing production technologies to reduce their
environmental impact, again at a cost. The clean technology
approach is a more ambitious response to these purely reactive strategies. However, as we will see, precise definitions are difficult to achieve.

It has been argued further that the focus on technology misses the
point: The solution to environmental problems can often be organizational and attitudinal rather than technological. Clean *production*
might therefore be a more suitable concept:

[Clean production describes] a conceptual and procedural approach to production that demands that all phases of the life cycle of a *product or of a process* should be addressed with the objective of prevention or minimization of short- and long-term risks to human health and to the environment.

UNEP/Industry and Environment Office 1989,
quoted by Jackson 1993 (emphasis added)

Jackson criticizes the focus on production *processes*, rather than embracing redesign of products and, indeed, of consumption patterns. From the environmental point of view, disputes over the definition of clean technology might be thought irrelevant: What really matters is that, overall, materials are used more efficiently, reliance on nonrenewable energy sources is reduced, and pollution (defined as releases to the environment that interfere with sustainable functions) is eliminated. However, while the notion of prevention as the key feature of the clean technology concept is a good starting point, how you apply it depends on which part of the "whole picture" you focus. Do you keep to production processes alone (and the process technologies they involve), or do you include the products of those processes throughout their life cycles? Consideration of consumption patterns moves the focus of clean production and clean technologies to a completely different level, beyond the sphere of intervention of one firm and, even, of one industry.

Clean Technology: The Definitions

It follows from this discussion that there is no generally accepted definition of clean technology. A recent report by the U.K. Government's Advisory Council on Science and Technology (ACOST 1992) noted 15 different definitions given over the previous five years by a range of supranational, European, U.S., and U.K. organizations.

The literature discusses a wide variety of methods for reducing the environmental impact of any industrial activity. These discussions can be related to the three levels of the production process, the products, and the industry itself (DTI/PA 1991; Ausubel and Sladovich 1989; Stahel and Jackson 1993).

Production Process Level

For the *production process*, the following options are available (though the boundaries between them may not always be as clear in practice):

- End-of-pipe treatment

- End-of-pipe recovery for use in the same process or for use elsewhere

- Efficiency improvements to the process (waste minimization) and substitution of process materials

- Radical redesign of the process

End-of-Pipe Treatment

Treatment responses initially involve converting one unintended output into another. After a range of treatments inside and outside the facilities that house the production process, the ultimate, processed result may be easier to handle, less toxic, of smaller volume (and thus easier to dump), or it may be in a form that is recyclable (such as heat, clean water, or sludge that can go back into the process as inputs). End-of-pipe technology implies equipment that can be added to a process to manipulate the waste stream into a more easily managed form. End-of-pipe treatment requires capital equipment and other inputs (such as added chemicals, energy) of its own. Consequently, end-of-pipe treatment technologies typically offer no return on investment on the initial capital outlay for the equipment. In fact, further costs may be incurred from the disposal of solid or aqueous waste created by the equipment.

A case can be made for using end-of-pipe treatment technologies where waste-reducing technologies are not available and may be some time in coming. Thus, in the short term, these technologies may be used to minimize the polluting potential of a waste without actually reducing the quantity of waste produced.

End-of-Pipe Recovery Systems

The case for using end-of-pipe technology is strengthened where components from the waste stream are treated for reuse rather than disposal. It is possible that some wastes can be extracted from the final effluent and treated in such a way that they can be used again and subsequently returned to the start of the process. For example, wastewater can be cleaned and reused rather than released into the rivers. This concept can also include closing the system to restrict solvent release to the environment so that the solvent is reused rather than just evaporated. While treatment systems imply no change in the product/waste ratio, recovery systems imply an increase in the ratio by virtue of reductions in the amount of virgin raw materials used and in waste created.

Waste Minimization

Waste minimization strategies illustrate one way of attempting to reduce the amount of waste at source, enabling a firm to reap rewards from both the reduction of raw material costs and the costs of waste disposal. As an alternative to adding equipment to the end of a process, waste minimization involves the redesign of manufacturing equipment used in the transformation process. The concept can be seen at different levels. With source reduction, a process can be modified to reduce the amount of energy (or other input) required or to increase the efficiency of material transfer from raw materials to final product. This type of redesign is embodied in the concept of integrated process control. In many cases, the use of information technologies and automation techniques have been especially important in enabling efficiency improvements. Another source reduction strategy involves reducing the potential environmental impact of a process waste rather than necessarily reducing the quantity produced.

Radical Redesign of Processes

However, it is also possible for companies to reduce the environmental impact of a production process by making their products in a different way. This approach involves bringing in a new process or replacing a particular stage of the manufacture. Due to the risk and costs associated with the R&D for these changes and the capital costs of replacing plant, radical redesign is likely to occur only in line with investment cycles. Even then it might be constrained by the particular technological regimes prevailing in a particular industry that limit the choice of technological directions a firm can in practice pursue.

The concept of technological regimes and trajectories and the associated notion of "lock-in" is explored by Kemp (1993, 1994).

Product Level

It is possible to change products so as to make them more environmentally benign. These changes include

- Changing the material composition of the product (substitution of the materials that constitute the product, without changing the basic design)

- Redesign of the product to reduce the environmental impacts associated with manufacture (fewer manufacturing steps, often resulting in a lower energy requirement)

- Redesign of the product to have a lower environmental impact while in use (redesign to be more energy efficient)

- Redesign of the product to be less environmentally damaging in the post-use phase of its life cycle (being more easily recoverable)

- Redesign of the product for durability (less frequent replacement and, consequently, reduction of disposal frequency)

Reducing the environmental impact of a production system in the longer term is likely to involve a combination of these strategies, with redesign of *both the process and the products* taking place at the same time, often based on completely new or refurbished technologies.

Industry Level

It is possible to draw the system boundary much wider than a particular production/product system so as to include the network of production-consumption activities that exist to satisfy a particular human need. When the environmental impacts of that network as a whole are considered, more radical changes might be identified that require the restructuring of complete industries and, indeed, of the ways in which particular human needs are met.

To illustrate: Automobile companies see the solution to the pollution problem caused by the gasoline-burning engine in terms of increasing fuel efficiency, changing the constituents of emissions, or even switching to electrically powered cars. All of these require a varying mix of product and process redesign along the lines we have listed above—toward cleaner processes and products. However, such solutions still assume the continued high-level use of the private automobile as *the* means of individual travel. A significant switch to public transportation—the result of a major techno-organizational change in the mode of satisfaction of a human need to travel—offers a solution to the automobile's pollution problem that actually threatens the existence of the automobile industry in its current form.

Conclusion

The notion that prevention is better than cure, or that clean technology is better than end-of-pipe clean-up, is now generally accepted as a goal, in rhetoric if not yet always in practice. However, there are many strategies for reducing the environmental impact of human production and consumption activity, and the disputes over which strategies are the "best" are visible in the differences of opinion as to what clean technology embraces.

From Clean Technology to Cleaner Technology to Waste Minimization

Given this range of possible definitions, it is important to consider how national and international bodies have defined clean technology. In the 1990s, official definitions relating to clean technology have tended to settle on strategies centered largely around processes and waste minimization (ACOST 1992). This emphasis on processes stems from and reinforces the fact that legislation has been more focused on processes than on products. However, some recommendations direct attention to the extension from processes to the products. For example, the U.S. Environmental Protection Agency's *Waste Minimization Opportunity Assessment Manual,* issued in 1988, classifies product changes under the source reduction category and includes product substitution, product conservation, and change in product composition. We might expect that this trend would be strengthened following the introduction of eco-labeling schemes that are concerned with the environmental impact of products over their whole life cycle (life cycle assessment).

Some of the earlier definitions of clean technology were explained in terms of "no-waste" technology. This, however, was considered an unreasonable target, since the manufacture of a product from raw materials through the use of energy implies at least the depletion of natural resources. Consequently, the more recent literature discusses options in terms of "low-waste" technology and often replaces clean technology with clean*er* technology (as in the DTI/PA report of 1991).

One of the main shifts has been the increased focus on *waste minimization* strategies. This reflects a reinterpretation of the strategies of five to ten years ago, which merely pointed out that pollution needed to be reduced and that companies would be required to meet more stringent legislation. For companies at that time, it meant increased costs through investment in pollution-abatement equipment. This message from government bodies was instrumental in the prevailing perception in industry that dealing with environmental problems was a burden to competitiveness, barely conceivable at a time when the economy was entering a recessionary period.

More recently, governments have begun to emphasize the business opportunities available to those companies willing to grasp the demands associated with reducing impact to the natural environment. The strategy has shifted to recommending the benefits of waste minimization techniques on the basis of their cost-saving potential in conjunction with meeting the challenge of the environment.

The last five years have seen a shift in the nature of strategies for reducing the environmental impact of products and processes from abatement to waste minimization. It may be that, in the next few years, opinions will shift further toward doing things differently to avoid causing the pollution or generating the waste in the first place. This will require long-term R&D strategies concerned with how products and processes can be rethought from first principles.

Policies and Strategies for Clean Technologies

The challenge for environmentalists (defined in the very broadest sense) is to develop policies and induce strategies that swing the balance in favor of clean technologies, to promote the positive aspects of clean technologies, and to reduce or remove obstacles preventing their adoption. Government policies to this end have been put forward for processes, and some changes in company strategy related to products and industrial systems have been induced.

Processes

In addition to improved environmental performance, the literature on clean technologies is in no doubt about the economic benefits accruing from their adoption: savings in raw materials and energy leading to increased profitability; reduction in the costs of pollution abatement; and the diffusion of new processes, creating new market opportunities and further stimulating innovation (Irwin and Hooper 1992; Dielemann and de Hoo 1993).

If the benefits of clean process technologies are so obvious, why has their adoption been so limited? Since the mid-1980s, it has been observed that the majority of investment expenditure for environmental purposes is devoted to end-of-pipe treatment technologies, with only a small fraction to clean technologies (Dielemann and de Hoo 1993). A number of factors appear to be contributing to this phenomenon.

Advantages to Firms of Alternative End-of-Pipe Technologies

End-of-pipe technologies are cheaper, give easily visible proof of commitment to environmental protection, involve far less disruption to the production process than clean technologies, and can be readily purchased. The market in clean technologies is less developed and is often specific to a particular industrial plant.

Emphasis on Emission Standards

Most pollution regulation authorities place excessive emphasis on emission and engineering standards, both of which tend to favor end-of-pipe technological solutions because they focus attention on adjustments to the waste stream itself rather than on the processes generating the waste in the first place.

Time Scale

The long-term return on investment in the radical innovation(s) often thought necessary for the development of clean technologies inhibits firms from making the necessary initial R&D commitment.

Lack of Knowledge

There appears to be widespread ignorance of the potential of clean technologies, which may be due to a lack of the necessary technical expertise and limited dissemination of information.

Cost-effectiveness

Cost-benefit analysis of a private project is usually restricted to those costs and benefits directly experienced by the firm. These narrowly defined economic criteria ignore the benefit derived from the reduction in the social cost of pollution damage achieved by the adoption of clean technologies, as this is not a cost directly borne by the firm. The result is that many firms do not find clean technologies cost-effective.

Government agencies at national and international levels have been very active since the mid-1980s in seeking to convince firms that clean technologies *can* be cost-effective, through a variety of schemes such as information dissemination programs, demonstration projects, and R&D subsidies (Yakowitz and Hamner, in Jackson 1993; Georg, Røpke, and Jørgensen 1992). Combined with regulatory regimes and public pressure for better monitoring of environmental performance, such schemes have had some success in convincing some firms of the effectiveness of source reduction and waste minimization technologies. However, any success has been restricted for the most part to the larger firms in a few industries. For some commentators, this is inevitable in the absence of much tighter regulatory regimes and more profound changes in corporate responsibility (Cannon 1994) or in the very structures of governance and ownership of capitalist industry (see Jones 1988).

Products

There is much literature on the redesign of products to incorporate "clean" principles, to minimize the product's environmental impact either during production or while in use and/or post-use (North 1992; Stahel and Jackson 1993). Such redesign has been partly driven by public information and education programs encouraging consumers to choose greener products. However, demand-side pressures of this kind, often orchestrated by retailing chains seeking competitive advantage, have often been confined to trivial practices of green marketing.

Recently, many large firms have begun to include green criteria in the management of product development and, backwards, into research and development (see ENDS 1993). The development of schemes for eco-labeling and of techniques for life cycle assessment will no doubt stimulate more companies to reexamine their product development and R&D activities to "clean" and "green" their products.

Industrial Systems

Reorganizing entire production-consumption systems that late 20th-century developed economies have become locked into is hardly susceptible to simple changes in policy. The relatively simple act of phasing out one small class of chemicals, CFCs, required international political action unprecedented in the history of environmental management. Radical changes in yet more complex industrial systems (such as reductions in the use of the automobile or the phasing out of the whole range of chlorine-containing chemicals) imply much more difficult policy changes. Major decisions are needed on social choices that have national, regional, and global dimensions beyond the scope of this chapter. However, whatever specific policies might be pursued to encourage clean production and clean consumption, their purpose has to be to change technologies (Cairncross 1991).

There is clearly a role for governments in long-term technological change, given their sponsorship of much scientific and technological R&D. The high-risk, long-term nature of investment in radical technological innovation has, so far, severely limited the extent of private R&D in the area of clean technologies. Thus the onus is on governments, as in other fields of technology, to take the initiative by either giving financial aid or stimulating joint projects between public bodies such as universities and research institutes and industry. (See Heaton *et al.* 1992.)

Conclusion

By its nature, clean technology offers a number of challenges. The point of this review has not been to argue that a clear typology of the concept exists. On the contrary, the technological possibilities are varied. Equally, the lack of definitional clarity is not necessarily a weakness. The whole point is to stimulate new ways of thinking as well as to promote unconventional approaches to technological development. There can be no single solution to the environmental challenge. Instead the concept of clean technology should encourage us to consider the panoply of responses.

At another level, however, the clean-technology notion challenges us to rethink the relationship between industrial development and environmental protection. It is important to step outside technical details to consider the wider social and cultural challenges in making technology "clean." Beck (1992), for example, argues that there is a public perception of a growing incompatibility between technology and nature, such that a wider reappraisal of technology is required. Cultural approaches, such as that of Schwarz and Thompson (1990), suggest that attention must also be paid to critics outside industry who feel that current technological priorities are excessively limited. In considering the best technological strategies for "cleaning" production and consumption, we need to keep in mind these wider questions concerning the direction of technological change.

Annotated Bibliography

Advisory Committee on Science and Technology (ACOST). 1992. *Cleaner Technology.* London: Her Majesty's Stationery Office.

ACOST is an advisory committee to the U.K. government, influential in formulating governmental policy on support for the development and exploitation of new technologies. This report explores the concept of clean technology, drawing on previous reports from international and other U.K. organizations. It settles on the concept as a purely relative term (hence clean*er*) and discusses policy options for applying it in the U.K.

Ausubel, J., and H. Sladovich (eds.). 1989. *Technology and Environment.* Washington, DC: National Academy Press.

This collection of articles by U.S. engineers and analysts of technology policy examines the "paradox of technology"—that environmental disruption is brought about by industrial technological developments, but that advancement in such developments "will be a main route to environmental quality." It includes some papers on clean "technological solutions" in power generation and the protection of the ozone layer and on the (positive) role of engineers in solving the paradox. For our purposes, the most interesting papers are those that present frameworks within which it is possible to consider the systemic environmental impacts of technological developments. In "Industrial Metabolism," Robert Ayres considers mass flows for key industrial materials of environmental significance and the waste emissions associated with them; his analysis suggests that cleaner technological systems would have to be based on the reduction of virgin materials extraction, reduced loss of wastes, and increased recycling of useful materials. In "Dematerialization," Robert Herman *et al.* advocate reductions in the amount of waste generated per unit of industrial products as a key goal of cleaner technological solutions.

Beck, U. 1992. *Risk Society: Toward a New Modernity.* London, Newbury Park, and New Delhi: Sage Publications.

A highly influential sociological account of the significance of risk and environmental issues within contemporary society. Beck argues that the broad social consensus over "modernity" has broken down—with a consequent loss of faith in Science, Truth, and Progress. Industry is under social pressure because it is so bound up with these "myths"— and is widely seen as the source of environmental problems ("the gain in power from techno-economic progress is being increasingly overshadowed by the production of risks"). Science likewise is under attack for its role in technological development. While much discussion of "cleaner production" assumes that the same scientific and industrial framework that got us into environmental problems will also get us out of them, Beck's account raises more fundamental questions about the direction of that framework's development. In "late-modern" society, a more far-reaching reappraisal of "progress" may be necessary. In particular, the environmental crisis may necessitate changes beyond new industrial products and processes so that new ways of living are also required.

Cairncross, F. 1990. "Cleaning Up: A Survey of Industry and the Environment." *The Economist* September 8, Supplement.

————. 1991. *Costing the Earth.* London: Business Books.

————. 1993. "Waste and the Environment." *The Economist* May 29, Supplement

————. 1995. *Green, Inc.: A Guide to Business and the Environment.* London: Earthscan.

In her books and occasional articles in *The Economist* (a weekly British magazine that strongly supports free-market economic solutions to environmental problems), Cairncross argues that a "clean world" can only come about with the cooperation of industry. The task now facing industry is to find ways to reduce the many forms of pollution. Part of this effort will entail devising new industrial processes that squeeze more output from each unit of input. Further, the world will need products that, during their lifetime, do minimal damage to the planet and that, at the end of their lives, can either be safely thrown away or put to new uses. Industrial innovation is therefore the key: Developing products that use nature most frugally at both ends of their lives will call forth whole new generations of technology. The great engineering projects of the next century will not be the civil engineering of dams or bridges, but the bio-engineering of sewage works and waste tips. Industry has before it that most precious of prospects: a spur to innovate.

Cairncross favors regulations that are "technology-forcing" (as in Germany and Japan); in her view the United States and United Kingdom see regulations as something to fight over rather than something "to build the business around." However, the best way to make sure that industry applies technology to solve environmental problems is for governments to give the right *price* signals.

Cannon, T. 1994. *Corporate Responsibility: A Textbook on Business Ethics, Governance, Environment: Roles and Responsibilities.* London: Pitman Publishing.

Issues of cleaner production need to be seen as part of a larger movement concerning business ethics and corporate responsibility. Cannon raises the value issues of "sustainability" and the central role of industry within such a change toward environmental protection and development. The stages of corporate response to the environmental challenge can move from the offensive ("environmental demands threaten our business, they should be attacked") through the defensive ("these demands will undermine our competitiveness") to the indifferent ("we will ignore these demands and hope they disappear") to the innovative ("our best strategy is to look for ways to capitalize on the demands and opportunities"). The "search for environmental excellence" is seen to incorporate all levels of the firm (senior management, operations, marketing, finance). Every aspect of current and future operations is affected by environmental issues.

Cannon also discusses the relationship between the firm and the built environment, including the urban environment of our major cities.

Department of Trade and Industry/PA Consulting Group (DTI/PA). 1991. *Cleaner Technology in the UK.* London: Her Majesty's Stationery Office.

According to this report, growing regulatory demands as they affect British industry have usually led to end-of-pipe pollution abatement technologies. The U.K. government's Department of Trade and Industry (DTI) has, however, advocated a longer-term solution in the form of cleaner technology. The broad objectives of this study are, first, to review certain key industrial sectors in terms of the environmental problems being faced; second, to assess relevant industrial research on clean technology that addresses these problems; and third, to review the barriers to and the forces driving the uptake of cleaner technologies in U.K. industry. A major goal of the report was to identify "hub technologies"—applications of basic science that have a potential for application in more than one sector of industry (for example, membrane separation and photo (electric) chemistry). The report suggests only moderate levels of activity in the conscious development and adoption of cleaner technologies by U.K. companies. The concept of cleaner technology is not well known—especially among SMEs—nor are its benefits known. However, there is also a need to address the shortages of skills, resources, and facilities that create barriers to the adoption of unfamiliar technologies. The report was influential in the formulation of policy for support of cleaner technology innovation in the United Kingdom.

Dielemann, H., and S. de Hoo. 1993. "Toward a Tailor-made Process of Pollution Prevention and Cleaner Production: Results and Implications of the PRISMA Project." In *Environmental Strategies for Industry.* 245–275. K. Fischer and J. Schot (eds.). Washington, DC: Island Press.

This essay reports on the Dutch PRISMA project, which sought to demonstrate whether it was possible to develop a pollution-prevention methodology and approach that could be a model for pollution control in the Netherlands (and elsewhere). Ten Dutch industrial companies participated in the project in the late 1980s to early 1990s; waste and emission reductions over two years were between 30 and 80 percent, usually without any financial problems in implementation. However, Dielemann and de Hoo observe that, despite these economically and environmentally favorable results, most companies are still reluctant to develop preventive strategies.

The reasons for this are conceptual (the widespread, if erroneous, view that waste prevention will be expensive); organizational (barriers between different functions and departments inside companies); lack of information about available prevention technologies; technical obstacles (because, sometimes, the necessary technologies are *not* available); and economic obstacles (the low cost of waste disposal, lack of detailed internal knowledge of the real costs of waste production). The paper makes recommendations for government action based on the need for more effective dissemination of knowledge—environmental, technical, and financial—about pollution prevention and cleaner production methods.

ENDS. 1993. "Philips: Integrating Eco-design into Product Development." No. 224 (September): 22–24.

This news report records the design principles being adopted by Philips for its electronic products—namely, design for cleaner production cycles, enhanced disassembly, longer life—and the entailed reduction of materials and energy (such as by miniaturization) and increased use of service carriers (for example, telecommunications rather than transportation). A design handbook lists criteria for designers to consider. This includes general rules, such as "develop long-life products," as well as specifics such as "redesign battery packs" or "avoid cadmium plating"; the manual includes a scoring chart that can be used to rate proposed projects. Similar methods of appraisal are being tried out in numerous companies and may well be a viable strategy for embedding environmental concerns into R&D.

Forester, W.S., and J.H. Skinner (eds.). 1992. *Waste Minimization and Clean Technology: Waste Management Strategies for the Future.* San Diego: Academic Press.

This book focuses on a number of areas of governmental and industrial activity where waste minimization and clean technology development is currently taking place. Chapter coverage includes a discussion of current experience in Denmark, China, Cuba, France, the Netherlands, the United States, and the United Nations Environment Program's Industry and Environment Office (UNEP/IEO). There is a presentation of the special issues faced by certain industrial sectors: electroplating, heavy-metal generating industries, the Italian leather industry, pulp and paper, chemical, and oil. Specific chapters also deal with the role of engineers in waste minimization, employee incentives, and household hazardous wastes.

Geiser, K. 1991. "The Greening of Industry, Making the Transition to a Sustainable Economy." *Technology Review* (August–September): 65–72.

Clean technology cannot be the answer by itself to achieving sustainable industry. A sustainable industry encompasses the entire social, economic, and technological system in which production takes place. This expansive context is also called "clean production." The system-wide perspective of clean production and sustainable industry merges prevention policies, the precautionary principle, and clean technology.

Georg, S., I. Røpke, and U. Jørgensen. 1992. "Clean Technology—Innovation and Regulation." *Environmental and Resource Economics* 2: 533–550.

Governments must address the issues of how firms can be given the necessary incentives to develop environmentally sound products and processes. Using five examples from the Danish Clean Technology Program, the authors analyze how appropriate technological innovation has been stimulated by government grants and financial aid. They conclude that, although such subsidies have been effective in stimulating the development of cleaner technologies in Denmark, other measures are required to ensure *diffusion* of these technologies. In addition, measures need to be taken to provide firms with information about cleaner production strategies and to construct networks of firms (especially for small and medium-sized firms).

Heaton, G.R., R. Repetto, and R. Sobin. 1992. *Back to the Future: U.S. Government Policy Toward Environmentally Critical Technology.* Washington, DC: World Resources Institute.

This report, by a U.S. policy research center, lists generic technologies that are "critical to the achievement of environmental sustainability," and on which public policy should be focused. It points out that many analysts have compiled lists of technologies deemed vital for national security and U.S. economic competitiveness. A similar list of environmentally critical technologies (ECTs) needs to be compiled: "If environmental technology is segregated and regarded narrowly as remediation and pollution treatment equipment, environmental concerns will inevitably be neglected in the promotion of critical technologies, and the potential of many emerging technologies for environmental improvement will be overlooked." The ECTs include those for *energy capture* (photovoltaics and, controversially, nuclear fission); *energy storage* (superconductors); *energy end-use* (electric vehicles); *agricultural biotechnology, catalysis, information technologies,* and *contraception.* The report briefly reviews the programs for supporting ECTs in the United States, Japan, Germany, and the Netherlands. It advocates, among other things, the establishment in the United States of a federal institute for environmental technology.

Irwin, A., and P. Hooper. 1992. "Clean Technology, Successful Innovation, and the Greening of Industry." *Business Strategy and the Environment* 1 (2): 1–12.

In addition to a review of the existing literature on the incentives and obstacles to clean technology development, this paper offers a categorization of end-of-pipe technology (R), recycling with a minor process adjustment (R+), and "integrated technologies" (I). Several case studies of "successful" clean technology (as identified by a British award scheme) are then considered. Environmental innovation is seen to be linked to technological excellence, long-term investment, and company-wide efficiency programs. However, this sample from the late 1980s demonstrated little sign of "corporate greening." Instead, regulatory pressure was particularly important in encouraging clean technology innovation.

Jackson, T. (ed.). 1993. *Clean Production Strategies: Developing Preventive Environmental Management in the Industrial Economy*. Boca Raton, FL, Ann Arbor, MI, London, Tokyo: Lewis Publishers.

This broad-ranging international collection discusses clean production strategies in 18 chapters. The goal of clean production is seen as coterminous with that of "sustainable development": production processes, product cycles, and consumption patterns that allow for human development and the provision of basic needs, without degrading and disrupting the ecosystems within which that development must occur. Part I of the book presents the "scientific and economic context," including the economic problems of hazardous waste and a discussion of environmental management and the "precautionary principle." Part II discusses the "preventive strategy" itself, including the operational principles for clean production, product lifestyle assessment, and the particular example of a Swedish program in this area. Part III shifts to the "policy framework"; a chapter by Yakowitz and Hanmer gives a broad overview of the available policy options (including regulatory programs, economic instruments, information and training, eco-labeling, voluntary agreements, strict liability, and full disclosure). In an epilogue to the discussion, the new environmental paradigm is discussed as a shift in underlying social and cultural values.

This useful collection brings together European and North American contributors from a variety of institutional locations; it also includes both theoretical and empirical accounts. The editor argues against gradualist notions implied in "clean*er*" as opposed to "clean" production. "Clean," he says, allows for "the expression of a vision of compatible eco-systems."

Johansson, A. 1992. *Clean Technology*. Boca Raton, FL: Lewis Publishers.

This book adopts an engineering approach based on the notion of "sustainable development." Particular emphasis is placed on the application of thermodynamic principles to human and natural systems. The possibilities for cleaner production in engineering systems (such as liquid membranes and biosorbents), waste, systems analysis, and materials and products are briefly introduced. The policy questions arising from clean technology are considered (including environmental audits, regulations, and market mechanisms). Overall, the book offers a number of specific engineering possibilities for cleaner technological systems.

Jones, T. 1988. *Corporate Killing: Bhopals Will Happen.* London: Free Association Books.

While it is possible to offer various optimistic scenarios concerning the "greening of industry" and cleaner production, this book argues that industry will be reluctant to make any changes in production processes since there is little economic incentive for it to do so. Thus, "toxic capital" is inherently antithetical to the demands of human and environmental welfare. This problem will be especially great in developing countries, where external controls will inevitably be less strong. Drawing on the example of Bhopal, but also other accidents worldwide, Jones stresses the limits to capitalist improvement in this area without firm political and economic action.

Kemp, R. 1993. "An Economic Analysis of Cleaner Technology: Theory and Evidence." In *Environmental Strategies for Industry.* K. Fischer and J. Schot (eds.). 79–113. Washington, DC: Island Press.

Kemp (an economist) explores the factors that promote and obstruct the development and use of cleaner technologies, defined as "environmentally sound consumer products, low-emission processes, pollution control devices, recycling systems, or environmentally friendlier materials." He presents a theory of environment-saving technological change, building on neo-Schumpeterian theories of technological change, following the work of Nelson and Winter. He argues that the process of "greening of industry" will be gradual and slow, despite strong public demands, due to the dominance of prevailing technological "trajectories" that have long-accumulated dynamic learning and scale effects and will be difficult to replace with "cleaner" trajectories.

This is explored with reference to three case studies: substitutes for CFCs, low-solvent paints and coatings, and membrane technologies in the metal-plating industry. He concludes that not enough is known about firms' strategies with respect to cleaner technologies and that this should be a priority for further research.

Kemp, R. 1994. "Technology and the Transition to Environmental Sustainability: The Problem of Technological Regime Shifts." *Futures* 26 (10): 1023–1046.

This article is from a Dutch-U.K.-Norwegian study of large-scale technological transitions, part of the Commission of the European Communities' research program on social and environmental aspects of environmental change. The article examines the possibility of achieving radical change in technology, such as a shift away from hydrocarbon-based energy technologies. Radical technologies often have long lead times and require for their operation special skills, infrastructure, and all kinds of institutional changes. Furthermore, the short-term costs are likely to be high, because the new technologies have not yet benefited from the dynamic scale and learning effects that result in cost reductions per unit of output and evolutionary increments in the technology. The article also suggests how firms with restricted technological capabilities might be able to bring about a shift into a new technological regime—emphasizing the importance of early market niches, institutional support, and the role of expectations.

Kirkwood, R.C., and A.J. Longley (eds.). 1995. *Clean Technology and the Environment.* Glasgow: Blackie Academic and Professional.

The 11 chapters by mainly British authors explore clean technology as a new approach to environmental protection essential for sustainable development. The first four chapters deal in technical terms with the ecological principles governing the function of ecosystems, sustainability and diversity and the problems resulting from atmospheric pollution, water pollution, and land pollution. Two chapters on the economics of pollution and on the basic concepts of clean technology are followed by detailed technical presentations of the principles of clean technology applied to five industrial sectors, with an emphasis on process industries: agricultural and pharmaceutical chemicals, plastics, food manufacture, organic chemical synthesis, and energy supply and use. There are many references to the scientific and technological literature.

The discussion of clean technology by Roland Clift and Anita Longley (Chapter 6) is notable for its stress on the relationship between technological and broader commercial and consumption changes:

> Clean technology depends at least as much on re-thinking commercial and social habits as on introducing technological developments. For example, . . . a clean technology for cleaning clothes would introduce completely different relationships between the manufacturers of detergents and washing machines: they would combine to provide the service, rather than each selling their own product.

However, this insight is inadequately developed in the industrial sector chapters.

Linnerooth, J., and G. Davis. 1990. "From Hazardous Wastes to Clean Technologies: Creating an Economic and Organizational Infrastructure." In *Industrial Risk Management and Clean Technology*. S.P. Maltezou, A.M. Amir, and W. Irwin (eds.), 327–344. Vienna: Verlag Orac.

An important conclusion of this paper is that the private competitive model cannot be expected to provide the infrastructure for the higher cost treatment and incineration technologies for a large number of regulated wastes, even if government regulation requires this type of management.

MacGarvin, M., and P.A. Johnston. 1993. "On Precaution, Clean Production, and Paradigm Shifts." *Water Science and Technology* 27 (5-6): 469–480.

There are three main reasons why change toward clean production will occur: (1) There is a growing scientific recognition that questions of marine ecology are much less understood than had previously been acknowledged. Thus scientific uncertainty is at such a level that "safe" levels of contamination cannot be currently specified. (2) Therefore, policy can no longer be based on the assimilative capacity of the environment and must move instead toward simple *ad hoc* reduction targets—which can only be achieved by waste prevention rather than waste management. (3) A number of examples are presented, demonstrating that clean production has the potential to deal with environmental problems. Finally, the consequences of this situation for the water treatment industry are assessed—with the precautionary principle, implemented by clean technology, opening up new opportunities for progressive companies.

North, K. 1992. *Environmental Business Management: An Introduction*. Geneva: International Labor Office.

An easy-to-read handbook, with many tables, diagrams, checklists, and case examples, for business managers who want to "make money and protect the environment at the same time." Examples are taken from multinationals as well as from small enterprises in developing countries. North discusses in more detail than is usual in such books how environmental principles can be incorporated into the research and development and technological design activities, sketching an "R&D methodology for environmentally friendly products" involving environmental impact analysis on the product's life cycle, suggestions on materials management, waste management, and energy saving.

Rushton, B.M. 1993. "How Protecting the Environment Impacts R&D in the United States." *Research—Technology—Management* (May–June): 13–21.

The author argues that the increasing use of R&D resources may well be the key to the technological solution of many present-day environmental concerns. The degree to which it is possible to direct R&D programs to produce environmentally friendly products via environmentally clean processes will be a determinant of how fast industry can grow and, in turn, how fast society can progress. According to the author, R&D must play a key role in this progression.

Schmidheiny, S. 1992. *Changing Course: A Global Business Perspective on Development and the Environment.* Cambridge, MA: MIT Press.

Schmidheiny chairs the Business Council for Sustainable Development, a network of top world business leaders from developed and developing countries, who proclaim: "progress toward sustainable development makes good business sense because it can create competitive advantages and new opportunities."

The book presents a number of cases of good global environmental practice in all aspects of management of business, including "managing cleaner production." Examples are *Smith and Hawken* (U.S.A): promoting products of sustainable forestry; *Procter and Gamble* (U.S.A): using life cycle analysis to cut solid waste; *Migros* (Switzerland): using life cycle analysis in retail operations; *Henkel* (Germany): developing substitutes for phosphates in detergents; *Laing* (U.K.): energy-efficient housing; *Volkswagen* (Germany): recycling the car; *Pick'n'Pay* (South Africa): retailers and sustainable development; and *Eni* (Italy): Developing a replacement for lead in gasoline.

Chapter 7 discusses cleaner technologies in the context of the innovation process in which "environmental considerations must be fully integrated into the heart of the production process, affecting the choice of raw materials, operating procedures, technology, and human resources. Pollution prevention means that environmental efficiency becomes, like profitability, a cross-functional issue that everyone is involved in promoting."

Schwarz, M., and M. Thompson. 1990. *Divided We Stand: Redefining Politics, Technology and Social Choice*. London: Harvester Wheatsheaf.

A cultural theory approach argues that the environment does not simply impact on industry; rather, different organizations define the environment according to their own sets of assumptions. The authors—drawing on the previous work of anthropologists such as Mary Douglas—identify four "myths of nature" that correspond to four major organizational forms. Nature is seen as *benign, ephemeral, perverse/tolerant,* or *capricious*—these definitions corresponding to the positions of the *individualist, egalitarian, hierarchist,* or *fatalist.* It follows that the culture of organizations will be important in the kinds of environmental response that is pursued. Thus, individualist (or entrepreneurial) organizations may focus solely on the "bottom line," while hierarchical (or bureaucratic) forms may be led to impose order (a place for everything . . .). This categorization may also be significant for information campaigns designed to encourage cleaner production.

Smith, D. (ed.). 1993. *Business and the Environment: Implications of the New Environmentalism*. London: Paul Chapman.

Cleaner production sits at the interface of a range of pressures and concerns as they affect industrial development. This book offers an overview of this new climate for innovation and attempts to outline the much-vaunted "paradigm shift" for industry and the environment. Two chapters are particularly relevant in this context. Tombs reviews the strategic responses of the chemical industry toward environmentalism largely in terms of "cleaning up" its negative image. Such strategies include process innovation—but this is in turn linked to attempts at avoiding increased governmental regulation. Overall, Tombs calls for greater access by public groups to information about environmental innovation and industrial decision-making processes. Green and Yoxen review the biotechnology sector and see scenarios in this area as being shaped both by the relationship between mass production/flexible specialization and by that between greenism and industrialism. In that sense, steps toward cleaner production will be shaped by other commercial and technological concerns.

Stahel, W., and T. Jackson. 1993. "Optimal Utilization and Durability." In *Clean Production Strategies. See* T. Jackson 1993.

Stahel is director of Geneva's Product Life Institute. During the last 15 years, he has persistently pressed the need to consider the environmental impact of products in use. This includes product redesign to minimize the use of toxic materials and the impact of the product in its manufacturing phase. More important, think Stahel and Jackson, is *extending* the product life of goods through the "4 Rs": *re*conditioning, *re*pair, *re*use, and *re*cycling. They contrast the so-called optimal utilization economy based on these self-replenishing product principles with our current system—the "fast replacement" linear production-consumption system of the Industrial Revolution. The advantages of an optimal utilization economy would not only be environmental; the expansion of reconditioning and repair services would also stimulate employment growth and decentralization. The authors discuss a variety of policy reforms, focusing on tax systems to encourage product life extension and durability rather than depreciation and obsolescence.

United Nations Environment Program (UNEP). 1993. *Cleaner Production Worldwide.* Paris: UNEP.

This booklet illustrates the various approaches to clean technology and production in a variety of developed and developing countries, including Singapore, Greece, Denmark, Indonesia, the Netherlands, France, India, Poland, the United Kingdom, Austria, Sweden, and the United States. The 14 examples include "low" and "high" technology in small, medium, and large industrial enterprises in both rural and urban locations.

van den Akker, F. 1990. "Recycling and Clean Technologies: The Challenge for the 21st Century." In *Industrial Risk Management and Clean Technology.* S.P. Maltezou, A.M. Amir, and W. Irwin (eds.). 183–190. Vienna: Verlag Orac.

The author works at the Ministry of Housing, Physical Planning, and Environment in the Netherlands. He argues that the next century needs an alternative approach to add-on technologies and waste-treatment technology to overcome problems and to prevent irreversible environmental degradation. Industries should cooperate with scientists, citizens, and governments to close the life cycle of products as much as possible. In many instances this can be realized by using cost-effective clean technologies.

Winter, G. 1988. *Business and the Environment*. Hamburg: McGraw-Hill.

Subtitled "A handbook of industrial ecology with 22 checklists for practical use and a concrete example of the Integrated System of Environmentalist Business Management"; the checklists include those that bear on clean technology, namely "economizing on energy and water," "product development," "materials management," "production technology," and "disposal and recycling." The lists are a mixture of the general ("develop long-life products") and the specific ("replace arsenic oxide by antimony trioxide"). Some of the subheadings for the various lists amount to a list of guiding propositions for clean technology; thus for *product development:*

• Use value analysis for ecological as well as economic purposes.

• When deciding on the material composition and design of products bear in mind the ecological repercussions of production, use, and disposal.

And for *production technology:*

• Use ecological materials and processes.

• Use technologies that achieve a better input-output ratio.

• Recover useful materials and heat.

The ideas presented in the book have been extended and updated in Winter, G. (1995), *Blueprint for Green Management,* London: McGraw-Hill. The "production technology" checklist now includes the recommendation "use clean technologies," listing a few two-line examples.

Chapter 8

Transnational Companies and Industrial Pollution in the South: An Overview

Jan Hesselberg

Transnational Companies in the North–South Context

In the 1970s, a debate started on the possible impact on industrial location of stricter environmental legislation in the United States. Attention was called to scenarios such as an exodus of manufacturing firms to poor countries in the South, where industrial pollution was relatively low (so-called pollution havens). B.I. Castleman is a leading researcher and writer in this debate on what became known as the industrial flight hypothesis.[1] The driving force behind this flight was thought to be the growing gap in strictness of environ-

---

1. B.I. Castleman, "How We Export Dangerous Industries," *Business and Society Review* (Fall 1978): 7–14; B.I. Castleman, "The Export of Hazardous Factories to Developing Nations," *International Journal of Health Services* 9 (1979) (4): 569–606; B.I. Castleman, "Occupational Safety and Health Regulations—An International Labour Perspective—Response," *International Journal of Health Services* 11 (1981) (2): 311–313.

mental laws and regulations between countries in the North and those in the South. The lack of financial resources and expertise to control existing legislation in the South was seen to add weight to the argument. A major point made and criticism directed at transnational companies (TNCs) was that although some firms complied with government-set standards on effluents and emissions, other firms decided to move part of their production to the South. By continuing industrial production with pollution in other countries, such TNCs then had a double standard in their technological and pollution-abatement levels. An ethical issue was easy to raise here—the habitat and working conditions of poor people, who have less resistance physically and politically to pollution, became dumping grounds of hazardous production and waste due to profit-seeking TNCs. Furthermore, sparsely populated regions often exhibited particularly fragile ecosystems (Walter 1975, 1976).

A counterargument to this line of reasoning is that the countries in the South are in need of direct foreign investments in order to industrialize. Additionally, they must go through a heavy-industry phase, with its related pollution, that countries in the North have experienced. Moreover, since the South has relatively little heavy industry, nature's capacity to assimilate pollution is still underutilized in most parts of their countries, according to this argument. Furthermore, the technological level of TNCs' production would in most cases be above similar local production in the South, and thus TNCs would at least pollute less per unit of production than would local firms (Ives 1985).

Industrial Flight

Starting near the end of the 1970s, documentation was sought on industrial flight to the South. A number of cases have been described where pollution-intensive types of production either were relocated to the South or expanded there with a parallel decline in similar production in the North. TNCs were involved in some way or other in this expansion. The conclusion drawn, however, was that no massive movement of manufacturing was occurring (Pearson 1987).[2]

Castleman was heavily criticized, and the exodus idea was refuted. To this, Castleman replied that he had never predicted an exodus, only warned about the danger of losing manufacturing employment in the United States and of a worsening health situation in poor countries. Since the late 1980s, it seems that the conventional wisdom is that there is no shift of industrial pollution to the South and that there are few, if any, cases of hazardous industrial pollution with the participation of TNCs (UN 1992).[3] Low (1992) in a World Bank study comes to the following conclusion: "Pollution abatement and control expenditures by firms do not appear to have had a significant effect on competitiveness in most industries, since these expenditures represent a modest share of total costs. This suggests that national differences in environmental regulations have not been a major explanatory factor in changing international patterns of location of dirty industries." However, he also concludes that "dirty industries have expanded faster in developing countries than the average rate for all industries over the last two decades, and faster than in industrial countries. It is uncertain whether this international pattern merely reflects growth, or industrial migration as well."

The United Nations Center on Transnational Corporations (UNCTC) produced together with the Economic and Social Commission for Asia and the Pacific (ESCAP) two important reports on the issue of industrial pollution in the South and the involvement of TNCs from the North (ESCAP/UNCTC 1988, 1990). In these reports, and in UNIDO's Global Report,[4] a number of cases of pol-

---

2. H.J. Leonard and C.L.J. Duerksen, "Environmental Regulation and the Location of Industry: An International Perspective," *Columbia Journal of World Business* (Summer 1980): 52–68; C. Levenstein and S.W. Eller, "Are Hazardous Industries Fleeing Abroad?" *Business and Society Review* 34 (1980): 44–46; H.J. Leonard, "Confronting Industrial Pollution in Rapidly Industrializing Countries: Myths, Pitfalls, and Opportunities," *Ecology Law Quarterly* 12 (1985) (4): 779–816.

3. Worldwatch Institute, *State of the World* (London: Earthscan, 1992).

4. UNIDO, Industry and Development, Global Report 88/89 (Vienna: UNIDO, 1988).

lution in Asia are documented. The level of technology in production in the subsidiaries is generally lower than that of the plants in the home country. The best available technology at reasonable cost is evidently not used. Many TNCs adhere to local environmental standards only. They do not transfer to their subsidiary in the South the best technology and environmental practice they use at their home plants. Moreover, for many of the types of production the TNCs engage in, there are no specific environmental laws in the South. Furthermore, the extensive pollution in some nations with rapid industrial growth, such as the newly industrialized countries (for example, South Korea and Mexico), is now getting more attention in international literature (Bello and Rosenfeld 1990). Many today fear that although a major disaster such as the Bhopal tragedy is less likely to happen now, the numerous instances of industrial pollution in several countries in the South may together result in future disasters. That is, a "Bhopal in slow motion" is occurring.[5]

Environmental Management Practices in TNCs

Several studies have been done on the environmental management practices of TNCs (Rappaport *et al.* 1991; Willums and Golüke 1992; UN 1993). According to these reports, the large international corporations are taking the issue of environmentally sound production seriously. Numerous firms have voluntarily adopted environmental policy statements, for example. However, the degree to which such statements are fully implemented is still unclear. Another undecided aspect is whether all the TNCs see to it that the new "green image" is applied in all their activities worldwide. The Keidanren group in Japan is in the front line of this issue with its advocacy of implementing the same environmental standard in all operations of a firm, globally. Similar business groups working for improved environmental awareness among industrial management and plant directors are the International Environmental Bureau of the International Cham-

---

5. B.I. Castleman and V. Navarro, "International Mobility of Hazardous Products, Industries, and Wastes," *Annual Review of Public Health* 8 (1987): 1–19.

bers of Commerce and the Responsible Care Program of the chemical industry.

The UN (1993) found, however, that there is still a lot to be improved, especially regarding European industry. TNCs admit that it is the imposition by governments of laws and regulations that change their environmental practice. The pressure from possible lawsuits is efficient in this respect. Ruud (1992) found in a study of Norwegian TNCs that environmental investments were postponed in the subsidiaries in the South during periods of reduced profitability in the parent company. Double standards in pollution abatement technology were also observed.

Rappaport *et al.* discuss environment, health, and safety (EHS) strategies in United States–based TNCs. The existence of systematic EHS policies varies widely among firms. Some firms say they delegate such responsibilities to their subsidiaries in the South. This is seen to be inadequate, and more effective control systems should be developed throughout a firm's activities worldwide. Another major point made is the need for a closer integration of EHS policies and practices in the firms' general strategies, policies, and practices.

International Trade

A recent discussion on the use of international trade restrictions to force countries and firms to become more environmentally benign includes empirical evidence and viewpoints relevant for the North's role in industrial pollution in the South (Anderson and Blackhurst 1992; Congress of the United States 1992; GATT 1992). It is maintained that unilaterally imposing special duties on imports of goods produced in countries with lower environmental standards is likely to be very divisive for the multilateral trading system in particular, and for international relations in general. Free trade, owing to its positive impact on economic growth, is seen as more important than using trade as a weapon to enforce similar standards and costs on pollution-abatement technology. Still, it is likely that the environmental argument will be used by pressure groups also for protectionist reasons.

The movement of pollution-intensive industries, which are not labor intensive, to the South documented in the World Bank report edited by Low, may be explained only partially by stricter environmental legislation in the North. The markets in the South may be the key cause for such a move, perhaps anticipating harder trade wars in the future. Moreover, TNCs may in fact welcome stricter environmental regulations in the South, since they are in a better position to comply with such regulations than local firms, owing to their control over technology and huge investments in R&D. The market for the products may then be found only in the South. This may result in a displacement of local production. When both plants and markets are shifted to the South, one may speak of a "double export of pollution."[6]

Evaluating the Evidence

Generally speaking, deciding on the relative importance of the various factors in industrial location decisions is extremely difficult. Likewise, it is not easy to assess the degree to which the opportunity to pollute replaces cheap and nonunionized labor as a comparative advantage for countries in the South in the 1990s. Moreover, to base a conclusion of the influence of environmental considerations (such as the opportunity to pollute) solely on interviews with business management, as Knödgen (1982) for example, does, is insufficient. Subjective data may be useful in some respects in this field of inquiry, but the high public awareness of environmental issues and the commercial importance of green images today underline the need for objective information. Such information is, however, very difficult to obtain. National and international statistical sources are too aggregate to allow for instance analyses of specific firms and subsectors of industries. Leonard's (1988) study is a case in point. By using aggregate data, his findings may not be valid since the data may hide possible trends within subgroups of industries. Important shifts may thus not be noticed. To get valid data, fieldwork and sample surveys must be conducted. This is time consuming and does not allow for an overall view of the role and impact of TNCs in industrial pollution in the

---

6. B. Bergsto and S.B. Endresen, "From North to South: A Locational Shift in Industrial Pollution?" *Norsk Geografisk Tidsskrift* 46 (1992) (4): 175–182.

South. To arrive at clear empirical conclusions in this complex field of research is, at best, difficult. Further analyses are required for conclusive statements.

If transnational corporations are widely seen as major sources of environmental degradation, they are also widely seen as potential—indeed essential—contributors to environmental restoration and management in developing countries. TNCs are, or may be, in a position, among other things, to "build clean" in the first place, self-regulate at the industry level, and transfer environmental clean-up and management technology and technical expertise (World Resources Institute 1984). Other important actors in the task of ameliorating existing and preventing future environmental degradation are host-country governments, many of which no longer see themselves as fundamentally weaker than TNCs. Home-country governments—reacting to, or acting in cooperation with, home-country environmental advocacy groups—are in a position to encourage more responsible behavior by "their own" TNCs.

Of the many books on suggestions of solutions to pollution, those by Cairncross (1992) and Schmidheiny (1992) deserve mention in our context. Cairncross discusses a wide range of central issues in the debate on industrial pollution in a North-South perspective. One conclusion is that government taxes are necessary to induce private enterprises to adhere to the "polluter pays" principle. Regulation of and taxation on effluents and emissions is required to make TNCs internalize the external costs stemming from their pollution. More generally, public involvement in the use of market forces in getting the relative prices right should force the private sector to act in an environmentally sound way. It is also seen to be important to obtain an international level playing field for industry and to solve the free-rider problem, as well as not to increase the total tax burden on businesses and individuals. The catch phrase is: "Instead of taxing good things, why not tax bad things?" Governments in OECD countries have shown an overwhelming preference for direct regulations over market-based policies, although the former are frequently more costly in terms of efficiency (Low 1992).

Environmental expenditures in industry are small. In most types of manufacturing the cost per unit of output in pollution abatement technology is also small. The overall effects on a country's economy of making manufacturing "clean" or "green" is and will be insignificant. In fact, environmental expenditures may have a favorable impact on productivity in general. The enforced disclosure of information on the materials used by TNCs and the wastes they create is rightly underlined by Cairncross to be of vital importance in changing the attitude among business leaders toward environmentally sound production.

The second book (Schmidheiny 1992), based on the work of the Business Council for Sustainable Development, emphasizes that the best knowledge of today's pollution rests in most cases with plant managers. Moreover, solutions depend on active participation of business leaders in reducing pollution at home and abroad, and on their willing cooperation with governments. In general, government regulations through markets is the way forward to achieve a greener industry. This is, however, not possible for all types of industrial pollution. There is now a widespread agreement that markets are not, and will not by themselves, reflect the price of environmental destruction and resource degradation. Mechanisms must thus be established to ensure that reduction in pollution benefits the individual firm. Furthermore, measures should be found to stimulate innovations toward a change from end-of-pipe solutions to savings in raw material and energy and less-polluting technology in the production processes. It is essential for the South to use the market forces in this way, because efficient enforcement of environmental legislation is often difficult.

Industrialization and Growth

Existing literature conveys a clear message of extensive industrial pollution with serious health effects, particularly in the South (WHO 1992a; 1992b). Moreover, the South may receive much damaging pollution and yet not achieve real industrialization with self-sustaining economic growth as a result. The important question seldom raised is whether today there is in the long run a conflict between industrialization with heavy pollution and economic growth. The negative side effects on climate and soils, on people's health, and on tourism, to mention but a few factors, may become very costly in both human and financial terms. At the same time there are positive signs of growing understanding of the problems and willingness to rectify them. The fundamental unanswered questions are whether international political agreements can be reached soon enough to avoid major calamities, and whether such agreements must include rather radical changes in the present competitive, industrial world system. The essential question to ask is whether the present extremely intense international competition among TNCs for markets leaves sufficient room for individual firms to take on the initial cost increases necessary to reduce pollution.

Acknowledgments

The author would like to acknowledge additional contributions supplied by George Mitchell, Tufts University, Medford, Massachusetts.

Annotated Bibliography

Anderson, K., and R. Blackhurst (eds.). 1992. *The Greening of World Trade Issues.* Hemel Hempstead, UK: Harvester Wheatsheaf.

Anderson and Blackhurst discuss the links between the environment, government policies, and international trade. International agreements are seen to be essential to avoid adverse effects on trade of the welcome efforts to reduce global industrial pollution. Using the "trade weapon" does not lead to a long-term solution for environmental problems.

Bello, W., and S. Rosenfeld. 1990. *Dragons in Distress.* San Francisco: The Institute for Food and Development.

Bello and Rosenfeld present data on industrial pollution in South Korea and Taiwan, among other aspects of the rapid industrial growth in these countries. The lessons of these experiences would be important for aspiring newly industrializing countries.

Braithwaite, J. 1984. *Corporate Crime in the Pharmaceutical Industry.* London: Routledge and Kegan Paul.

Braithwaite discusses the case of drug companies in the South. Focusing on production and marketing of dangerous products, his discussion of safe manufacturing practices elaborates on the extent to which pharmaceutical manufacturing affects the health of workers and surrounding communities.

Cairncross, F. 1992. *Costing the Earth: The Challenge for Governments, the Opportunities for Business.* Boston: Harvard Business School Press.

Cairncross, environment editor of *The Economist,* argues that environmentally sound economic growth requires government intervention. The essay advocates the use of market forces to achieve growth in a cost-effective way. This is a very useful book that discusses strategies to reduce industrial pollution. Differences between North and South are included for all issues discussed throughout the book.

Choucri, Nazli. 1991. "The Global Environment and Multinational Corporations." *Technology Review* (April): 52–59.

In the context of environmental change, multinationals are part of the problem. According to the author, cooperation between multinationals and smaller indigenous firms is central to the solution. Corporations need to address environmental factors and arrest environmental deterioration in order to compete effectively. Their technological capabilities and edge can shape new modes of economic performance. Three types of global corporations—the oil, chemical, and construction industries—illustrate the basic dilemma: Almost any action generates environmental effects that can only be reduced, managed, minimized, or contained. These three industries all contribute in particular ways to ubiquitous environmental degradation, and all confront the necessity of major corporate response.

Clarke, R. 1985. *Science and Technology in World Development.* Oxford: Oxford University Press.

In this book about science and technology, Clarke includes a discussion on TNCs and their environmental management practices in the South.

Congress of the United States. 1992. *Trade and the Environment: Conflicts and Opportunities.* Washington, DC: Office of Technical Assessment.

A highly useful report, produced by the Congress of the United States, presents several important debates regarding trade and the environment. Included are the consequences of various trade measures and policies on sustainable development in the South.

Davis, L.N. 1984. *The Corporate Alchemists: The Power and Problems of the Chemical Industry.* London: Temple Smith.

Davis presents the growth and global dispersal of the chemical industry and its main subsectors. He discusses the troubles with dangerous chemical products, accidents, and waste and ways to regulate and meet these troubles.

Dembo, D., *et al.* 1990. *Abuse of Power: Social Performance of Multinational Corporations: The Case of Union Carbide.* New York: New Horizons Press.

Dembo gives a detailed description of the TNC Union Carbide and its activities in the South. Environmental aspects are highlighted.

ESCAP-UNCTC. 1988. *Transnational Corporations and Environmental Management in Selected Asian and Pacific Developing Countries.* Publication Series B, No. 13. ST/ESCAP/608. Bangkok: ESCAP-UNCTC.

This report deals with manufacturing, the environment, and the role of TNCs. It concludes that relocation from North to South of pollution-intensive industries has taken place, and that TNCs often have better health and safety standards at home than in their subsidiaries in poor countries.

ESCAP-UNCTC. 1990. *Environmental Aspects of Transnational Corporation Activities in Pollution-Intensive Industries in Selected Asian and Pacific Developing Countries.* Publication Series B, No. 15. ST/ESCAP/857. Bangkok: ESCAP-VNTC

This report is a comprehensive work on manufacturing and environmental issues in Asia and the Pacific. As in the previous report, there are separate chapters for a number of countries. The report shows a rapid growth in pollution-intensive industries in Asia with a high rate of participation of TNCs. The TNCs have not transferred the best available technology to their factories there.

French, H.F. 1993. *Costly Tradeoffs: Reconciling Trade and the Environment.* Worldwatch Paper 113. Washington, DC: Worldwatch Institute.

In this short report, French discusses some of the central issues in the debate on trade and the environment. This is an up-to-date presentation of policies and measures regarding the trade aspect of industrial pollution in a North-South perspective.

GATT. 1992. *International Trade 90–91, vol. 1*. Geneva: GATT.

This GATT report on international trade includes a very useful discussion on the pros and cons of using trade regulations to reduce pollution. The role of GATT in this context is reviewed.

Gladwin, Thomas N. 1987. "Environment, Development, and Multinational Enterprise." In *Multinational Corporations, Environment, and the Third World: Business Matters*. C.S. Pearson (ed.). Durham, NC: Duke University Press.

In his introductory essay to Pearson's edited volume (discussed below), Gladwin describes the evolution of corporate, national, and international views and practices regarding the interactions of environment, development, and multinational enterprises. The chapter considers what is known about multinational corporations' environmental management policies and practices and offers an explanation of the major patterns observed. The chapter also focuses on the need for, and forms of, intergovernmental cooperation regarding the environmental behavior of multinationals.

Gladwin, T.N. 1977. *Environment, Planning, and the Multinational Corporation*. Greenwich, CT: JAI Press.

Gladwin's book examines the role of TNCs and their interest in transferring environmentally sound technology to the South and the effects of host-country government policies. He concludes that TNCs often are reluctant to transfer their most advanced technology, fearing diffusion to competitors.

ILO. 1984. *Safety and Health Practices of Multinational Enterprises*. Geneva: ILO.

This ILO report deals with occupational health and safety issues in TNCs. The standards "at home" are compared to those in subsidiaries in the South. A number of examples are given for selected firms and countries.

ILO. 1990. *Environment and the World of Work.* International Labor Conference 1990, report of the Director-General. Geneva: ILO.

This report presents some of the critical issues in the linkage between environment and development. Its main focus is on the role of ILO, workers' unions, and employers' organizations in pollution reduction and improvement of health and safety.

Ives, J.H. (ed.). 1985. *The Export of Hazard: Transnational Corporations and Environmental Control Issues.* London: Routledge and Kegan Paul.

Ives has edited one of the very few books dealing extensively with the question whether pollution-intensive industries have a tendency to relocate from North to South. This is an essential book both regarding the arguments used in the debate and the empirical data presented in some of the articles.

Knödgen, G. 1982. *Umweltschutz und industrielle Standortentscheidung* (Environmental protection and decisions on industrial location). Frankfurt: Campus Verlag.

From interviews with 150 German industrial leaders, Knödgen concludes that stricter environmental regulations in Germany are not seen by them as being important for location decisions.

Leonard, H. Jeffrey. 1984. *Are Environmental Regulations Driving U.S. Industries Overseas?* Washington, DC: Conservation Foundation.

This book reports the results of the Conservation Foundation's 1979–1984 efforts to determine whether U.S. federal environmental laws and regulations have had the effect of driving United States–based industrial facilities out of business or out of the country and/or hindering the construction of new plants within the United States. The investigation showed, among other things, that U.S. federal environmental regulations had not caused a significant exodus of U.S. industries.

Leonard, H.J. 1988. *Pollution and the Struggle for the World Product: Multinational Corporations, Environment, and International Comparative Advantage.* Cambridge: Cambridge University Press.

Leonard looks at the possible relocation of polluting industries from the United States to Ireland, Mexico, and Spain. He does not find a massive shift by using aggregate international statistics. The book also includes a review of location theories and the role of TNCs.

Low, P. (ed.). 1992. "International Trade and the Environment." In *World Bank Discussion Papers No. 159*. Washington, DC: World Bank.

This comprehensive and highly useful World Bank report discusses environmental management and trade issues from a variety of perspectives. In several chapters, different methods are used to determine whether pollution-intensive industries are shifting to the South.

Norwegian Journal of Geography (Norsk geogr. Tidsskr.). 1992. "Exports of Pollution-intensive Industries to the South," Theme issue. 46 (4). Oslo: Scandinavian University Press.

This theme issue of the journal, edited by Hesselberg, has both theoretical and empirical articles on the question of a shift in industrial pollution from North to South.

OECD. 1991. *Environmental Management in Developing Countries*. Paris: OECD.

OECD presents a number of articles read at the 1990 conference "Coping with Environmental Threats." Several articles deal with the issue of the relevance of OECD experiences for countries in the South. Other articles are about environmental problems and management in specific countries.

Pandya, C.G. 1987. *Hazards in Chemical Units*. Ahmedabad: Gandhi Labor Institute.

Pandya provides a case study of working conditions in chemical production in Gujarat, India. This is a thorough empirical analysis that is useful as an example of research in the field of industrial pollution in the South.

Pearson, C.S. (ed.). 1987. *Multinational Corporations, Environment, and the Third World: Business Matters*. Durham, NC: Duke University Press.

Pearson has edited an important book dealing with industrial location, hazardous exports, and the role of TNCs. Empirical examples are given from selected countries in the South.

Rappaport, A., et al. 1991. *Global Corporate Environment, Health, and Safety Programs: Management Principles and Practices.* Medford, MA: The Center for Environmental Management, Tufts University.

Through the presentation of case studies, this comprehensive report examines TNCs' health and safety policies. Five U.S. companies with production facilities outside the country were selected for detailed analysis. In addition, persons from 11 other companies based in the United States, Latin America, and Europe were interviewed. Two of the five companies had affiliates in Mexico, while the others had affiliates in Brazil, Britain, Canada, and France. The companies represented the following subsectors of industry: oil and gas, pulp and paper, manufacturing of instruments, and manufacturing of household goods.

Ruud, A. 1992. *Transnational Corporations and Environmental Considerations in Developing Countries: A Study of Environmental Issues Related to Norwegian FDI in Developing Countries.* Oslo: Center for Development and the Environment, University of Oslo.

Ruud presents the environmental management views of some Norwegian TNCs and their environmental management practices in their subsidiaries in the South. The study found that the more profitable subsidiaries have standards comparable to those at the home factories.

Sahabat Alam Malaysia. 1985. *The Bhopal Tragedy One Year After.* Penang, Malaysia: Sahabat Alam Malaysia.

The NGO Sahabat Alam Malaysia has put together an insightful book on the Bhopal disaster and the ensuing struggle for compensation.

Schmidheiny, S. 1992. *Changing Course: A Global Business Perspective on Development and the Environment.* Cambridge, MA: Business Council for Sustainable Development, MIT Press.

Schmidheiny reports on an essential problem of educating and motivating industrialists to take responsibility for their own pollution. The Business Council for Sustainable Development, started in 1990, is an important global actor in this process. The book includes a range of specific issues and the contributions that business itself is making toward sustainable development.

Ui, J. (ed.). 1992. *Industrial Pollution in Japan*. New York: United Nations University Press.

Ui has edited a very useful book on Japan's experiences of environmental destruction. Detailed descriptions of the most damaging pollution cases viewed are presented in an enlightening historical perspective. The long-term struggle of victims of pollution and community groups against both industrial management and state institutions is revealing reading. The book contains important lessons for countries in the South today.

UN. 1992. *World Investment Report: Transnational Corporations as Engines of Growth*. New York: United Nations.

UN's World Investment Report 1992 gives a broad overview of the role of TNCs in technology development, economic growth, the environment, and human capabilities. The chapter on environmental quality provides a comprehensive assessment of the impact of TNCs in the South.

UN. 1993. *Environmental Management in Transnational Corporations: Report on the Benchmark Corporate Environment Survey*. New York: UNCTAD, Program on Transnational Corporations.

This benchmark survey on TNCs, environmental management policies, and attitudes of corporate leaders provides a wide range of information from a sample of large firms. A questionnaire of 200 questions was filled out by 169 firms with sales above $1 billion. One-third of the firms were based in Asia, Europe, and North America. The subsectors of industry covered were agriculture, extractive, finished products, and services. The report deals with the South only to a limited extent.

UNCTC. 1985. *Environmental Aspects of the Activities of Transnational Corporations: A Survey*. ST/CTC/55. New York: United Nations.

UNCTC assesses the effects of TNCs on the environment in the South. Based mainly on literature available in the United States, this report emphasizes the role of the TNCs in reducing industrial pollution in the South.

UNIDO. 1988. *Global Overview of the Pesticide Industry Subsector*. Sectoral working paper. Vienna: UNIDO.

This overview of the global pesticides industry concludes that cooperation between companies in the North and South makes sense for environmental protection and safety reasons. International organizations may also assist in the process of improving the environmental management in this subsector.

UNIDO. 1990. *Industry and Development: Global Report 1990/91*. Vienna: UNIDO.

This report contains a chapter on industry and the environment as a special theme. Technical and economic aspects of pollution are discussed as well as recent pollution abatement technology.

Walter, I. 1975. *International Economics of Pollution*. London: Macmillan.

Walter discusses industrial pollution, international trade, comparative advantage of nations, and competitive advantage of TNCs. This is a basic text in the debate on a possible shift of industrial pollution from North to South.

Walter, I. (ed.). 1976. *Studies in International Environmental Economics*. New York: John Wiley & Sons.

This book contains several interesting chapters on industrial pollution. It reviews the environmental management policies of TNCs and the possible migration of pollution to the South due to stricter regulations in the North.

White, A.L., and S. Emani. 1990. *Environmental Regulation in Developing Countries: Case Studies of India, Thailand, and Venezuela and Priorities for a Capacity-building Program*. Boston: Center for Environmental Management, Tufts University.

White and Emani present valuable information on environmental regulations in India, Thailand, and Venezuela. The legislation dealt with concerns air pollution, standards for water pollution control, and waste handling.

WHO. 1992a. *Our Planet, Our Health*. Report of the WHO Commission on Health and the Environment. Geneva: World Health Organization.

WHO presents in this report the health problems connected to pollution in several sectors, industry among them. The report is rich in empirical detail and conveys a clear message of extensive occupational and environmental problems in the South.

WHO. 1992b. *Report on the Panel of Industry.* WHO/ EHE/92.4. Geneva: World Health Organization.

WHO has made an extremely useful report on the health effects of industrial activities. A number of issues are touched on, with empirical data from selected countries in the South.

Willums, J.O., and U. Golüke. 1991. *WICEM II: Second World Conference on Environmental Management.* Conference report and background papers. Seminar arranged by ICC in cooperation with UNEP and UNCED April 10–12, Rotterdam. Oslo: ICC.

Willums and Golüke have edited an extensive conference report on industry and the environment. This is industry's view, with proposals for action on reduced pollution and sustainable development in relation to the UNCED conference the following year.

Willums, J.O., and U. Golüke. 1992. *From Ideas to Action: Business and Sustainable Development.* The ICC Report on the Greening of Enterprise 92. A report prepared by the International Environmental Bureau of the ICC. Paris: ICC.

Willums and Golüke present numerous cases of efforts made by industry to reduce pollution. They examine the leading role taken by industrial organizations such as the International Chambers of Commerce as well as examples of positive action taken by individual companies.

World Resources Institute. 1984. *Improving Environmental Cooperation: The Roles of Multinational Corporations and Developing Countries.* Washington, DC: World Resources Institute.

This report was produced by a panel of business leaders and other experts convened by the World Resources Institute in 1983. Their goal was to gather the experience, perspective, and recommendations of selected experts concerning the role of multinational corporations in environmental and resource management in developing countries. The panel recommended a number of constructive steps that could be taken by corporations to avoid disputes and improve resource management. These include use of emission standards, self-regulation at the industry level, transfer of technology and technical expertise to host countries, codes of conduct or guidelines, and steps by host countries to improve environmental management.

Chapter 9

Greening of Small and Medium-sized Firms: Government, Industry, and NGO Initiatives

Kenneth Geiser
Marcel Crul

Introduction

In most economies small and medium-sized firms make up the largest share of most industrial sectors. In the United States, it was estimated in 1992 that there were 5.7 million businesses and of these about 14,000 had more than 500 employees. This means that, by number, small to medium-sized firms in the United States make up about 99.7 percent of all firms with employees.[1] The U.S. Environmental Protection Agency classifies hazardous-waste generators as large-quantity generators and small-quantity generators. In 1991, large-quantity generators in the United Sates produced 294.5 million tons of haz-

---

1. U.S. Office of the President, *The State of Small Business: A Report of the President* Washington, DC: U.S. Government Printing Office (1993): 36–37.

ardous waste (97 percent) compared with 10.7 million tons of hazardous waste (3 percent) released by small-quantity generators.[2]

In the European Union there were 15.8 million enterprises in 1990 and of these 13,000 had more than 500 employees. This means that small and medium-sized firms make up 99.9 percent of all firms. Of the total, 93.3 percent were microenterprises (fewer than 10 employees) and 6.2 percent had between 10 and 100 employees. Although no exact figures are available on environmental impact, it can be expected that also in Europe the largest part of the environmental impact is caused by the larger firms.[3]

Thus, in some industrial sectors such as chemicals, steel, and transportation equipment, the largest share of industrial pollution comes from a small number of very large facilities. Yet, in many other sectors the total amount of pollution and waste from small and medium-sized firms still makes up a significant share of the total. Even where the total share of emissions and waste is low, the broad geographic spread of these small and medium-sized firms across countries amplifies the effects of these pollutants on the environment. The large number of small and medium-sized firms and the wide dispersion of these firms suggest that these facilities should be of high interest to organizations promoting more environmentally sound production.

The Literature on Small and Medium-sized Firms

Although several topics of the greening of industry are being analyzed by governments, industrial groups, and research institutes, little analysis has been carried out with respect to small and medium-sized firms. A sizable body of anecdotal and prescriptive literature is focused on the smaller firms. Yet, most of this literature is descriptive and educational in format. Published analytical material on the "greening of small and medium-sized firms" is limited or nonexistent.

---

2. U.S. Environmental Protection Agency, Office of Solid Waste and Emergency Response, *Biennial Annual Hazardous Waste Report from RCRA,* EPA #53-OR-94039C (Washington, DC: September, 1994).

3. European Network for SME Research, *The European Observatory for SME's, Second Annual Report,* DG XXIII (Brussels European Union: 1994).

As far as the descriptive and educational material is concerned, a distinction can be made among three types of literature: case studies, manuals and guides, and government and nongovernmental organization reports.

A substantial number of case studies focus singularly on a specific firm or more likely a specific process within a firm. The substance is of varying levels of detail, but it is written primarily to report on the successful adoption of some technical change that has resulted in a lessened environmental impact and, often, some cost savings. Most of these case studies are from the United States.

The guides and manuals are far more general, typically written as instructional as well as promotional pieces. They often focus less on specific technologies and more on the processes that management might find useful to identify, assess, plan for, and implement some particular process change that would lead to a reduction in environmental impacts.

In many countries, special programs or projects have been initiated, focused on the greening of small and medium-sized firms. Many of these projects have been initiated by local or regional governments or nongovernmental organizations. These projects usually focus on the introduction of pollution-prevention, cleaner-production, or waste-minimization programs. Typically, these projects are reviewed periodically with interim and, eventually, final reports documenting the problems and successes.

Most of these case studies and guides and manuals are published independently or appear in local and national media that are not catalogued. Therefore, while examples of these materials are easy to acquire, assessing the total body of work is nearly impossible. The limited publication aspect of these documents also means that most appear in the native language of the country and most are never translated.

Besides the case studies, manuals, and local and regional projects, many industrial branches have started up environmental improvement programs that usually focus on specific topics like office paper recycling, the reduction of volatile organic compound emissions, the conservation of packaging materials, or the dissemination of specific technologies. Unfortunately, however, many of these programs are not well documented, documented only in native languages, or kept in a proprietary state. For these reasons, these items are not covered by this review.

Case Studies

Much of the sense of progress among small and medium-sized firms is accounted for by the ever increasing number of successful stories appearing in case study form. These case studies appear in many different forms. Some are published independently as freestanding reports from firms, trade associations, government technical assistance agencies, private consulting services, or universities. Others appear as published articles in trade magazines or professional journals. Many more appear as conference papers. The National Roundtable on Pollution Prevention and the European Roundtable on Cleaner Production Programs provide forums for company case studies. Over 100 initiatives, including many case studies and demonstration projects, were presented at the 1994 European Roundtable in Graz, Austria.

The United Nations Environment Program (UNEP), Cleaner Production Program based in Paris, collects facility case studies from around the world and enters them into the International Cleaner Production Information Clearinghouse (ICPIC). The ICPIC database, which is linked to the U.S. Environmental Protection Agency's Pollution Prevention Information Exchange System (PPIES), is accessible to anyone with a personal computer linked into a telephone line. Occasionally, these case studies will be compiled in independently published collections edited by an academic or a professional. An early example of such a compilation is that done by Donald Huisingh in 1986 (Huisingh *et al.* 1986). This compendium brings together short case studies from a wide range of industrial sectors to demonstrate the many opportunities for resource conservation and waste reduction. The UNEP Cleaner Production Program has compiled a collection of short case studies from countries throughout the world and published them in a brief publication called *Cleaner Production Worldwide* (UNEP 1993). Both of these compilations present information of the various enterprises in common formats so as to facilitate easy comparison among the cases. In summarizing the cases, the UNEP publication concludes for both of these compilations:

The applications here range from low to high technology. They show examples from small and medium-sized enterprises, large industrial companies, and from plants in rural locations to those in overcrowded and highly industrialized cities, in a variety of countries. They show how seriously the concept of cleaner production is being taken by some governments, industries, and individuals. The fundamental point is this: It is better for society to prevent than to cure.[4]

To examine specific case studies, this review has sought to bring together a number of case studies that have appeared in the journal *Pollution Prevention Review* over the past three years. This survey identified six articles containing 10 case studies that involved or appeared to involve small and medium-sized firms.

Included is a case study on woolen yarn and fabric (Calfa *et al.* 1994); a case study on writing instruments (Houseman 1993); a collection of case studies on automobile mirrors, military furniture, and aluminum extrusions (Kirsch *et al.* 1993); a case study on electronic processing equipment (Hamilton 1992-1993); a case study on synthetic fibers (Kikta 1994); and a collection of case studies on automobile parts, pumps and valves, military tanks, and air-powered fasteners—nails and staples (Kohler and Sasson 1993).

The typical case study is short and descriptive. Little effort is made to analyze the material from a conceptual perspective, to review the case in comparison with other similar cases, or to review the relevant literature and place the case into a broader context. Indeed, if there is any generalized material in the case study, it typically appears in conclusions, and then more as summaries than as lessons or propositions.

From Firms to Industries

Most of these case studies focus on individual firms and not on industrial sectors or groups of firms. For instance, only one of the articles (Kirsch *et al.* 1993) contained several case studies involving a common industrial process—in this case, surface painting. But the cases ranged

---

4. United Nations Environment Program, Cleaner Production Program, *Cleaner Production Worldwide* (Paris: Industry and Environment Program Office, 1993): 1.

from furniture painting to the painting of car and truck mirrors and did not focus on painting operations in a single industry, such as automobile assembly. Indeed, the first European (often national) demonstration projects around 1990, like the PRISMA (Project on Industrial Successes with Waste Prevention) project in the Netherlands (Dieleman *et al.* 1991), the Media project in Spain (MEDIA 1992a), and the PREPARE (Preventive Environmental Protection AppRoaches in Europe) projects in Finland (TEKES 1994) and in Austria (BMFW 1994) focused on individual firms, often the larger and more proactive companies.

There are signs that this focus on individual firms is shifting. A sectorwise approach is now common throughout the Netherlands where all important industrial sectors are targeted for comprehensive programs in cleaner production (VROM 1993; Tweede Kamer 1994). In the United States, the U.S. Environmental Protection Agency (U.S. EPA) launched a special "Design for the Environment" in 1992 that focused on pollution prevention opportunities in specific sectors. Recently, the U.S. EPA convened five industry sector focus groups under its "Common Sense Initiative" to identify and correct regulatory barriers to pollution prevention.

The interest in "chains of companies" in the Netherlands and the attention to vendor certification and "product stewardship" in the United States offer opportunities for examining how the greening process may work on interdependent groups of firms. The Dutch first pioneered the new direction in "integrated chain management," where environmental improvements are pursued over the total sequence of companies involved in the manufacture, distribution, and sale of a product in order to optimize the environmental performance taken across all companies (Roth *et al.* 1994). Pilot projects have now been set up in Austria, the Netherlands, and Scandinavia.

The concept of "industrial ecology" provides another means of linking firms together. Companies located in close proximity work together to improve the use of wastes produced among them. In Europe, the Danish project on "industrial symbiosis" in Kalundborg optimizes environmental performance by linking together four companies to exchange wastes and share in the use of heat generated by a local utility (Christensen and Christensen 1994).

Finally, there is a growing movement toward full regional approaches. Government programs may target all firms within one city, as in Graz, Austria (Okoprofit 1992); or in one province, as in the PROGRES (Prevention in Industry in Gelderland: Reduction of Emissions and Waste) project in the Netherlands (van Berkel *et al.* 1992); or in one county, such as the SPURT project in Storstrohm County in Denmark (SPURT 1993). These projects tend to include more of the medium-sized and often quite small firms. Especially where the region is relatively small in geography (as in Graz or Storstrohm County), there is likely to be a tight connection and functional relationship among firms, often in the form of service cooperatives and information exchange. Close connections among facility managers encourages the spread of initiatives among firms. Local government award schemes (such as those found in Graz and Storstrohm County) further enhance close working relations.

From Production Processes to Products

Most of the case studies surveyed deal with production processes and not with products. The design of products is still fairly segregated from the design of the production processes and consideration of the environmental impacts of those processes. However, some changes can be seen in this respect. In Europe there have recently appeared several case studies focusing on cleaner products.

In the Netherlands, a demonstration program called PROMISE has produced eight case studies where products differing from transport packaging materials to office chairs and coffee vending machines were redesigned with environmental aspects in mind. The results demonstrated 30 to 50 percent reductions in the use of materials (including toxic materials) and the consumption of energy (te Riele 1994). Another program in Denmark has focused on the redesign of five electronic products to reduce environmental impacts (NOH 1992). Many of these so-called ecodesign projects have focused on commercial electronic products, packaging, and to a lesser degree, automobiles, because there is increasing government pressure on the disposal of these products.

These product-oriented projects encourage attention to management issues. Ecodesign company projects are more conceptual in nature than projects focused solely on production processes. Because of the central position of the product in business planning, strategic thinking, and marketing, the organization of the processes and the

selection of product materials and production methods has a much
more fundamental starting point in the firm.[5]

From Technology to Management Focus

The case studies covered here focused on production processes and
considered a range of technological and procedural changes that
include process redesign, input chemical substitution, process equipment modernization, improved process control, internal recycling of
process chemistries (so-called closed-loop systems), and improvements in general housekeeping practices, including improved maintenance and repair. Only one of these case studies covered changes
in company organizational structure or decision making. Internal
corporate constraints that are often important impediments to the
"greening process" therefore get little attention.

Results from many of the early technical assistance programs in
the United States and demonstration programs in Europe show that
without attention to organizational and management changes in the
firms the initial efforts toward pollution prevention and cleaner production will not endure. In the United States, many firms voluntarily
are adopting some form of total quality management (TQM) to mod-
ernize manufacturing management. There is even a special form
called total quality environmental management (TQEM), focused
directly on improving the environmental performance of the firm.
These programs typically provide for team-based analyses of production systems to identify weak areas of performance and develop
programs for improvement based on iterative steps toward numeric
goals.

In Europe, the mandatory adoption of an "environmental management system" (EMAS) will certainly spur increased attention to
organizational issues. The first step in implementing an EMAS
program will be to develop the internal organization necessary to
maintain the system. If these EMAS programs are well coupled
with cleaner production activities in the form of "working programs"

---

5. M. Crul. *Environmentally Conscious Product Development in Practice*, A PROMISE Report (The Hague: NOTA, 1994).

this could be a powerful combination (van der Steen *et al.* 1992). However, neither the EMAS approach nor the TQEM approach guarantees cleaner production or pollution prevention, because improvements in environmental performance by the company can still be achieved through traditional end-of-pipe technologies.

From End Results to Social Processes

Most of the case studies focused on company results, whereas the process of change can be inhibited or encouraged by external factors in the government or economy. If the case studies described the process of change at all, they typically described it as a simple linear process within the firm with no account of government or market factors. Indeed, many states in the United States have set up specialized technical assistance services to assist companies in adopting pollution-prevention approaches.

In the case of the Dutch PRISMA and PROMISE projects, social processes were an explicit part of the government approach. As the programs were implemented, parallel studies were performed concerning the impediments encountered, both inside the firms and in existing government policies (Dieleman *et al.* 1991; Crul 1994; Cramer *et al.* 1994). The results of those studies were presented at the same time as the reports on the firm's progress, together with recommendations for change, both in industry and in government policy. These reports were integrated into follow-up activities already planned at the beginning of the PRISMA and PROMISE projects and placed in the hands of public organizations such as the National Environmental Center (NMC 1994). Because both programs were performed by order of the Dutch Parliament, direct political action followed from these programs.

Manuals and Guides

In aggregate there are an enormous number of guides and manuals to assist firms in implementing waste reduction, waste minimization, pollution prevention, toxics-use reduction, eco-efficiency, or clean production. Historically, these manuals can be seen as evolving through several generations.

The first generation of manuals appeared in the late 1980s. One of the most influential of these was the U.S. EPA's *Waste Minimization Opportunity Assessment Manual,* first published in 1988 (U.S. EPA 1988). While this was not the first manual of its kind, it was so widely distributed and so often copied that it tended to serve as an archetype. This manual opens with an introduction noting the benefits of waste minimization and the need to integrate the waste minimization perspective throughout the firm. In the second section the manual lays out a conceptual scheme that has become the template for many subsequent manuals.

The template lays out an idealized greening process as a series of four phases:

• Phase 1: Planning and Organization

• Phase 2: Assessment

• Phase 3: Feasibility Analysis

• Phase 4: Implementation

Each phase is described in some detail, and the need for a cyclical and iterative approach to the whole process is stressed. This template is followed by a compendium of worksheets that are meant to be filled out in the book or torn out to serve as guides in conducting facility visits.

Beginning in 1990 in the United States there appeared a second generation of manuals less generic and more focused on specific industrial sectors. For example, between 1990 and 1992 the U.S. EPA produced 16 *Guides to Pollution Prevention* written for specific industrial sectors (U.S. EPA 1990-1992). These guides to pollution prevention cover industrial sectors ranging from paint manufacturing and commercial printing to the fabricated metal and auto repair industries.

A review of these guides demonstrates that they are fairly rigid in their construction and suffer from a lack of internal integration. Each section, including the case study appendix, stands alone, without reference to any other section. The conceptual introduction and the worksheets are similar in each of the 16 guides. Thus, the only differences are found in the industry profiles, the description of waste minimization options, and the appended case studies. In these sections there is wide variation among the guidebooks. The descriptions of waste minimization options are, arguably, the most useful sections, as the ideas provided here are, at minimum, a healthy checklist for beginning a more detailed search for solutions.

State Technical Assistance Manuals

Many of the more industrialized states in the United States have established government-supported technical assistance offices that are organized to provide free consultative services to small and medium-sized firms on waste reduction, pollution prevention, or toxics-use reduction. These offices are typically financially constrained and struggling for visibility and legitimacy. Many have found that the publication of a generic industry assistance manual raises awareness among firms and provides guidance for self assistance where state resources are limited.

While many states have published such manuals, four are reviewed here as relatively typical. These include (1) New York State Department of Environmental Conservation's *New York State Waste Reduction Guidance Manual* (New York Department of Environmental Conservation 1989); (2) Texas Water Commission's *Pollution Prevention Assessment Manual for Texas Businesses* (Texas Water Commission 1992); (3) the Massachusetts Office of Technical Assistance's *A Practical Guide to Toxics Use Reduction* (Massachusetts Office of Technical Assistance 1992); and (4) Washington State Department of Ecology's *Pollution Prevention Planning* (Washington State Department of Ecology 1992).

Each of these is a self-published document of roughly 100 pages directed toward industrial managers seeking to reduce waste or prevent pollution within the context of state laws. Two of the manuals start out with motivational sections describing reasons for improving environmental performance. The Washington manual begins by describing the state waste reduction law. From there on the manuals are fairly similar. Each has a section on "starting up," conducting a facility audit or assessment, selecting appropriate wastes or pollutants, identifying reduction options, carrying out "feasibility analyses," and implementing programs. The Texas and Washington manuals include a specific section describing planning and the proper elements of a plan. Both of these manuals also include model worksheets for setting goals, facility audits, feasibility assessments, and so on.

Neither the Massachusetts nor the New York manual relies on worksheets. The New York manual is livened up with numerous short case studies in small boxes. All of these state manuals rely on appendices to present lists of relevant publications and directories of technical resources that might assist the manual users in implementing their programs. The Massachusetts manual closes with a description of the state law in a final appendix. The New York manual includes a list of applicable rules and regulations and a glossary of terms among its extensive appendices.

European Technical Assistance Manuals

In Europe, a line of first generation manuals became available in 1990-1992. The first was the Dutch PRISMA manual, which was an adaptation of the U.S. EPA *Waste Minimization Opportunity Assessment Manual* (de Hoo *et al.* 1990). Similar adapted versions of the U.S. EPA manual became available soon afterward in most European languages, many of them based on the English version of the PRISMA manual (PREPARE 1991). Although the general outline was still followed in those manuals, some flexibility was brought into the system by introducing a "pre-assessment" or preliminary study or survey in the beginning. This provided the opportunity to quickly select and implement some easy, successful solutions without going through the entire procedure. Other adaptations included early introduction of regulations and specific legal requirements, and more attention toward the economical and financial aspects of company programs. While these early manuals were useful, they were criticized because of their rigid structure, their inappropriateness for small and medium-sized firms, and the amount of effort required to fill in all the worksheets.

A second generation of manuals similar to the sector manuals in the United States also appeared in Europe, notably in Norway, Denmark, Spain, and the Netherlands, following 1992. However, this proved to be not as successful because the manuals were not specific enough. Practically every company had to make up its own adaptation. The sector-specific approach focused heavily on material-intensive industries, such as chemical, food, and electroplating, and not on information-intensive industries such as communications and services (Nilsen *et al.* 1994).

A third generation and more promising line of manuals is developing now. These are simpler guides, tailored to specific sectors, but focused on small and medium-sized firms. They are often intended to be used as aids in training programs. This training-oriented approach is increasingly important. Fifteen industry-sector training programs have been developed in the Netherlands, where the overall approach is translated into specific course modules, coupled with take-home work to be conducted between classes in the participants' specific companies. The manual in these cases is worked directly into the course workbook. Sometimes a consultancy-oriented approach, or a so-called train-the-trainer approach is followed, in which consultants, government authorities, or intermediaries are trained in the approach first; they then take this training along with them in their work with companies.

A separate but important new line of manuals is emerging from the introduction of the EMAS, environmental management systems. The first steps in this approach—particularly the inventory and materials balancing—is comparable to cleaner production approaches, but the later steps focus more on organization and management. Because of the mandatory character of EMAS in the future, there is the potential for increasing integration of these two approaches.

Finally, there has appeared a series of manuals focused on product design. There are at least 10 new ecodesign manuals from Austria (IOW 1993), Denmark, Canada, the Netherlands (Brezet 1994), and elsewhere. The variation among these manuals is much broader than among the process-oriented manuals. Clearly the starting point for ecodesign is much broader and also there is less consensus over the use of particular tools and procedures. Generally, a distinction can be made between a design orientation (ecodesign is a specific case of conventional product design) and an environmental orientation (ecodesign is a new tool of environmental policy). The environmental orientation requires much more attention on life cycle analysis and other environmental-impact-assessment tools. In an effort to keep product and process orientations compatible, the step-by-step procedures laid out in the Dutch PROMISE manual have been organized as much as possible in the same pattern as those found in the older U.S. EPA manual.

From Material to Functional Orientation

The first and second generation manuals are based either implicitly or explicitly on an input-output analysis, or "materials balance," as it is often called. Quite simply, this refers to the engineering axiom that for any production process (or production facility) "materials in" must equal "materials out." Firms are encouraged to inventory their material purchases on an annual basis and then account for all those materials not sent out as products during the year. Such analyses indicate the wastes and emissions, both those accounted for and permitted and those unaccounted for and in need of attention.

The use of a materials balance as a foundation for analyzing current processes, and later for seeking options for improvement, grounds these manuals in issues of materials management, resource conservation, chemical substitution, internal materials recycling, and waste prevention. By contrast, little is offered as advice on a functional analysis of each process that might lead to nonmaterial efficiencies or on product redesign or changes in the services offered by the firm.

The generic state manuals do not urge users to reconsider their products or the functions of production, largely because they are not specific to any one industry or product. The more industry-specific U.S. EPA guides are so tightly defined and unimaginative that they would little encourage more speculative or fundamental thinking about the business, the products, or the clients of the firm.

The third generation manuals in Europe are less materials-focused and more tailored to the functions of the small and medium-sized firms. Combining these manuals with the impending EMAS requirements will certainly expand the focus to more functional considerations of the firm. Also, the ecodesign manuals are more functional by nature. These manuals tend to place a strong emphasis on considering and reconsidering functions of products and processes and the company's marketing orientation as a whole.

From Technologies to Organizational Structure

The emphasis in the first and second generation manuals was placed on a "process-flow-diagram point of view." This contrasts sharply with the limited attention given to the "organization-diagram point of view." The object of interest in these manuals is the linear process flow system, rather than the more complex internal communication and decision-making system. There are no worksheets on organization structure and no discussion of the role that corporate culture, communication, or governance play in encouraging or discouraging environmentally conscious solutions. Where manuals do refer to work organization the discussion is typically limited to task-oriented team-building or techniques for acquiring upper-level managerial commitment.

As a result, much of the analysis and opportunity identification is focused on technologies and production practices, rather than on ways to change the structure of the firm or its culture and thus nurture more creative and fundamental changes. Again, much of this may be changing as total environmental quality management becomes more accepted in the United States and the EMAS system comes on line in Europe.

From Prescriptive to Descriptive Analysis

Most of the early manuals include worksheets within the text or as appendices. Such worksheets cover facility descriptions, waste inventories, options identification, technical evaluations, and financial analyses and are designed to be filled out by the reader. But many of these manuals fail to encourage creative and spontaneous thinking, because the worksheets lead to a prescriptive form-filling approach. Instead, some practitioners recommend a descriptive approach that requires industrial staff to identify and describe their production processes and problems in a fully fresh and unassisted manner.[6] While a worksheet approach may be quick and low cost, the insights available from a more fundamental reconsideration of the production system has the potential to prove more effective over the longer term.

---

6. Robert Pojasek and Lawrence Cali, "Contrasting Approaches to Pollution Prevention Auditing," *Pollution Prevention Review* 1 (3) (Summer 1991): 225–235.

The third-generation manuals in Europe are much more descriptive in their approach. No long appendix of worksheets is included. It can be argued that the optimal number of worksheets proposed for a cleaner production project for a small firm is two: one blank page on which to sketch the process and problems of the company and a second blank page on which to write down all the innovative ideas. A recent Danish guide uses only these two sheets, and another example from Austria includes only five worksheets.

Government and NGO Reports

Government Initiatives

Local and regional initiatives in the greening of small and medium-sized firms first appeared in the early 1980s. During this period several American states, notably Minnesota, New York, and North Carolina, set up promotional and technical-assistance programs to encourage industrial waste reduction. While underfunded, focused on waste alone, and engaging firms only on a voluntary basis, these programs encouraged the first programmatic experimentation in greening processes.

In Europe, similar projects started toward the end of the 1980s. By 1990 experimental and demonstration projects had appeared in Sweden, Denmark, Germany, France, and the Netherlands. While the state and local programs in the United States tended to focus on specific industrial sectors, the European projects tended to focus more on specific geographic regions, such as Landskrona in Sweden; the provincial projects like PROGRESS in the Netherlands; the Catalyst project in England (Catalyst 1994); the Ecoprofit project in the region of Graz, Austria; and the SPURT and CARTA projects in Denmark. These regional projects generally have a more comprehensive form including not only demonstration but also policy initiatives (both regulatory and communicative), training courses, financial support, and follow-up and dissemination programs. This comprehensive approach is now fairly well accepted among the 18 countries participating in the European PREPARE working group that promotes research and development projects on the greening of industry.

Canada has followed both the American and European models. A good example of the regional approach has been the pollution prevention demonstration project in Hamilton, Ontario. Begun in 1991 by Environment Canada and the Ontario Ministry of the Environment and Energy, the project focused on identifying small-quantity hazardous-waste generators, presenting pollution-prevention options to them, and assessing their progress in adopting "behavioral changes" leading to reduced generation of waste (Cave et al. 1993).

Nongovernment Organization Initiatives

Nongovernmental organizations have played an important role in promoting the greening process by documenting and publicizing the environmental and public health risks of irresponsible industrial practices, by identifying and disseminating information about cleaner technologies, by compiling case studies of successful firms, and by promoting legislation and government programs to encourage the greening process.

An early and seminal example of nongovernmental organization promotion was the relatively sophisticated compilation of brief cases put together by the Canadian environmental organization Pollution Probe in 1982 (Cambell and Glenn 1982). This paperbound production chronicled scores of environmentally conscious process changes implemented by Canadian and U.S. firms by industrial sector.

In some cases, nongovernmental organizations have produced industrial guidance manuals that are quite similar to the state manuals and may come to be used in place of a state manual. The Ontario (Canada) Waste Management Corporation, a quasi-public authority, prepared a manual for in-plant waste audits (OWMC 1987). In Alaska, the Alaska Health Project, a private organization providing information about hazardous materials, produced a simple but quite effective manual (Wigglesworth 1988).

In 1986 the Environmental Defense Fund and the Metropolitan Water District of Southern California established a unique joint government/nongovernment organization project, called the Source Reduction Research Partnership, to study techniques for reducing the release of halogenated solvents in the Los Angeles region (Source Reduction Research Partnership 1990). While not filled with particular case studies of program implementation, the project reports are full of specific technical options that are well targeted to adoption by small and medium-sized firms. The range of options is broad and well described, and the technical, regulatory, and financial analyses appear sound and encouraging.

From Voluntary to Mandatory

Most of the local and regional government-initiated projects have been voluntary in nature. Voluntary programs are praised because they cost governments less and because they provide the flexibility for firms to apply well-planned solutions that are the most cost effective. In the state programs, firms voluntarily approach the state for technical and programmatic assistance. In the European projects, firms in a targeted region have the option to avoid participation in the project. Thus, these programs are limited by the willingness of firms to participate and the amount of resources and commitments they will voluntarily contribute.

While most of the cleaner production programs in the Netherlands are voluntary, the PRISMA approach is mandatory for certain industrial sectors such as plastics production and shipyards. However, in general the approach taken by the Dutch government takes the form of consensus building and the signing of (voluntary) covenants. Environmental targets take the form of 50 to 70 percent reductions in emissions by the year 2000. For many of the sectors, these goals will be met by a mixture of end-of-pipe and preventive measures. For instance, in the packaging industry's emissions-reduction covenant, up to 75 percent of the reductions will come from preventive approaches.

Norway has taken a more mandatory approach. As part of the permitting process, all firms must start a cleaner production program. To date over 300 large and medium-sized firms have complied. Attention is now turning to smaller firms. Some states in the United States have followed a similar approach. Massachusetts, Washington, New York, Minnesota, Oregon, Maine, and others require firms to prepare pollution-prevention plans for each facility in the state. While these plans are typically confidential business documents, they must project goals and schedules for reducing pollution, and reports on progress must be released annually.

While volunteerism may well encourage the more innovative and cooperative firms, it does little to motivate the more recalcitrant. Voluntary programs may be justified by the substantial participation rates that may appear in the first years of a program's implementation; but eventually, after much has been learned about how best to conduct the program, more mandatory requirements may be necessary to reach the less cooperative firms so as to "level the playing field" with the firms that took the lead voluntarily. Indeed, a recent study in the Netherlands suggests the high level of participation in voluntary programs is partly due to the threat of regulations if targets are not met.[7]

From Demonstrative to Comprehensive Programs

Many of the government and, particularly, the nongovernment projects are designed as demonstration projects to display the technical and economic benefits of pollution prevention or environmentally sound production. As demonstration projects, the successes are promoted as examples for firms in other regions or industrial sectors. The voluntary nature of these demonstration projects cannot guarantee comprehensiveness, because not all potential participants may participate.

In none of the American projects is an industry or a region as a whole targeted in a comprehensive and all-inclusive manner. Even the Southern California research project that covers the Los Angeles region focuses on only one set of chemical substances, not the greening of a whole region of industries.

However, a number of good examples of comprehensive programs for a region have started now in Europe. The Graz 2000 program is

---

7. M. Crul and F. Schelleman, *Long Term Planning and the Use of Integrated Environmental Technology: The Dutch Experience,* Report for the Office of Technology Assessment (Bonn: German Parliament, 1995).

very well developed and takes into consideration all activities—industry, transportation, tourism, and so on. Several regional sustainability efforts have also begun in places like Storstrohm County in Denmark. This project was well recognized in 1992 with a prize from the United Nations Conference on Environment and Development for the best regional sustainability initiative in the world.

Conclusions

There is a growing body of literature on the greening of small and medium-sized firms. Much of it is in the form of manuals, guides, reports, and compendia published by government agencies or non-government organizations. There are many case studies in professional and trade journals. Most of these reports are fairly descriptive in nature and there is seldom much conceptual or theoretical material involved.

Most of the literature can be divided between early material and more recent writing. The early material tended to be fairly narrowly focused. Significant attention was given to changes in the technologies—the materials and equipment—of production. Little attention was given to management organization and practices, processes of change, products, networks of firms, or industrywide developments. During the past few years this has begun to change as the focus on pollution prevention and clean technologies has increasingly been broadened to cleaner production and environmentally conscious manufacturing.

This management focus needs to be extended and broadened. More research and more projects need to be targeted at changes in management, corporate culture, internal communication, and employee rewards and incentives. Much of this should be encouraged by integrating the environmental and safety orientation with the product and service orientation of the firm. Environmental and industrial outcomes must become parallel. Closer integration of cleaner production and EMAS in Europe and pollution prevention and total quality management in the United States would encourage this. Finally, all of these process programs should be integrated with the new ISO (International Standards Organization) standards on product quality and environmental management.

More research and program attention needs to be directed at products, "product chains," and life cycle analysis, particularly in the United States. Ecodesign needs to be tailored to smaller enterprises. Eventually, small and medium-sized firms should consider the service-oriented approaches that go beyond commodity production.

Regional approaches that include local government entities need to be further developed. Programs need to be developed to respect and enhance linkages among networks of small and medium-sized firms. The "industrial symbiosis" or "industrial ecology" offers rich possibilities for small and medium-sized firms within regions, but this should include more than mere waste recycling.

Finally, more research is needed on firms in industrializing countries. The UNEP program has identified the opportunity to integrate industrial development and cleaner production in developing countries (UNEP 1993, 1995). This requires more research and project attention to the smaller enterprises there.

Annotated Bibliography

Books, Articles, and Papers

Calfa, L., J. Holbrook, C. Keenan, and T. Reilly. 1994. "The Descriptive Approach to Pollution Prevention in a Woolen Mill." *Pollution Prevention Review* (Spring): 179–189.

This case study derives from a team of students employing the descriptive approach promoted by Robert Pojasek in developing a facility-auditing guidance manual for the Northern Textile Association. The case study uses a cause-and-effect diagram to identify pollution prevention opportunities in the five basic steps of wool fabric manufacturing.

Chistensen, J., and V. Christensen. 1994. "Industrial Symbiosis." Paper prepared for the European Roundtable on Cleaner Production Programs, Graz, Austria, October 1994.

This article provides a description of "industrial symbiosis" on an industry site in Kalundborg, Denmark, where exchange of waste and heat takes place among several large firms, an electricity generator, and some local agricultural companies.

Dieleman, J., *et al.* 1991. "Choosing for Prevention Is Winning." In *PRE-PARE Experiences.* The Hague: SDU.

This is a comprehensive and policy-oriented report of the first Dutch demonstration project, PRISMA (Project on Industrial Successes with Waste Prevention). On the basis of 10 case studies of wide variation and scope, more generic conclusions are drawn, barriers are identified, and solutions to overcome them are formulated. An integrated set of policy recommendations for government and other social sectors is included.

Hamilton, A. 1992. "An Ecologically Responsible Design for NCR's Personal Image Processor." *Pollution Prevention Review* (Winter 1992–93): 73–86.

This case study describes the manner in which sound ecological product design and good business sense were combined in redesigning the production of a desktop document-imaging processor. The new design process relies on checklists to promote design for disassembly and to improve the selection of environmentally sound materials.

Houseman, J. 1993. "Parker Pen's Total Quality Management Strategy to Prevent Pollution from Solvents." *Pollution Prevention Review* (Spring): 187–195.

This case examines the results of using a total quality management approach to significantly reduce trichloroethelyene emissions. The pen manufacturer used quality-improvement teams and statistical quality control to identify and implement a program that reduced emissions with little capital investment, a 36,000-pound decrease in hazardous waste generation, and a $30,000 savings in operating cost.

Huisingh, D., and V. Bailey. 1982. *Making Pollution Prevention Pay: Ecology with Economy as Policy.* New York: Pergamon Press.

This is an early but still quite useful analysis written in the form of an argument about the economic benefits of environmentally conscious manufacturing.

Kikta, A. 1994. "Using a Six-Step Organizational Framework to Establish a Facility P2 Program." *Pollution Prevention Review* (Spring): 199–208.

This study examines the implementation of a pollution-prevention program in a synthetic fiber and resin production facility. The study follows over a three-year period the sequence of steps leading to implementation and then presents a useful evaluation of the results achieved by the pollution-prevention program.

Kirsch, F.W., G.P. Looby, and M.C. Kirk Jr. 1993. "How Four Manufacturers Improved Painting Operations to Reduce Waste." *Pollution Prevention Review* 3 (4): 429–436.

This article draws four case studies from a broader study of waste reduction assessments implemented at 70 small and medium-sized firms. The four case studies presented here involve surface coatings on automobile mirrors, military furniture, and aluminum extrusions. The case studies are brief, but include process diagrams, technical descriptions, and cost data. There is no discussion of process implementation or managerial issues.

Kohler, K., and A. Sasson. 1993. "Multi-Industry Success Stories to Reduce TCA Use in Ohio." *Pollution Prevention Review* 3 (4): 407–415.

This article contains brief case studies covering the efforts of four Ohio firms in reducing or eliminating the use of trichloroethelyene in degreasing and cleaning. The case studies cover electrical parts assembly, metal castings, welding, and lubricating. Each case identifies only the technical changes made and the results achieved.

NMC. 1994. "Draft Report on the Dutch Cleaner Production Programme." Paper presented at the European Roundtable on Cleaner Production Programs, Graz, Austria, October 1994.

This article provides an overview of several follow-up initiatives in the Netherlands after the demonstration projects on cleaner production. Information materials, education, and support schemes central to the approach to small and medium-sized firms are identified.

Roy, M., and L. Dillard. 1990. "Toxics Use Reduction in Massachusetts: The Blackstone Project." *Journal of the Air Waste Management Association* 4: 1368–1371.

This case study reviews the experience gained from a special state program to combine multimedia regulatory initiatives with intensive technical assistance to reduce the volume and toxicity of wastewater discharges in an industrial region in Massachusetts. The majority of firms involved were metal platers or finishers. The results achieved over a three-year period were important in demonstrating the effectiveness of multimedia inspection programs for other industrial sectors.

Government Manuals and Guides

Brezet, J. (ed.). 1994. *PROMISE Handleiding voor milieugerichte Produktontwik-keling* (PROMISE manual for environmentally conscious product development). The Hague: SDU.

> This manual is the first systematic manual on ecodesign published in Europe. The manual describes a series of phases that follow the formal product development procedure and attempts to use the same phrases and terminology as in the process-oriented cleaner production approach. Several easy-to-use analytical tools are included.

Center for Hazardous Materials Research. 1987. *Hazardous Waste Minimization Manual for Small Quantity Generators in Pennsylvania*. Pittsburgh: University of Pittsburgh Applied Research Center.

> An early manual focused on small and medium-sized firms.

de Hoo, S., *et al.* (eds.). 1990. *Handleiding voor Preventie van Afval en Emissies* (Manual for the prevention of waste and emissions). The Hague: SDU.

> This is the first European adaptation of the U.S. EPA *Waste Minimization Opportunity Assessment Manual*. This Dutch manual was used in the PRISMA project, and adaptations were used in many follow-up projects. As with its American predecessor, this manual was criticized for its rigid structure and high complexity; therefore, it was not used widely with small and medium-sized firms.

Massachusetts Office of Technical Assistance. 1992. *A Practical Guide to Toxics Use Reduction: Benefitting from TUR at Your Workplace*. Boston, MA: Massachusetts Office of Technical Assistance.

> This is the only state manual written to promote toxics-use reduction. It differs from the other state manuals on pollution prevention and waste reduction because it focuses on analyzing the role that toxic chemicals play in creating the costs and hazards of production. The manual sets up a series of stages and provides examples and illustrations that assist the user in understanding the value of each stage.

New York State, Department of Environmental Conservation. 1989. *Waste Reduction Guidance Manual*. Albany, NY: New York State, Department of Environmental Conservation.

> This is one of the oldest state manuals. It follows the conventional out-

line, but there are many helpful matrices of options and sidebar illustrations drawn from New York State firms.

PREPARE. 1991. *PREPARE Manual for Waste and Emission Prevention.* The Hague: SDU.

PREPARE (PReventive Environmental Protection AppRoaches in Europe) is a EUREKA and European Union working group involving representatives from 18 European countries. This manual was an adaptation of the Dutch PRISMA manual used as a template for many other European manuals.

Texas Water Commission. 1992. *Pollution Prevention Assessment Manual for Texas Businesses.* No. LP92-03. Austin, TX: Texas Water Commission.

This is one of the manuals that relies heavily on worksheets. Much of the manual is taken up in describing how to use the worksheets. There are no examples or case studies.

U.S. Environmental Protection Agency. 1988. *Waste Minimization Opportunity Assessment Manual.* No. EPA/625/7-88/003. Washington, DC: U.S. EPA.

This is the original U.S. EPA manual initially developed under contract by Jacobs Engineering.

U.S. Environmental Protection Agency. 1990–1992. *Guides to Pollution Prevention.* Office of Research and Development NTIS No. PB-87-114–328. Washington, DC: U.S. EPA.

Sixteen independent manuals are available as a five-volume set from the National Technical Information Service. These guides, produced under contract by Jacobs Engineering, follow a standard format that includes, first, the waste minimization template outlined above, followed by a profile of the specific industrial sector, a description of identified waste minimization options for that sector, and a set of standard worksheets. Many of these guides include specific facility case studies in their appendices.

Washington State Department of Ecology. 1992. *Pollution Prevention Planning.* Waste Reduction, Recycling, and Litter Control Program. No. 91-2. Olympia, WA: Washington State Department of Ecology.

This manual is designed to assist Washington State firms to comply with the state Hazardous Waste Reduction Act. It is quite prescriptive, beginning with definitions and a review of legal requirements. The body of the manual relies heavily on 18 worksheets that are included in an appendix. While it is clear and direct, it provides no case studies, examples, or illustrations. This formulaic approach offers little encouragement to examine the process, managerial, or more creative aspects of pollution prevention planning.

Government Reports

BMWF. 1994. *PREPARE Osterreich, Results.* Vienna: Ministries for Science and Research and the Environment.

This report contains results of the first national cleaner production demonstration project in Austria that included several small and medium-sized firms. The Austrian government has been among the most active promoters of cleaner production.

Catalyst. 1994. *Project Catalyst.* Report to the Demos Project Event, June 1994. BOC March DTI/Aspects int./WS Atkins Report. Manchester, UK: Catalyst.

This is a report on the Catalyst project, which included 14 companies and was started in the Mersey River basin, one of the major concentrations of industry in the United Kingdom and a significant contributor to environmental pollution.

Cave, R., and Associates. 1993. *Small Quantity Hazardous Waste Generators Demonstration Project in Hamilton, Ontario: Final Management Report.* Contract No. KA401-1-0648/01-XSE. Oakville, Ontario: R. Cave and Associates.

A brief analysis of a regionally organized demonstration program involving certain demonstration programs in selected industries, such as photoprocessing, automobile services, and printing, and producing a long and encompassing "management plan."

Cramer, J. 1994. *Met beleid naar milieugerichte produktontwikkeling* (With policy toward product improvement). PROMISE report. The Hague: NOTA.

This is a very complete policy study into improvements of existing Dutch policy to stimulate the product approach. Separate attention is given to actions that companies can take themselves, actions as a part of technology and innovation policy, actions as part of environmental policy, and actions of other societal actors, especially the financial sector.

IOW. 1993. *Ecodesign: Fibel fur Anwender* (Ecodesign: User guide). IOW Report 20/93. Vienna: IOW.

Although one of the first ecodesign guides, it does not present a formal procedure. The guide presents several approaches in popular language without too much scientific complexity and offers good examples of industrial applications.

MEDIA. 1992a. *Ejemplo practico* (Practical examples). Madrid: MICYT (Ministerio de Industria, Commercio y Turismo).

This is a report on the first Spanish demonstration projects that involved five small and medium-sized firms.

MEDIA. 1992b. *Descripcion del Manual Media* (Description manual for MEDIA). Madrid: MICYT.

This is a Spanish adaptation of the PREPARE and U.S. EPA manuals. As an extra feature, how-to instructions are added to all the steps of the procedure. This is a useful manual for introducing cleaner production in Spanish-speaking countries and companies.

Nilsen, B., *et al.* 1994. *Waste Management: Clean Technologies, An Update on the Situation in EU Member States.* RENDAN/Kruger/TME Report. Brussels: European Commission, DG XI.

This is the first comprehensive survey of all the initiatives, programs, and policies on cleaner technologies in the European Union countries with a special emphasis on Denmark, the Netherlands, and Spain. The survey provides a good overview of the weak and strong points in each country and offers an elegant framework on the terminology and connection of different trends in cleaner production.

NOH. 1992. *First NOH European Conference on Design for the Environment* Nunspeet, the Netherlands, September 21–23. NOH Reports 9260-9264. Bilthoven/Utrecht: the Netherlands.

These proceedings give a good overview of many European initiatives on cleaner products research and product development, including a list of projects and contact persons.

Okoprofit. 1992. *Okologisches Project Fur Integrierte Umwettechnik* (Ecological project for integrated environmental technology). Industrial examples. Graz, Austria: City of Graz and BMWF.

This is an excellent example of a regional project on cleaner production. This publication is very attractive for the nonscientific public because of its clean presentation, examples, diagrams, and photographs.

Roth, H., *et al.* 1994. *Milieu—en energiebewuste Produktontwikkeling en ketenbeheer. Overzicht van Onderzoek—en Demonstratieprojecten* (Environmental and energy conscious product development and integrated chain management—overview of demonstration projects). *Vijde editie,* NOH rapport 9431 (5th ed., NOH Report 9431). Bilthoven/Utrecht, the Netherlands: NOH.

This is a useful annual survey of all public-financed demonstration projects in cleaner products and chain management in the Netherlands. Each project is briefly described, key words are noted, and publications and contact persons are identified.

SPURT. 1993. *Strostrohm County's Program for the Dissemination of Cleaner Production.* Strostrohm amt, Denmark: Strostrohm.

A good example of the regional approach, leading among other things to a good educational program for government workers and industry. Following Strostrohm, many Danish counties moved to promote their own cleaner production programs.

TEKES. 1994. *Results of the Finnish PREPARE Projects.* Reports 1-5. Helsinki: TEKES (Technology Development Center).

Presentation of five Finnish case studies on cleaner production, mainly in large companies in the chemical/petrochemical sectors, including many good examples of technical opportunities.

Tweede Kamer. 1994. *Vergaderjaar 1994–1995.* 23905 nrs 1–2. Milieuprogramma 1995–1998 (Environmental program, 1995–1998). The Hague: SDU.

Yearly, updated program for the Dutch National Plan, including an interesting presentation of aggregated indicators for each environmental theme for each target sector based on policy goals for the years 2000 and 2010.

United Nations Environment Program (UNEP), Cleaner Production Program. 1993. *Cleaner Production Worldwide*. Paris: Industry and Environment Program Office.

Compendium of brief (two-page) case studies of cleaner production at 14 quite varied facilities around the world, presented in common format for easy comparison.

United Nations Environment Program (UNEP), Cleaner Production Program. 1995. *Cleaner Production in the Asian Pacific Economic Cooperation Region*. Paris: Industry and Environment Program Office.

This compendium of 12 case studies, following the format of the earlier UNEP compendium, demonstrates that industries in developing countries can leap over pollution-control approaches directly to cleaner production.

U.S. Environmental Protection Agency. 1993. *Building State and Local Pollution Prevention Programs*. Washington, DC: National Advisory Committee on Environmental Policy and Technology.

Brief description of the state pollution-prevention programs.

U.S. Environmental Protection Agency, Office of Solid Waste and Emergency Response. 1994. *Biennial Annual Hazardous Waste Report from RCRA*. EPA #53-OR-94039C. Washington, DC: U.S. EPA, September.

van der Steen, J. *et al.* 1992. *De Relatie tussen de PRISMA Methodiek en het Bedrijfsinterne Milieuzorssysteem* (The relation between the PRISMA methodology and EMAS). TNO IMET, report 92-354. Apeldoorn, the Netherlands: TNO.

This report describes the two systems and the similarities and differences between them. Two scenarios are developed, one starting with PRISMA and continued by EMAS and the other vice versa. Regrettably, no explicit choice is made between the two systems, although PRISMA seems to be the better choice for continuous improvement.

VROM. 1993. *The Netherlands National Environmental Policy, Plan 2*. The Hague: Ministry of VROM.

Second five-year integral Environmental Plan for the Netherlands. The descriptions include many valuative parts on the famous first plan of 1989 and a good overview of all industry-oriented policy actions.

NGO Reports

Campbell, M.E., and W.M. Glenn. 1982. *Profit from Pollution Prevention: A Guide to Industrial Waste Reduction and Recycling.* Toronto: Pollution Probe Foundation.

This is one of the first compendia of case studies to appear in North America. It is divided by industrial sector and full of brief cases, photographs, and illustrations from Canada and the United States. While it is not technical nor very detailed, this publication served an important role in popularizing the idea that there were many opportunities for pollution prevention well before most governments had made any such programmatic commitments.

Crul, M. 1994. *Environmentally Conscious Product Development in Practice.* PROMISE Report. The Hague: NOTA.

An analysis of the first Dutch ecodesign case studies, providing an overview of practical experiences and an evaluation of the barriers and solution options to overcome them. The official report is in Dutch, but an English translation is available.

Crul, M., and F. Schelleman. 1995. *Long Term Environmental Planning and the Use of Integrated Environmental Technology: The Dutch Experience.* Bonn: Office of Technology Assessment, German Parliament.

This is a study of the effect of long-term environmental planning in the selection of cleaner technologies by industry. The study concludes that there is no direct and easy link between long-term planning and the selection of cleaner technologies. Industry tends to select technologies that are "on the shelf," both end-of-pipe and preventive, within economic possibilities. However, there is a recent trend toward cleaner technologies, especially in research and development investments.

Huisingh, D., *et al.* 1986. *Proven Profits from Pollution Prevention: Case Studies in Resource Conservation and Waste Reduction.* Washington, DC: Institute for Local Self Reliance.

This is an early compendium of case studies and includes 46 separate cases among different industry sectors from around the United States, organized by industry type. The cases are presented in a systematic format to permit comparisons that include a category on benefits achieved.

A separate section presents a cross-referencing of abstracts of the cases by type of waste and type of pollution-prevention technique.

OWMC (Ontario Waste Management Corporation). 1987. *Industrial Waste Audit and Reduction Manual: A Practical Guide to Conducting an In-Plant Survey.* Toronto: OWMC.

This is an example of an early manual prepared for Canadian facilities, but used extensively in the United States. While the primary focus of this well-presented manual is on audits and waste inventories, later sections of the manual provide guidance on waste-reduction options and option assessment.

Source Reduction Research Partnership, Metropolitan Water District of Southern California and the Environmental Defense Fund. 1990. *Potential for Source Reduction and Recycling of Halogenated Solvents.* Pasadena, CA: Jacobs Engineering Group.

This is a report on a multiyear project that united an environmental advocacy organization and a water utility in a well-documented, 12-volume study of options for reducing and recycling solvents. Each volume examines a particular use such as dry cleaning, paint stripping, parts cleaning, and so on. Each volume describes the use characteristics and the source reduction opportunities, concluding with quantitative analyses of the "source reduction potential."

te Riele, H., *et al.* 1994. *Ecodesign: acht voorbeelden* (Ecodesign: eight examples). PROMISE Report. The Hague: NOTA.

This report describes the first Dutch ecodesign case studies on products such as an office chair, car dashboard, potplant tray, and gas cooker. The product-development process and related environmental issues are described in detail, although this report lacks the sufficient economic data that appears in a subsequent report.

van Berkel, C., *et al.* 1992. *Preventie van Afval en Emissies in Gelderland eindrapport* (Prevention of waste and emissions in the Province of Gelderland), IVAM Report 53. Amsterdam: IVAM.

PROGRESS (Prevention in Industry in Gelderland: Reduction of Emissions and Waste) was one of the first regional projects in the

Netherlands. This report offers a good example of the further development of the research methodology and integration of policy aspects
into the study.

Wigglesworth, D. 1988. *Profiting from Waste Reduction in Your Small Business.*
Anchorage, AK: Alaska Health Project.

This manual is pitched to the smallest of enterprises and is organized in
the same manner as the state manuals, providing step-by-step guidance
to those operating small enterprises. The text is enriched with boxes
containing brief case studies of dry cleaners, sign painters, photofinish-
ers, and automobile repair services. It is short, encouraging, and filled
with concrete illustrations drawn from commercial activities that are
likely to be found in local neighborhoods.

About the Contributors

Caron Chess is director of Rutgers University's Center for Environmental Communication, which conducts research and training to improve communication about environmental issues. She coauthored two risk-communication manuals that are used widely, and she routinely provides risk-communication training to government agencies and industry.

Marcel Crul is director of Aries Environmental Consultancy in the Netherlands. He performs national and international strategic studies on preventive approaches for industry, like cleaner technologies, cleaner products, and environmental marketing studies.

Kurt Fischer is senior research associate at the George Perkins Marsh Institute, Clark University in Worcester, Massachusetts; and U.S. coordinator of the Greening of Industry Network. His research interests concern the social meaning of "greening" and "sustainability."

Kenneth Geiser is associate professor of work environment at the University of Massachusetts at Lowell and the director of the Toxics Use Reduction Institute there. He is involved in research on new environmentally appropriate materials and new clean technologies. Currently he is an advisor to the U.S. Environmental Protection Agency on pollution prevention and the Toxics Release Inventory and is an advisor to the United Nations Cleaner Production Program.

Mark Gijtenbeek is an economist and holds a master's degree in environmental sciences from the University of Amsterdam. He has done research on environmental management information, environmental reporting, and environmental performance indicators. Currently he is editor for an environmental management study book at the Institute of Environmental Control Sciences of the University of Amsterdam, and he has his own agency for environmental publications.

Kenneth Green is a senior lecturer in technology management at the Manchester School of Management, University of Manchester Institute of Science and Technology (UMIST). His research at the school's Center for Research on Management, Organizations, and Technical Change (CROMTEC) is concerned with social, economic, and political influences on the development of new technologies.

Peter Groenewegen is a chemist and holds a doctorate in science studies from the University of Amsterdam. He has done research on company strategy and technology development, as well as on research and development cooperation between corporations and universities. Currently he is coordinator of the Research Program on Science, Technology, and the Environment at the Free University of Amsterdam in the Netherlands.

Sue Hall is a former Charles Williams Fellow at Harvard University Graduate School of Business Administration and more recently founded Strategic Environmental Associates, a specialist consulting company. Her work focuses on developing leading-edge environmental strategies for corporations by building innovative partnerships with other stakeholder groups. She has been appointed board member and executive director of the Institute for Sustainable Technology, a nonprofit group designed to help catalyze sustainable market transformations.

Julie L. Hass is currently a doctoral researcher at Manchester Business School in Manchester, England. Her research focuses, from an interorganizational network perspective, on why and how companies are changing by incorporating "green" or environmental issues into their companies.

Jan Hesselberg is professor in human geography, University of Oslo, Norway, and holds a post at the Center for Development and the Environment at the same university. He has been involved in research on development problems in the South for nearly 20 years. He is presently in charge of a research program on international location of pollution-intensive industry, particularly focusing on a possible shift in industrial pollution from the North to the South.

Alan Irwin is reader in sociology at the Department of Human Sciences, Brunel, University of West London. His current research focuses on environmental sociology, the social management of environmental change, and the development of regulatory science.

Peter James directs the Environmental Leadership Program at Ashridge Management College, U.K. He was previously professor of management at the University of Limerick. He has published a number of works on quality and the environment, environmental accounting, and the environment and comparative environmental management in Europe, Japan, and North America.

Edith G. Jenkins is a doctoral candidate in management policy at the Boston University School of Management. She holds a master's degree in urban and environmental policy from Tufts University. Her research focuses on the interface between consumers and industry and the goals of democracy and sustainable societies.

Frances Lynn is director of the Environmental Resource Program and research associate professor in environmental sciences and engineering at the University of North Carolina at Chapel Hill. Her research focuses on citizen participation and collaborative decision making. The organization she directs promotes citizen participation and collaborative decision making on environmental issues.

Johan Piet is an environmental accountant at Deloitte & Touche (member of the European Directing Board of Environmental Management and Auditing Services) and part-time professor at the Institute of Environmental Control Science, University of Amsterdam. He is president of the Environmental Task Force of the European

Federation of Institutes of Chartered Accountants (FEE) and of the Dutch Institute for Environmental Accountancy. His specialties include environmental information, reporting, and auditing.

Nigel Roome holds the Erivan K. Haub Chair in Business and the Environment in the Faculty of Administrative Studies, York University, Toronto, Canada. He directs the Faculty's Business and the Environment Program. He has published works on company strategy, technology management, the sustainable enterprise, and environmental education in the management curriculum. He advises several companies and has worked with the Canadian Standards Association and the British Standards Institute on environmental management systems.

Johan Schot is a historian and holds a doctorate in technology studies from the University of Twente, the Netherlands. He is involved in research and consulting on sustainable transport, constructive technology assessment, and environmental strategies for industry. Currently he is European coordinator of the Greening of Industry Network.

Ulrich Steger holds the Alcan Chair for Environmental Management at IMD, the International Institute for Management Development, in Lausanne, Switzerland. He also heads the Research Institute for Environmental Management. He has published extensively on management paradigms, strategy formulation, organizational learning and development, innovation management, and instruments of environmental policy.

Walter Wehrmeyer is lecturer in ecological management at the Durrell Institute of Conservation and Ecology of the University of Kent at Canterbury, England. He holds a doctorate in environmental management and is director of the Graduate Studies "Business in the Environment" Program. His research interest lies in evaluating corporate environmental cultures and in environmental performance assessment.

Name Index

Aarts, Thomas, 92, 105
Albes, W., 109
Allen, D., 116, 123
Allenby, Braden R., 14, 19, 24, 64, 67, 71, 77
Altman, Barbara, 27
Amir, A. M., 181, 190
Anderson, K., 199, 203
Annighofer, Frank, 25–26
Ansoff, H. I., 17, 18, 19–20, 21, 24–25
Argyris, Chris, 40, 45, 48, 53
Armstrong, S., 18, 25
Arnold, Matthew, 89, 105
Arnstein, Sherry, 88, 97
Atman, Cynthia, 106–107
Aucott, Michael, 115, 127
Auster, Ellen R., 38, 56
Ausubel, Jesse H., 71, 171, 181
Ayres, Robert, 67, 71, 77, 181
Azzone, G., 115, 122

Bailey, V., 234
Baram, Michael S., 65, 72, 74–75, 90, 97
Bartolomeo, M., 141, 153
Bartunek, J., 21, 25
Baumgartner, Thomas, 67, 82, 121, 122–23
Bebbington, Jan, 68, 77, 140, 147, 149, 157
Beck, U., 180, 181–82
Becker, M., 143, 165

Behmanesh, N., 116, 123
Bello, W., 198, 203
Bennett, Martin, 111, 112, 113, 114, 115, 117, 122, 123, 128
Bergsto, B., 200n.
Bingham, Gail, 88, 89, 94, 97–98
Blackhurst, R., 199, 203
Blumenfeld, Karen, 25–26, 67, 72–73
Blundell, W. R. C., 39, 44, 51, 53
Bostrom, Ann, 106–107
Botzler, R., 18, 25
Boulding, K., 19, 26
Bragg, Sara, 119, 123
Braithwaite, J., 203–204
Brezet, J., 225, 236
Brisson, Inger, 64, 73
Brock, Silke, 53
Brown, Halina, 103
Brundtland, G., 10, 26
Bryant, Bunyan, 92, 98
Busenberg, George, 89, 96, 105–106

Cairncross, F., 179, 182–83, 201, 204
Calfa, L., 217, 233
Cali, Lawrence, 227n.
Campbell, M. E., 229, 242
Cannon, T., 183
Carey, A., 158
Carley, Michael, 98
Carroll, A. B., 18, 26
Castleman, B. I., 195, 197, 198n.

Cave, R., 229, 238
Charlton, Carol, 73, 117, 124
Charter, Martin, 69, 73, 119
Chess, Caron, 20, 31, 66, 87–96, 98–99,
    102, 106, 245
Choucri, Nazli, 204
Christensen, J., 218, 233
Christensen, V., 218, 233
Christie, Ian, 98
Chynoweth, Emma, 64, 67, 73–74
Clark, I. D., 39, 44, 51, 53
Clarke, R., 204
Claudius, Mathias, 111
Clift, Roland, 190
Cluck, Victoria, 96
Cohen, Nevin, 96
Cooper, R., 154
Coyle, S. W., 53–54
Cramer, Jacqueline, 26, 65, 74, 221,
    238–39
Crowfoot, James E., 89, 99
Cruikshank, Jeffrey, 110
Crul, Marcel, 213–33, 242, 245
Curran, Mary Ann, 115, 125

Davis, G., 190
Davis, L., 45, 47, 54, 205
Dechant, Kathleen, 27
de Haes, Udo, 78
de Hoo, S., 177, 184–85, 224, 236
Dembo, D., 205
den Hond, Frank, 66, 75, 78
Dieleman, J., 218, 221, 234
Dielemann, H., 177, 184–85
Diependaal, M. J., 159
Dierkes, M., 39, 40, 48, 51, 54
Dillard, L., 235
Dillon, Patricia S., 65, 72, 74–75, 90, 97
Dozier, David, 92, 101
Drumwright, Minette E., 70, 75
Duerksen, C. L. J., 197n.
Durkee, Linda C., 90, 99

Earle, Ralph, III, 25–26, 67, 72–73
Eccles, Robert, 113, 124
Eckel, Len, 119, 125
Ehling, William, 92, 101
Eller, S. W., 197n.

Emani, S., 211
Emel, Jacque, 103
Endresen, S. B., 200n.

Fagg, B., 155
Fairclough, Sir John, 68, 76
Fairtlough, Gerard, 76
Fessenden-Raden, June, 92, 99–100
Fiorino, Daniel J., 88, 100
Fischer, Kurt, 1–7, 26, 27–28, 34, 74, 78,
    109, 184, 188, 245
Fischoff, Baruch, 91, 106–107, 110
Fisher, Kathryn, 119, 125
Fitchen, Janet M., 92, 99–100
Fitzgerald, Chris, 117, 119, 125, 130
Fitzgerald, Kevin, 92, 105
Forester, W. S., 170, 185
Fouhy, Ken, 67, 77
Freedman, Martin, 125, 141, 156
Freeman, Harry, 112, 115, 125
Freeman, R. E., 18, 28
Freese, E., 120, 126
French, H. F., 205–206
Freudenburg, William R., 92, 100
Friedman, Frank B., 55
Frosch, Robert A., 14, 19, 28, 77

Gallopoulos, Nicholas E., 77
Gandz, J., 39, 44, 51, 53
Geiser, Kenneth, 185–86, 213–33, 245
Georg, S., 178, 185–86
Gijtenbeek, Mark, 137–53, 246
Gilbert, D. R., 18, 28
Gilbert, Michael, 112, 119, 126
Gladwin, Thomas N., 18, 28, 206
Glenn, W. M., 229, 242
Gobel, Robert, 103
Golding, Dominic, 91, 104
Goldstein, J., 143, 165
Golüke, U., 198, 212
Gow, H. B. F., 90, 100–101
Gray, Barbara, 20, 28–29, 39, 47, 55, 89,
    101
Gray, Rob, 68, 77, 140, 147, 149, 151,
    157
Grayson, L., 140, 157
Green, Kenneth, 169–80, 246
Greenberg, Michael, 95, 96, 98–99

Greenberg, Richard, 115, 127
Greening, D. W., 39, 47, 55
Groenewegen, Peter, 1–7, 63–71, 75, 77–78, 246
Grunig, James E., 92, 101
Grunig, Larissa, 92, 101
Guinee, J. B., 67, 78
Guntram, Ulrich, 35

Haasis, Hans-Dietrich, 134
Habel, M. J., 39, 40, 49, 55
Hadden, Susan, 92, 101–102
Hafkamp, W. A., 158
Hahn, Walter, 68, 84–85
Hall, Sue, 9–24, 246
Hallay, Hendrick, 117, 120, 127, 131
Hamel, G., 16, 17, 24, 29–30
Hamilton, A., 217, 234
Hance, Billie Jo, 102
Hansen, Ursula, 62
Harten, Teresa, 115, 125
Hass, Julie L., 63–71, 246
Hastam, C., 43, 45, 50, 56
Hawken, Paul, 21–22, 30
Hearne, Shelley, 115, 127
Heath, Jenifer S., 92, 99–100
Heaton, G. R., 180, 186
Heijungs, R., 67, 78
Herman, Robert, 181
Hesselberg, Jan, 195–203, 247
Heyungs, R., 141, 167
Hinnells, Mark, 65, 81–82
Hochman, Stephen, 112, 114, 115, 133–34
Hocking, Roland, 119, 127
Hockman, Mark, 112, 114, 115, 133–34
Hodgkinson, Simon, 114, 115, 127–28
Hofer, C., 24–25
Holbrook, J., 217, 233
Hooper, Linda, 96
Hooper, Paul, 169, 177, 186–87
Hopfenbeck, Waldemar, 63, 78–79
Houseman, J., 217, 234
Howell, Belinda, 73, 117, 124
Howes, Helen, 119, 134
Huisingh, Donald, 216, 234, 242–43
Hulpke, Herwig, 62

Hunt, Christopher B., 38, 56
Huppes, G., 67, 78, 141, 167
Hutchinson, Colin, 30

Ingersoll, Eric, 16, 17, 18, 19, 20, 29
Irwin, Alan, 169–80, 181, 186–87, 247
Irwin, W., 190
Ives, J. H., 196, 207

Jackson, T., 171, 178, 179, 187–88, 192–93
Jaggi, Bikki, 112, 125
Jakobs, Evelyn, 53
James, Peter, 111–22, 123, 128, 247
Jasanoff, Sheila, 90, 92, 102
Jenkins, Edith G., 1–7, 247
Johansson, A., 186–87
Johnson, Branden, 92, 102
Johnston, P. A., 190
Jones, T., 178, 188
Jørgensen, U., 178, 185–86

Kahane, Adam, 30
Kaplan, R. S., 154
Kaplan, Robert, 116, 128–29
Karch, K. M., 43–44, 49, 50, 56
Kartez, Jack, 93, 103
Kasperson, Jeanne X, 91–103
Kasperson, Roger E., 90, 91, 103
Keenan, C., 217, 233
Kemp, R., 188–89
Kennedy, Gary, 119, 134–35
Kieser, A., 50, 57
Kikta, A., 217, 234–35
Kirchgeorg, M., 38, 44, 45–46, 49, 51, 57
Kirk, M. C., Jr., 217, 235
Kirkwood, R. C., 189–90
Kirsch, F. W., 217, 235
Klafter, Brenda, 118, 129
Klassen, Robert D., 68, 79
Kleiner, Art, 94, 104
Kloock, J., 120, 126
Knapp, Philippa, 119, 123
Knight, Alan, 69, 79
Knödgen, G., 200, 207
Kohler, K., 217, 235
Kooijman, Jan M., 68, 79–80

Kreikebaum, H., 38, 40, 46, 50, 57
Krimsky, Sheldon, 89, 91, 93, 104,
    108
Krozer, J., 141, 147, 158
Kunreuther, Howard, 92, 105

Lascelles, David, 112, 122, 129
Lave, Lester, 92, 106–107
Lent, Tony, 30–31
Leonard, H. Jeffrey, 197n., 200, 207–
    208
Leroy, P., 159
Levenstein, C., 197n.
Lewis, Sanford, 94, 95
Lichtenstein, Sarah, 91, 110
Linneroth, J., 190
Long, Frederick, 89, 105
Longley, Anita J., 189–90
Looby, G. P., 217, 235
Lovins, Amory, 17, 31
Low, P., 197, 199, 201, 208
Lynn, Francis, 20, 31, 66, 87–96,
    105–106, 247

MacGarvin, M., 190–91
McLean, Ronald, 119, 123
McMeekin, Andrew, 169
McQueen, J. R., 39, 44, 51, 53
Macve, R., 158
Mahoney, Joseph T., 80
Maltezou, S. P., 190
Manzini, R., 115, 122
Meffert, H., 38, 44, 45–46, 49, 51,
    57
Milne, M. J., 147, 158–59
Mitchell, George, 203
Mitroff, Ian, 38, 57–58, 66, 80
Moch, J., 21, 25
Mogezomp, H. G., 159
Mohai, Paul, 92, 98
Morgan, G., 23, 32
Morgan, M. Granger, 92, 106–107
Morton, D., 39, 44, 51, 53
Müller-Wenk, Ruedi, 120, 129
Murphy, Anthony, 169

Navarro, V., 198n.
Neely, Andy, 114, 116, 129

Nelkin, Dorothy, 108
Newall, J. E., 39, 44, 51, 53
Nielsen, Larry, 119, 129–30
Nilsen, B., 225, 239
Norgaard, Richard B., 58
North, K., 179, 190-91
Norton, David, 116, 128–29

Oakley, Brian T., 68, 80–81
O'Connell, Patricia, 112, 114, 115,
    133–34
Oliff, Michael P., 36
Orlin, Judy, 117, 130
Otway, Harry, 90, 100–101
Owen, D., 140, 149, 159

Pandian, J. Rajendran, 80
Pandya, C. G., 208
Peacock, Marcus, 119, 130
Peapples, G. A., 39, 44, 51, 53
Pearson, C. S., 197, 206, 208
Pearson, Christine M., 58
Pfriem, Reinhard, 120, 131
Piet, Johan, 137–53, 159–60, 161,
    247–48
Plough, Alonzo, 89, 93, 104, 108
Pojasek, Robert, 227n., 233
Porter, Michael, 13, 15, 24, 31, 32, 41,
    42, 58
Power, Shaked, 119, 127
Prahalad, C., 16, 17, 29–30

Rappaport, A., 198, 199, 209
Ratick, Samuel, 91, 103
Reilly, T., 217, 233
Reisch, Marc, 90, 93–94, 96, 108
Relph, G., 39, 44, 51, 53
Renn, Ortwin, 103
Repetto, R., 180, 186
Repper, Fred, 92, 101
Rest, Kathleen, 93, 108
Rice, F., 118, 131
Richards, Deanna J., 14, 19, 24, 64, 67,
    71, 77
Roberts, Michael, 64, 67, 73–74
Roome, Nigel, 9–24, 32–33, 65, 66,
    81–82, 84, 248
Røpke, I., 178, 185–86

Roque, J., 116, 123
Rosenfeld, S., 198, 203
Rosenstiel, L. V., 39, 40, 48, 49, 50, 51,
    54, 59
Roth, H., 218, 240
Roy, M., 235
Rubik, Frieder, 67, 82, 121, 122–23
Ruffle, Betsy, 71–72, 90, 97
Rushton, B. M., 191
Russel, Grant, 119, 125
Ruud, A., 199, 209

Sachmann, S., 51, 59
Sahabat Alam Malaysia, 209
Salter, Malcolm, 29
Sandman, Peter, 102
Sasson, A., 217, 235
Savage, D., 144, 147, 166
Saville, Alex, 95, 98–99
Schafhausen, Franzjosef, 134
Schaltegger, S., 160–61
Schelleman, F., 231, 242
Schendel, D., 24–25
Schmidheiny, Stephan, 10, 13, 20, 33,
    64, 65, 82, 191, 201, 202, 209
Schmidt-Bleek, Friedrich, 82
Scholtens, A. M., 140, 141, 161
Schot, Johan, 1–7, 26, 27–28, 34, 65, 66,
    74, 78, 83, 109, 184, 188, 248
Schreiner, Manfred, 113, 115, 116, 120,
    131–32
Schulz, Erica, 59, 115, 132
Schulz, Werner, 59, 115, 132, 134, 140,
    142, 147, 161–62
Schwartz, Peter, 16, 33
Schwarz, M., 180, 192
Schwing, R. C., 109
Seidel, Eberhard, 38, 40, 46, 50, 57, 112,
    120, 132, 162
Senge, P., 17, 33
Serageldin, I., 60
Sethi, S., 13, 33
Shillito, David, 45, 50, 60
Shirley, R. S., 53–54
Shopley, Jonathan B., 67, 72–73
Shorthouse, Barry, 115, 132
Shrivastava, Paul, 19, 33–34, 90,
    108–109

Sietz, Manfred, 45, 46, 51, 60–61
Simmons, Peter, 20, 34, 91, 92, 109
Skinner, J. H., 170, 185
Sladovich, Hedy E., 71, 171, 181
Slot, R. J., 162
Slovic, Paul, 91, 92, 103, 109–10
Smart, Bruce, 34, 119, 133
Smith, D., 192–93
Smith, J. K., 155
Sobin, R., 180, 186
Springer, Johny, 115, 125
Stagliano, A. J., 156
Stahel, W., 171, 179, 192–93
Stallen, P. J. M., 90, 91, 103
Stead, J. G., 21, 34
Stead, W. E., 21, 34
Steger, Ulrich, 16, 34, 37–52, 54, 61–62,
    131, 248
Stern, Alissa, 34–35
Stokke, P., 16, 35
Sturm, A., 160–61
Surma, J. P., 162–63
Susskind, Lawrence, 110
Swallwell, Peg, 117, 130

Talbot, N., 144, 147, 166
Tamuz, Michal, 95, 98–99
Taselaar, H., 141, 167
Taylor, Geoff, 69, 83
Teichler, Thomas, 53
te Riele, H., 219, 243
Thain, D. H., 39, 44, 51, 53
Thayer, Ann M., 83–84
Thayer, J. M., 39, 44, 51, 53
Thompson, M., 180, 192
Todd, R., 139, 142, 163–64
Trist, E., 20, 35

Ui, J., 210
Unger, Cynthia, 115, 127

van Berkel, C., 219, 243–44
van den Akker, F., 193
van der Linde, Claus, 31
van der Steen, J., 221, 241
Vandermerwe, Sandra, 36
Varchol, B. D., 53–54
Vaughn, Elaine, 91, 110

Congress of the United States, 199,
    204–205
Control and motivation, 139
Cooperation and network formation,
    19–20, 65–66
    see also Strategic cooperation
Corporate relationships with communi-
    ties, see Industry relationships with
    communities
Costs, see Environmental costs
Council on Economic Priorities, 118
Creativity and integrated environmental
    management, 49–51

Decentralized organizations, 45
Decision support, 139
Deloitte, Ross, Touche, 27
Deloitte Touche Tohmatsu International
    (DTTI), 140, 142, 149, 150–51,
    154–55
Department of Trade and Industry
    (DTI), 171, 176, 183–84
Dow Chemical, 138

Eco-balancing, 67, 113, 120, 121
Eco-controlling, 113, 120, 121
Eco-efficiency, 11, 13
Economic and Social Commission for
    Asia and the Pacific (ESCAP), 197,
    205
Ecoprofit project, 228
Eco-rating method, 141
Education and qualification, 50–51
EMAA Research Contact Group, 151
Emergency Planning and Community
    Right to Know Act (EPCRA), 90
End-of-pipe technologies
    alternative, 177
    recovery systems, 172–73
    treatment, 172
ENDS, 115, 125, 179, 184–85
Environment, health, and safety (EHS)
    strategies, 199
Environmental accounting, 113–14
    see also Greening of corporate account-
        ing
Environmental business strategy, 11,
    15–16

Environmental costs, 142–48
    capital budgeting and, 143–47
    as challenges to accounting practices,
        142
    clean technologies and, see Clean
        technologies
    cost "drivers" and, 146
    misallocation of, 145–46
    technology continuum and, 143–44
Environmental Defense Fund, 94–95,
    106, 229
Environmental information, 137–40
    systems of, 140–42
    see also Greening of corporate
        accounting
Environmental management information
    system (EMIS), 117
Environmental management systems
    (EMAS), 14, 232
    implementation of, 220–21, 226,
        227
    manuals from, 225
    organizing for, see Organizing for envi-
        ronmental management
    sustainable corporation and, 38–40
Environmental Performance Indicators
    (EPIs), 141, 142
Environmental performance measure-
    ment (EPM), 111–22
    benchmarking studies and, 118
    Canadian, 119
    comparability of data and, 117–18
    European, 119–20
    factors to account for, 121–22
    forces driving organizations to, 111–12
    future challenges to, 120–22
    general principles of, 114
    individual performance measures,
        114–16
    as influencing behavior, 120–21
    for internal use, 117
    introduction, 111–12
    key themes, 112–14
    managerial and scientific approaches
        to, 121
    national approaches to, 118–20
    relationship with the external environ-
        ment, 117–18

standardized forms of, 122
system of, 116–17
Total Quality Management and,
    118–20
Toxic Release Inventory and, 115,
    116, 117
U.S., 118–19
Environmental policy, stages in the devel-
    opment of, 38
Environmental Protection Agency (EPA),
    64, 67, 68, 75–76, 89, 138–39, 143,
    147, 152, 164–65, 175, 213–14,
    216, 218, 222, 237
Environmental reporting, 148–51
    companies that publish, 149
    dimensions of, 149
    five-stage model of evolution of,
        150–51
    freestanding, 149–50
    scale of, 150
Environmental self-assessment program
    (ESAP), 116
Environment Canada, 229
ESCAP-UNCTC, 197, 205
European Community's Fifth Action Pro-
    gram on the Environment, 138
European Green Table (EGT), 140, 142,
    155
European Roundtable on Cleaner Pro-
    duction Programs, 216
European technical assistance manuals,
    224–25

Facility-sustaining activities, 146
FEE (Federation des Experts Comptables
    Européens), 138, 140, 155–56
Financial accounting, 113
Function-oriented organizations, 45

GATT (General Agreement on Tariffs
    and Trade), 199, 206
Gemini Consulting, 29
General Electric Corporation, 140,
    156–57
Global Environmental Management Ini-
    tiative (GEMI), 115, 119, 126–27,
    138, 152
Good Neighbor Agreements, 94

Governmental initiatives, 63–64, 228–29
Graz 2000 program, 231–32
"Green" design, 68
Greening of corporate accounting,
    113–14, 137–53
    accounting profession and, 137–39
    "data" versus "information," 140–42
    environmental costs and, see Environ-
        mental costs
    environmental reporting, see Environ-
        mental reporting
    future research directions, 151–53
    internal versus external matters and,
        139–40
Greening of Industry Network, 16, 26,
    27, 31

Hazardous waste, 213–14
Hierarchic organizations, 45
Human resource management (HRM),
    37–52
    in integrated environmental manage-
        ment, 38–40, 48–51
    introduction, 37–38
    organizing for, see Organizing for envi-
        ronmental management
    sustainable corporation and, 38–40,
        51–52

ILO, 206–207
Industrial ecology, 14–15, 218
Industrialization and growth, 202–
    203
Industry relationships with communities,
    87–96
    antecedents to, 88–89
    Citizen Advisory Panels, 93–94
    collaborative efforts, 94–95
    conclusion, 96
    Good Neighbor Agreements, 94
    history of corporate efforts, 90–92
    innovative approaches to, 95
    introduction, 87–88
    Local Emergency Planning Commit-
        tees, 93
    mediation, 94
    risk communication and, 92
    risk perception and, 91–92

Information, 137–40
  data versus, 140–42
  see also Greening of corporate
    accounting
Innovation-oriented environmental man-
  agement, 39–40
Institute for Environmental Control Sci-
  ence, 148
Institute for Management Accountants
  (IMA), 151–52
Integrated environmental management,
  38–40
  human resource management in,
    48–51
Integrated Process Control, 173
Integrated substance chain management,
  68
Integrative functions, 46–48
International Chambers of Commerce,
  198
  Charter for Sustainable Development,
    115–16
International Cleaner Production Infor-
  mation Clearinghouse (ICPIC), 216
International Environmental Bureau, 198
International Standards Organization,
  150, 232
International trade, 199–200
Investor Responsibility Research Center,
  118, 128
IOW, 225, 238–39

Keidanren group, 198

Legitimacy, 18
Life cycle analysis (LCA), 64, 67–71,
  75–76
  cooperation and, 68–69
  eco-balances and, 67
  eco-rating method of, 141
  "green" design and, 68
  management and, 67–68
  research and management decisions,
    69–71
Life cycle management, 64, 67–68
Limperg Institute, 151
Local Emergency Planning Committees
  (LEPCs), 93

McDonald's Corporation, 94–95, 106
McKinsey and Company, 31
Management accounting, 113
Management Institute for Environment
  and Business (MEB), 13, 31
Manuals and guides, 215, 221–28
  European technical assistance, 224–25
  from material to functional orienta-
    tion, 226
  from prescriptive to descriptive analy-
    sis, 227–28
  state technical assistance, 223–24
  from technologies to organizational
    structure, 226–27
Marketing and environmental manage-
  ment, 44
Massachusetts Office of Technical Assis-
  tance, 223, 224, 236
MEDIA, 218, 239
Mediation, 94
Metropolitan Water District of Southern
  California, 229
Monitoring, 139
Motivation and integrated environmental
  management, 49–51

National Environmental Policy Plan
  (NEPP), 63, 65, 80–81
National Research Council, 92, 107
National Roundtable on Pollution Pre-
  vention, 216
Network formation, 19–20, 65–66
New York State, Department of Environ-
  mental Conservation, 223, 224,
  236–37
Nikkei Research, 118, 130
NMC, 221, 235
NOH, 219, 239
Nongovernmental organization (NGO)
  initiatives, 229–30
Norwegian Journal of Geography, 208

ÖBU (Ökobilanz für Unternehmen),
  120, 130
OECD, 208
Okoprofit, 219, 240
Ontario Ministry of the Environment
  and Energy, 229

Ontario Waste Management Corpora-
    tion (OWMC), 229, 243
Organizational change, 20–21
Organizing for environmental manage-
    ment, 40–48
    integrating environmental issues,
        45–46
    integrative and additive functions,
        46–48
    marketing and, 44
    Porter's value chain and, 41–43
    in production, 43–44
    product life cycle and, 44–45
Overlaid organization, 47

PA Consulting Group, 171, 176, 183–84
Performance measurement, see Environ-
    mental performance measurement
Personal and professional evaluation,
    50
"Polluter pays" principle, 201
Pollution Prevention Information
    Exchange System (PPIES), 216
Pollution Probe, 229
Portfolio analysis, 16
"Power promoter," 45–46
PREPARE (PReventive Environmental
    Protection AppRoaches in Europe),
    218, 224, 228, 237, 238
President's Commission on Environmen-
    tal Quality, 118, 131
President's Council for Sustainable
    Development (PCSD), 13
PRISMA (Project on Industrial Successes
    and Waste Production), 218, 221,
    224, 230
Production and environmental manage-
    ment, 43–44
Production process, clean technologies,
    172–74
    end-of-pipe recovery systems, 172–73
    end-of-pipe treatment, 172
    policies and strategies for, 177–78
    radical redesign of processes, 173–74
    waste minimization, 173
Product life cycle, 44–45
Product-sustaining activities, 146
"Professional promoter," 45–46

PROGRESS (Prevention in Industry and
    Gelderland: Reduction in Emissions
    and Waste), 219, 228, 243–44
PROMISE, 219, 221, 225

Regulations, environmental, 143
Responsibility for the Future, 63, 68,
    81
Responsible Care program, 198
Risk communication, 92
Risk perception, 91–92
Rollins Environmental Services, 94

Scenario planning, 16–17
Seveso Directive, 90
Shell Corporation, 15–16
Small and medium-sized firms, greening
    of, 213–33
    case studies of, 215, 216–21
    conclusions, 232–33
    from demonstrative to comprehensive
        programs, 231–32
    from end results to social processes,
        221
    from firms to industries, 217–19
    government initiatives, 215, 228–29
    introduction, 213–14
    literature on, 214–16
    manuals and guides, see Manuals and
        guides
    nongovernment organization (NGO)
        initiatives, 215, 229–30
    from production processes to products,
        219–20
    from technology to management focus,
        220–21
    from voluntary to mandatory, 230–31
Society for the Promotion of Life Cycle
    Development (SPOLD), 67, 83
Source Reduction Research Partnership,
    229–30, 243
SPURT, 228, 240
Stakeholders, 20, 66
"Standard Dutch" life cycle approach,
    141
State technical assistance manuals,
    223–24
Stone, Kenneth, 115, 125

Strategic choices and sustainable strate-
     gies, 9–24
  collaboration, alliances and networks,
     20
  compliance, 11–13
  definitions, conditions, and assump-
     tions, 10
  eco-efficiency, 13
  emerging themes, 19–21
  environmental management systems,
     14
  environmental strategies versus sus-
     tainable strategies, 23
  environmental strategy, 15–16
  industrial ecology, 14–15
  introduction, 9
  list of, 12
  organizational change, 20–21
  portfolio management, 16
  "practical," 22
  real challenge for, 21–24
  scenario planning, 16–17
  stakeholders and, 20
  summary, 18–19
  systems concepts, 19–20
  total quality environmental manage-
     ment, 14
  value-based strategies, 17–18, 22–24
Strategic cooperation, 19–20, 63–71
  introduction, 63–65
  life cycle analysis and, see Life cycle
     analysis (LCA)
  network formation and, 19–20, 65–66
Sustainability, 10
  see also Strategic choices and sustain-
     able strategies
SustainAbility Ltd., 67, 83
Sustainable corporation, 38–40
  barriers to the development of, 51–52
  research questions for, 52
Sybron Chemicals, 95
Systems concepts, 19–20

Technical assistance manuals, 223–25
Technology continuum, 143-44
TEKES, 218, 240

Tellus Institute, 145, 152, 163
Texas Water Commission, 223, 237
Total quality environmental management
     (TQEM), 14, 21
Total Quality Management (TQM),
     118–20, 220, 221
Toxic Release Inventory (TRI), 115, 116,
     117
Transnational companies (TNCs),
     195–203
  environmental management practices
     in, 198–99
  evaluating the evidence, 200–202
  industrial flight of, 196–98
  industrialization and growth, 202–203
  international trade and, 199–200
  in the North–South context, 195–96
Tweede Kramer, 218, 240

UNIDO, 197, 210–11
United Nations (UN), 197, 198, 199, 210
United Nations Center on Transnational
     Corporations (UNCTC), 197, 205,
     210
United Nations Conference on Environ-
     ment and Development, 232
United Nations Environment Program
     (UNEP), 36, 170, 193, 216–17, 233,
     241

Value-based strategies, 17–18, 22–24
Value chain, 41–43
VNCI (Association of the Dutch Chemi-
     cal Industry), 68, 84
VROM, 218, 241–42

Washington State Department of Ecol-
     ogy, 223, 237–38
Waste minimization, 173
  from cleaner technology to, 175–76
World Bank, 197, 199
World Commission on Environment and
     Development, 10
World Health Organization (WHO), 202,
     211–12
World Resources Institute, 152, 201, 212

The Greening of Industry Network Coordinators

Kurt Fischer
The George Perkins Marsh Institute
Clark University
950 Main Street
Worcester, Massacusetts 01610-1477 U.S.A.
Telephone: 508-751-4607
Fax: 508-751-4600
E-mail: kfischer@vax.clarku.edu

Johan Schot
Centre for Studies of Science Technology and Society
University of Twente
TWr.RC 302, P.O. Box 217
7500 AE Enschede, The Netherlands
Telephone: 31 53 489 3344
Fax: 31 53 489 4775
E-mail: j.w.schot@wmw.utwente.nl